THIS TREMENDOUS LOVER

This Tremendous Lover

DOM EUGENE BOYLAN, O.C.S.O.

Christian Classics™

A Division of
RCL · Resources for Christian Living
Allen, Texas

First published April, 1947

Reprinted 1987 by Christian Classics, Inc.,
with permission from Paulist Press

Cum permissu superiorum

Nihil Obstat: Josephus Rogers
Censor Theol. Deputatus

Imprimi Potest: Michael
Ep. Laonensis
die 23 Julii, 1946

Copyright © 1964 by the Mercier Press

Send all inquiries to:
CHRISTIAN CLASSICS
200 East Bethany Drive
Allen, Texas 75002-3804

Telephone: 877-275-4725 / 972-390-6400

Fax: 800-688-8356 / 972-390-6560

Visit us at: **www.thomasmore.com**

E-mail: **cservice@rcl-enterprises.com**

Printed in the United States of America

6981   ISBN 0-87061-138-0

37 38 39 40 41   07 06 05 04 03

to Mary

THE MOTHER OF THE WHOLE CHRIST
AND THE WOMAN THOU GAVEST ME
TO BE MY COMPANION

Preface

THERE is a phenomenon in the natural order which illustrates a great principle of the supernatural order: it is the structure and the growth of crystals. Each crystalline substance has its own characteristic shape; wherever complete crystals occur, not only the whole crystal, but also each unit of it, has that particular shape. If a crystal be suspended in a suitable solution of the substance of which it is composed—the "mother liquor" as it is called—that crystal will grow by drawing to itself material from the solution, forming it to its own image and likeness, and then uniting it to itself, yet so that the new and greater unity is an exact replica of the original nucleus and of each of the component units.

So it is with Christ. Lifted up on the cross, He draws all things to Himself; as St. Irenæus says, "He recapitulated in Himself the long history of men, 'summing us up' and giving us salvation, that we might receive again in Christ Jesus what we have lost in Adam, that is the image and likeness of God."[1]

On the cross, Christ "summed up" in one sacrificial act His whole life and His whole love. In His life and death, He "sums up" the whole life and destiny of His Church, and also the whole life and death of each member of that Church. There is, of course, individual diversity between the members but there is also a fundamental unity of pattern. To see it, one must first look below

[1] St. Irenæus: *Adv. Hær.* iv, 38 and 2. Many of our quotations from the fathers are taken from Fr. Kelly's translation of that splendid work on the Mystical Body by Fr. Mersch, S.J. The English translation is published by Bruce under the title *The Whole Christ.*

the surface of the individuating differences to observe the common pattern, and then stand back far enough from the complete unity to see it as a whole; for unless something of the consummation be glimpsed, there is difficulty in seeing the full significance of the individual destiny and of the common bond.

For the common bond—the bond of all perfection—is love, and the magnificence of the whole is the unity of love. The model according to which the whole is designed is the Blessed Trinity itself—*that they may be one as we also are one.*[2] And the final consummation and achievement of the whole is summed up in one daring pregnant phrase of St. Augustine: *And there shall be one Christ loving Himself.* For "no one can love the Father unless he love the Son and he who loves the Son . . . loves also the members of the Son. And by loving he too becomes a member; through love he enters into the unity of the Body of Christ—*and there shall be one Christ loving Himself*—for when the members love one another, the body loves itself."[3]

This book is an attempt to outline that love story of God and man, which achieves its consummation in the unity of the whole Christ; and to show that the spiritual life is a partnership of love between God and man which can be summed up in one word: Christ. Instead of describing a *mere* union of companionship, we have attempted to use St. Paul's concept of an organic unity in one body—in one Christ. Because of the resemblance of the nucleus to the whole and to each constituent part, as implied in the illustration of crystal structure, such a treatment may, at times, seem to lead to confusion, even to contradiction. All the more so, as our main object is not to write a theological exposition of the doctrine of the Mystical Body, but to show how that doctrine can be used as a basis of the spiritual life, and to draw from it some ideals and principles that will serve to animate that life in the souls of ordinary Christians.

[2] John xvii, 22.
[3] St. Augustine, *Epist. ad Parthos.*, P.L. 35, 2055.

After the manner of St. Paul, we speak sometimes of Christ as an individual who is the Head, as distinct from the society of the individual members who form the Body; at other times, we speak of Christ as the whole Body composed of Head and members. We speak, too, of our being "in Christ" and also of Christ's being "in us." Yet a further difficulty arises when we consider the individual member already incorporated in Christ by baptism, in relation to Christ considered as an individual quite separate from him; for example, as He is in the Blessed Sacrament. Such confusion is inherent in any attempt to discuss and depict in two dimensions what is really a four-dimensional entity, defying as it does the limitations of space and time, and ranging from time to eternity and back again.

To avoid adding to this confusion we have reluctantly limited to one chapter the consideration of the part played by our Lady in the formation of the whole Christ in our spiritual life. She really has an important—one could almost say essential—part in every chapter. So much so, that we hope with God's grace to consider her part as the Mother of the whole Christ elsewhere at greater length. If for the moment we return to the illustration of the crystal growing in the mother liquor, we may notice that the substance to be added to the growing crystal must first be dissolved in the liquid surrounding the crystal. Here we have an illustration which, with limitations, can well be applied to our Lady. If Christ be the crystal, Mary is the mother liquor, at least insofar as all comes to us through her, and through her we all go to Christ. There is no more certain or more easy way of being united to Christ than by "dissolving" ourselves in Mary. But we must remember that all her power of "dissolving" us is due to her intimate union with Christ. Yet, the chemist who remembers the part played by the solvent in promoting chemical action and union between two substances, cannot help being reminded of Mary's part in the process of uniting men with God. And the illustration of "solution" is even more obviously applicable to our entering into union with God. For, *Behold, a virgin shall conceive, and bear a son, and his name shall be called Emmanuel—which being interpreted is 'God with us.'*[4]

To foster the development of that union with God in the lives of the faithful is the purpose of this book. Our aim is devotional rather than didactic. We believe that the proper foundation of devotion is dogma, and that the best way to lead Catholics to live their Catholic life in its fullness is to try to make clear to them what a Catholic really is, and what the plans and the principles underlying Christianity are. Believing that most of the evils of the day arise from the neglect of metaphysics in the world of thought and from the neglect of the interior life in the practice of religion, we try to show how the interior life is the logical sequence of the nature of the Christian, who, as someone has said, is composed of "a body, a soul, and the Holy Ghost."

Since, however, we are writing for everybody—for the layman as well as the priest and the religious—to the end that each may put into practice what we preach, we have no hesitation in sacrificing the unity of exposition and the logical development of the idea, in order to put some practical ideals before the reader: and we hope, by discussing the practices of the interior life, to indicate the practical possibility and the natural necessity of such a life for every Christian.

The book resembles, somewhat, the general sketch of a building under construction, whereon details of special features are given at certain points which, at times, obscure the main drawing. The sketch is not the complete plan, and the notes of details are not working drawings. Exact working drawings of the various features of the construction must be sought for elsewhere, and the scientific exposition of the theology of the Mystical Body and of the mystical life is already available from more competent pens.

On one point we would like to sound a warning note.

[4] Cf. Isaias vii, 14; Matt. i, 23.

There is today a school of psychology which is said to interpret all vital striving in terms of one unique urge, which those who betray its originators, by translating imperfectly-comprehended scientific terms into popular catchwords, assume to be that intense sense appetite which man shares with the brute animal and which is all that our materialistic philosophy can find to correspond to the concept of love. All else is interpreted by these second-hand dealers in popular psychology as a "sublimated" form of that lower instinct.

Apart from the possibility that this doctrine may itself be the fruit of a deep-seated neurosis originating in the racial and academic difficulties of its inventors, it would be fatal as well as foolish to read such an interpretation into the scheme of this book. It would be foolish; for in the first place, the love of man for God presupposes a new nature, a sharing of the divine nature, an elevation of the whole being of man to a new order by grace. This love further supposes what is almost a new faculty, or, to be more exact, the infusion of a supernatural virtue, by which the human will is enabled to perform a superhuman act. There can be no question of the "sublimation" of any natural appetite here. Further, even in the natural order, there is a sharp distinction between the two natural appetites of man; between his intellectual appetite, which is called the will, and his sense appetite, which is referred to above. The will is a voluntary and a free faculty; the sense appetite is automatic and is determined by its nature.

An error of this sort would be fatal, for it would blind one to the true significance of the mutual connection and the resemblance that can be traced in all the different works of nature. So far from being evolutions or sublimations from below, they are rather reflections and images from above, more or less faintly showing forth in prismatic fashion the wonders of the Creator who designed them all; and it is quite a lawful proceeding to use the natural order as a means of knowing and finding the higher good—which alone is fully real.

It would also be a grievous error to conceive the love of God as anything which essentially involves sense-emotion or feeling. The love of God lies in the grace-aided will; it presupposes the intellect insofar as the will needs its co-operation to love, for the will is a blind faculty; but in practice one need only attend to the will. A very high degree of love of God is quite compatible with an absence of any feeling of emotion, and even with the presence of a feeling of distaste for the service of God. We have only to remember our Lord's prayer in the Agony at Gethsemani to realize that. In fact, if one is going to achieve the heights of the spiritual life, it is necessary to pass through a stage where one's apparent spiritual activity is reduced to a dry act of willingness to conform one's self to God's Will, in the darkness of a sheer decision to *believe* in God without light of any sort. This does not mean that the emotions have not their part to play in the spiritual life. On the contrary, they can be a most effective aid to the real agent, which is the will working by faith.

There is, however, one conclusion that follows from our principles which seems to be in full agreement with the prescriptions of modern psychology. This science finds, as we do, that the source of much mental trouble and anguish lies in one's incomplete adaptation to reality. Our discussion, starting from the principle of our incorporation in Christ and our vocation to everlasting union with Him in heaven, leads to a practical program of humility, charity, and abandonment to the will of God. By humility, one accepts oneself with all one's deficiencies; by charity, one "adjusts" oneself to other members of society and lives for them as well as for oneself; by abandonment, one strives to fulfil one's allotted task, and to accept willingly all that Providence allows to happen in one's life. This is in full agreement with modern scientific conclusions; our view has the further advantage of giving a sanction to, and a perfect reason for, such a loving acceptance of reality, and of explaining it in its true context and purpose.

If, in the course of this book, the summit of divine love is proposed to everybody, it need occasion no surprise. Such a height must be reached either here or hereafter. There is no choice finally except heaven or hell. Heaven supposes perfect love of God which must either be reached in this life, or else, with far more suffering, in the next life through the fires of purgatory. The easier way is to be sanctified here and now.

Given that view, the fact that apparently we do not make extensive demands on the reader in the way of spiritual exercises may occasion further surprise. What we regard as essential is that the soul should put itself in daily contact with our Lord; and what we suggest in this book is an outline of the way to achieve that end and to make that daily contact a fruitful one. If that much is done, we feel that the rest can be safely left to the guidance of our Lord. In any case, abandonment to the divine will and complete humility form no small program. It should be noted that we use the word abandonment in an active as well as in a passive sense, to imply not only a generous acceptance of all that the divine will allows to happen to us, but also a prompt and generous performance of all that the divine will clearly asks of us. What we would emphasize is that it is the will of God which gives its value to what we do. For love is the conformity of our will to the will of God, and love eventually is all that matters.

In this book we have considered the importance of the interior life for the individual Christian. That it is also important for the Catholic body as a whole is just as certain. The only hope for civilization in its present crisis is that Catholics succeed in leavening society. Their success in doing so depends primarily not on their organization but on their interior life and personal love of God. Once Catholic Action puts the emphasis on the "Action," and forgets the real meaning of "Catholic"—which in its essence is the result of union with Christ—then the failure of Catholic Action has begun. And if we Catholics have not had the influence on society that our numbers and our harmony with the essential principles of Christian civilization should have produced, the reason is to be found in our lack of the interior life. All Catholicity—individual, social, secular, or regular—must begin and end in interior union with Christ. *For there is no other name under heaven given to men, whereby we must be saved.*[5]

Happily there is a short cut to that union with Christ for the individual and for society. For as Pius X. taught: *They are miserable and unfortunate who under the pretext of honoring Christ neglect Mary, for they do not know that the Child cannot be found except with His Mother.* And the same Holy Father quotes the text of the Apocalypse:

And a great sign appeared in heaven. A woman clothed with the sun and the moon under her feet and on her head a crown of twelve stars. And being with child, she cried travailing in birth and was in pain to be delivered.[6]

and applies it to our Lady, who, though blessed in heaven, is still laboring in a mysterious birth. *Whose birth?* asks the Holy Father:

Clearly ours, who are still detained in exile and have yet to be brought forth to the perfect charity of God and eternal happiness.[7]

The part played by our Lady in our sanctification is so important that it calls for a book itself. Here for the moment we have to be content to discuss the perfect love of God to which she brings us forth in Christ, but that reserve must not be taken to indicate any failure to appreciate her importance.

To her after her Son, is due any good in this book. That it is the result of the teaching and the example of those who live and have lived according to the Cistercian

[5] Acts iv, 12.   [6] Apoc. xii, 1, 2.
[7] Pius X, *Ad diem illum*, 1904.

Rule, does not lessen our indebtedness to her. To her, then, we offer it as an attempt to co-operate with her in her maternal work of bringing forth the whole Christ. *Nos cum prole pia benedicat Virgo Maria.*

December 8th, 1945.
Feast of the Immaculate Conception of
the Virgin Mary,

THE ABBEY OF MOUNT ST. JOSEPH,
ROSCREA.

Introduction

IT is beyond the power of any human mind to know or measure the depths of sorrow that filled the Heart of our Lord Jesus Christ. One thing, however, we do know: that His sorrows were begotten of love; of love for His Father so offended by the sins of men and of love for men so helpless in their sins. The pain of this love is so intense that even in the moment of His greatest earthly triumph when He rides in royal state into the city of Jerusalem amidst the acclamation of the people, His wounded heart bursts forth in tears, and His sacred lips utter that most tragic of all lamentations: *If thou hadst known, and that in this thy day, the things that are to thy peace: but now they are hidden from thy eyes;* and He goes on to foretell the destruction that was to come upon the city *because thou hast not known the time of thy visitation.*[8] His complaint is no new one. Twice we hear the utterance of this frustrated love that is breaking His Sacred Heart: *Jerusalem, Jerusalem, that killest the prophets, and stonest them that are sent to thee; how often would I have gathered thy children as the bird doth her brood under her wings, and thou wouldest not!*[9] And it is not His own loss that touches Him so much as the loss which those who reject Him would suffer: *Behold, your house shall be left to you desolate.*

These are but instances of a sorrow that ran through His whole life. It is the sorrow of a lover who knew that He, and He alone, could give real joy and happiness to

[8] Cf. Luke xix, 41–44.
[9] Luke xiii, 34 and Matt. xxiii, 37.

the heart of His beloved. It is the sorrow of a lover whose heart was on fire to give rather than to receive—whose ardent desire was that His beloved might have life and have it more abundantly. It is the sorrow of a lover who came down from heaven, and lived on earth and was to die in order that a share of His own divine joy might fill the heart of His beloved. He was the Way, the Truth and the Life. He knew that but one thing was necessary, and it was to give His beloved this one thing that He delivered Himself and emptied Himself, becoming *obedient unto death, even to the death of the cross.*[10]

Throughout the whole of His life and death, one can trace the desire to convince us of His love for us and of our need of Him. And one should remember that His intention is not merely directed to humanity in general. He loves us as individuals, and died for us as individuals. Each of us can truly say with St. Paul: *He loved me, and delivered Himself for me.*[11] If then our Lord thought it of such urgency for us to seek the kingdom of God which is within us, that He deliberately endured His terrible passion and death for each of us, we, on our part, must realize that for our own sake, as well as for His, it is of vital importance that we should endeavor to understand and to perform what He requires of us.

That is the purpose of these pages—to show what our Lord's plan for our happiness is and to indicate how we are to co-operate in its achievement. What is written in this book is addressed to every Christian, especially to those who have come to feel the limitations set by their own human self, and who feel the need of something more than their own unaided efforts can achieve. For this book is the story of a partnership—a partnership between God and the human soul, which begins at baptism—a partnership which should, by the joint action of both partners, lead to an ecstasy of perpetual union in heaven. To perform one's own share of the work, one must have knowledge. To live as a true Catholic one

[10] Phil. ii, 7, 8.
[11] Cf. Gal. ii, 20.

must have some idea of what a Catholic really is: to seek the kingdom of God, one must know something about it; to find Christ and live in union with Him, one must have the necessary knowledge, for knowledge must come before love. Knowledge, of course, is not enough; it must lead to action, to that action that is summed up in the two great commandments of love: the love of God for His own sake, and the love of our neighbor in God. But we are rational beings, and the service of God is a rational service. Too often do we find devotion based on mere sentiment and emotion, or on a foolish sort of faith that by defying reason approaches superstition. Moreover, God is supreme wisdom, and nowhere does His wisdom shine forth more remarkably than in His plan for our Redemption.

If then many pages of this book are given to an attempt to show the fundamental unity and connection of God's plan, it is because the effort to grasp the fundamental principles underlying His work is well worth while. Once one has caught a glimpse of the meaning of God's plan to restore all things in Christ, one has the key, not only to the whole history of the universe, but also to the history and destiny of one's own soul. All the details of the spiritual life fall into their proper perspective, and the quest of perfection is seen to be both possible and reasonable for every Christian.

But the plan is a complex one. It ramifies from time into eternity and from eternity into time. It involves both the natural and the supernatural, closely interwoven. It joins Eden to Calvary, and connects Calvary with each moment of time. It involves realities that have no parallel in the natural order. One can only speak of it in metaphors, and yet the reality signified is far more real than the symbols used for its signifying. It is, in truth, God's masterpiece. But our happiness here below and our eternal joy in heaven depend on it, and therefore, even if the plan be not an easy one to grasp, any trouble its comprehension may involve is well worth while.

The difficulty will be lessened if we note that this

plan of God is of a piece. It has a unity of purpose and a unity of pattern which give an order to all its variety. As we said in the Preface, it resembles a crystal. The pattern of the whole is found in each of its parts, and in fact the parts are only incorporated into the whole by being made conformable to the whole—who is Christ. For Christ is all and in all. The whole Christ—head and members—resembles Christ the Head. Each member is an image of the Head, for each Christian is another Christ. And the bond between the members is like the bond that unites the whole; so much so that St. Paul does not hestitate to compare the union of two single members in marriage to the union of the Head with the whole Body. In fact, there is something "sacramental" in all the units of the pattern, in the sense that each member, and each member's story, in some way and in some degree, resembles and reflects the Head and the story of the Head—and even the whole Christ and the story of the whole Christ. Each tiny chapter of the story re-echoes the end of the whole story so daringly summed up by St. Augustine: *And there shall be one Christ loving Himself*. For Christ saves us and sanctifies us by making us part of Himself, so that His story is our story also.

It is, in fact, a love story—the story of God's love for man, and therefore our own love story. But the happy ending of the story depends on ourselves, and we must make sure of our part in it. Journeys end, they say, in lovers' meetings; if so, life is, indeed, a journey, which ends not merely in the meeting of lovers, but in their eternal union. That eternal union which is the end of all, is modelled on the eternal union that is the beginning of all, and so to get a proper grasp of God's plan for us it is necessary to go back to the very beginning.

Contents

Et erit unus Christus seipsum amans.

St. Augustine

This Tremendous Lover

CHAPTER 1

The Beginning and the Fall

IN *the beginning*, St. John tells us, *was the Word, and the Word was with God, and the Word was God*.[1] All things began with God, who Himself has no beginning for He always *is*. Our life is limited in its extent and still more limited in its possession, for it comes to us bit by bit, in succession and not all at once. We have to let go of one moment to take hold of the next; it is like beads passing through devout hands. God's life is unlimited in any way; He possesses the whole of it all at once. He is the supreme and self-existent being, infinite in every respect, infinitely happy and completely sufficient for Himself.

We may not even think of Him as lonely, for in God there is a Trinity of Persons. In human knowledge one can distinguish a mind knowing, an object known, and an idea that represents in the mind the object known. There is, of course, a great difference between the idea and the object to which it corresponds. In divine knowledge we have the perfection of knowledge. God knows Himself, and His knowledge is so perfect that it corresponds exactly to the object known. The Idea, or the "Word" as St. John says, which God has of Himself is so perfect that it *is* God Himself, the Second Person of the Blessed Trinity. *And the Word was God*. There are not two Gods, but there are two Persons, the Knower and the Knowledge—the Father and the Son. And these two are one God. But in God there is Will as well as Intellect, and God loves according to His Knowledge. And the

[1] John i, 1.

mutual Love of the Father and the Son is so perfect, that that Love is also a Person—the Third Person of the Blessed Trinity, whom we call the Holy Ghost. And these three are one God.

Ordinary language fails us when we come to speak of the life and happiness of the divine Trinity, who share everything without dividing it. Each of the three is God, yet there is but one God. Their loving union is so intimate that They have but one nature, one existence, one life; everything except what pertains to their distinct personalities is common to each. In short, the life of God is an ecstatic union of knowledge and love—complete and infinite happiness. God has no need of anything more; His joy and happiness are such that nothing could increase them. Yet, in His infinite goodness, He decided to share them with somebody else. And so, out of the nothingness that was not God, He created us. It is true, that God could not without contradiction act for a motive less than Himself; being infinite Truth, He cannot deny His own supremacy. But, in planning all creation for His own glory, He decided to glorify Himself by making His creatures happy. And when His creatures revolted against His plan, He went further in beneficence and arranged to find His glory in His mercy. And that is a fundamental principle that must never be forgotten: *God made the world for His own glory; but He glorifies Himself in this life by His mercy.*

Of His creation of the angelic spirits and of the material universe, there is no need to treat at the moment. The angels were pure spirits, independent of matter, having the essential powers of knowing and loving, for these belong to all rational beings. The material universe was first created without life of any sort; then, came the lowest form of life which we call plant life, consisting of beings with the power of growth and of reproduction. The next addition was the animal creation, made up of beings which had the power of sensation and what is called sense-appetite, in addition to the powers found in plants. Finally God created man, as a single individual who was to be the head of the human race, and in him, God manifested His goodness in a special way.

The essence of human nature consists in two points, animality and rationality. Man thus is in a unique position in the universe for he shares in some way the natures of all creatures. His body is material like the rest of the universe; he feeds and grows as an individual, and multiplies as a race like the plants; he perceives with his senses and experiences sense desires like the brute animals: and he even has a share in the angels' nature, for he is a rational being, endowed with intellect and will. In a word, he can know and he can love; in this, he even resembles God. But this very complexity of his nature can lead to difficulty, for the animal nature in man has its own knowledge and desires, which may be opposed to, and even anticipate, the decisions of the higher intellectual nature which should rule his actions. And further, this complexity could mean that man's corporal life should come to an end; he is not by nature immortal.

It was in regard to these two points that God showed His goodness, for in the creation of Adam and his helpmate Eve to be the first parents of the human race, God was not satisfied merely with endowing them with the perfection of all that human nature called for, but He further added two gifts that were in no way due to it. The first was the privilege of immunity from death; the other was what is called the gift of integrity. To understand this latter gift, one must realize that, as an animal, man has the power of sense knowledge and can experience a desire of what is pleasing to his senses. He can desire food or pleasure; he can be moved to anger, in fact he is subject to all the animal passions. Now this sense life in man pursues its own good, which is by no means always identical with the real good indicated by man's rational faculties. And thus there can arise a conflict in man's own being; as St. Paul puts it: *the flesh lusteth against the spirit;*[2] and a difficult and painful effort may be necessary to assert the due supremacy of reason. Adam and Eve

[2] Gal. v, 17.

were given a special privilege called "integrity," by which their reason had complete control over their animal nature; they could not be carried away by sense desire to irrational action, nor could their judgment be blinded by passion. They had complete self-control and their nature worked with complete harmony in due subordination to their higher faculties.

But God's benignity was not satisfied even then. The whole of His work is replete with His mercy, and even in the formation of Adam and Eve, His generous goodness and magnificent mercy manifested themselves. Not content with making man share in all created nature, God deigned to raise him even to a participation in His own divine nature. It is true that this sharing in God's nature does not make man God; man does not share the divine nature as he shares, say, the animal nature; the change in him produced by this participation is accidental rather than substantial. But man was raised to a supernatural order, and given a life altogether above his natural end or natural powers; he was raised to the state of sanctifying grace.

One could write pages and still leave the meaning of grace a mystery; here we are merely summarizing. Let it be said, then, that love either finds equality or makes equality. For the proper love of friendship between two beings, some equality of nature is necessary. In order that man could be His friend and lover, God deigned to give him such a participation in the divine nature so that in some mysterious way, man has something corresponding to God's own power of knowing and loving God. In some extraordinary way man was destined to share—in a finite way, of course—in the life of the Blessed Trinity, and this sharing began even here on earth.

This was essentially a *super-natural* privilege—a privilege to which man's nature was in no way entitled—nor was there any reason in human nature which would call for it in any way. Adam and Eve were given a supernatural life; and all their faculties were endowed with new powers and qualities which would enable them to live this new life so much above their own nature as to be utterly impossible for their unaided natural powers. It was literally a superhuman state, calling for superhuman powers; is represented an elevation of man to an entirely new and superhuman order; and it meant that an entirely new and superhuman end or final happiness was set before him, which may be said to be a sharing in God's own happiness. Henceforth, natural happiness, even of the highest sort, could never suffice for him; he must eventually either be united to God and share His joy, or else remain forever in the hell of eternal loss.

The very nature of things laid certain obligations of worship and obedience upon man before God on whom he was so dependent. But God imposed a special precept on Adam and Eve, to remind them of their subjection to Him, and to enable them to honor Him; and He added the sanction of dire penalties if the precept were disobeyed. He had placed Adam and Eve in a garden of delights, where they had everything that made for complete happiness; but He had singled out one tree, and had commanded that they should not eat of its fruit: *For in what day soever thou shalt eat of it, thou shalt die the death.*[3] The story of the transgression of that order by Adam and Eve and their consequent expulsion from the garden are well known, but the tremendous issues that depended upon these events, the enormity of the offence, its motives and its consequences for us, are not so well understood. The first person who moved in the event was the devil, who, in the form of a serpent, spoke to Eve and urged her to defy God's command. Who was the devil?

To answer that question, one must recall that God had already created a number of rational beings called angels. They are pure spirits, existing in complete independence of matter, and persons of immense mental powers. They are far superior to man, belonging to a much higher order of being. Even the manner of their mental processes is quite different; for while we human

[3] Gen. ii, 17.

beings proceed step by step in the gradual process of reasoning, they see truth immediately—at a glance, as it were. The intellectual powers of even the lowest of the angels are far superior to the greatest human intelligence as such. It seems, that after their creation, the angels were given a choice of freely serving God and submitting to Him. One of the very greatest of them, Lucifer by name, with a host of followers, refused to submit. His attitude can be summed up in the classic phrase: *I will not serve.*[4] The result of this rebellion was that the rebel angels were condemned to hell, while those who obeyed God were confirmed in His friendship and entered into the permanent possession of the joy of heaven. It is not certain on what particular point the fallen angels rebelled. Some say that God showed them His plan of raising them to a participation in His own nature, which would involve the end of their primacy in their own order and a new dependence upon God. Others say that God's plans for the human race were shown to them, and that they rebelled against the proposal that they should be subject to the human natures of Christ and His Mother. Whatever the details were, their sin was one of pride and disobedience.

It would be wrong to imagine that the immediate condemnation of the rebellious angels, without any further time for reconsideration and repentance, is any reflection on God's mercy. The very excellence of the powers of the angelic mind is such, that reconsideration, as we understand it, is meaningless for them. They were in full possession of the facts of the case, completely undisturbed in their judgment by any earthly passions or by lack of reflection, and they saw their obligations and the heinousness of their crime with a clarity that is far beyond anything we can imagine. No amount of time for reconsideration would lead to a reversal of their decision. By their sin they lost the happiness of heaven and became subject to the unspeakable torments of hell. This involved the fearful pain of the loss of God, of the loss of all power

[4] Jer. ii, 20.

to love God or even to love anything else; and that was coupled with the clear knowledge that only in loving God could they find happiness, and that their own free act had made that love impossible forever. Their hatred for God and for all that belonged to Him, was then unspeakable; when they saw the beginning of His plan to create the human race and to raise its members to the exalted positions which they themselves had lost, their fury knew no bounds. From that moment, no effort would be spared by these mighty intelligences to destroy the human race.

And so their leader, whom we know as the devil, spoke to Eve under the form of a serpent, asking her why God had commanded that she and Adam should refrain from eating the fruit of one particular tree. To her explanation, he replied by denying that death would be the result of disobedience, and he stated that they would thereby become *as gods, knowing good and evil.* The exact meaning of this phrase is not easy to explain. It involves the idea of complete independence of God, and the power to determine what would be right and wrong for themselves. It was, in fact, an appeal to pride—that inordinate desire of one's own excellence. And it was as such that it was received.

All such colored and touching accounts as are given of Eve's weakness owing to the charm of the fruit, to her thirst on a sultry day, to her lack of consideration— are quite incorrect. Since Eve had the gift of integrity, there could be no question of any weakness caused by a rebellion of sense-appetite. On the contrary, she knew clearly—far more clearly than we can imagine—what such a transgression of God's law would mean for herself, for her husband, and for the whole human race of whom she was to be the mother. And yet, *She took of the fruit thereof, and did eat, and gave to her husband who did eat.*[5]

Not until Adam had sinned, were the awful consequences of the rebellion brought about, involving the

[5] Gen. iii, 6.

ruin of the temporal and eternal happiness of the whole human race. At first sight there seems to be no proportion between the sin and its consequences. The eating of an apple, and the ruin of the whole human race! So much so, that some are tempted to see in this story an allegory which covers a much greater sin, perhaps some sin of the flesh. Such a theory is quite unnecessary, for Adam and Eve were not only man and wife, but they also had the gift of integrity and no passion could mislead them. To find the real malice of their sin, we have to look into their minds and try to realize the enormity of their pride and disobedience.

For that was the sin of our first parents—pride and pride's offspring, disobedience. We must remember the perfection of Adam's nature. His mind was endowed with powers and with knowledge that have never been surpassed by any of his fallen children. Unclouded by passion, he saw life clearly; he understood thoroughly his dependence on God and his duties towards God. He knew quite well that God had raised him quite gratuitously to a special share in His own divine nature and had made him His friend. He knew further that he was to be the father of the human race, and he was endowed with the wisdom and knowledge necessary for the instruction of his offspring. He knew, too, that his sharing in God's life by grace was dependent on his obedience to God, and he clearly understood that if he lost that grace by the forbidden sin, it was lost not merely for himself, but for his children.

Knowing all that, he calmly and deliberately decided to rebel against God's express command; and by his pride and rebellion he rejected God's plan for the happiness of the whole human race. The first effects of that rebellion immediately became apparent, for the guilty pair immediately perceived the loss of their privilege of integrity. In the very moment when by rebellion they had asserted the independence of their human nature and rejected the subordination to God that was necessary for their sharing in the divine nature, their own animal nature was unleased from its complete subjection to their reason, and there began that unending rebellion of the flesh against the spirit, that is called concupiscence. More than that, the very chemical forces of the constituents of their body were allowed to rebel, inasmuch as the removal of the gift of immortality ensured the ultimate disintegration of the human organism in the decay of death. They were expelled from the garden of pleasure, and condemned to eat their bread "in the sweat of their faces," until, after a life of toil and labor, they should return by death to the earth from which they came.

The fact that Adam and Eve repented of their sin and were pardoned by God, did not save their children. Their offspring were born in a state of deprivation of the grace known as original sin and were subject to all the miseries attendant on the loss of God's friendship and subjection to the power of the devil. Their condition needs closer examination, for it is our own story we are considering.

CHAPTER 2

The Plan of Restoration

It was God's original plan that the new nature of grace given to Adam and Eve should have been transmitted to their offspring together with their human nature. Just as God creates each human soul and infuses it into the body formed by natural processes, so also He intended to give each soul the gifts of His grace. But the sin of Adam rejected that plan; and each child now comes into existence with nothing more than the human nature of his parents—a human nature lacking even those gifts of integrity and immunity from death, that were the privilege of Adam and Eve. But the lack of supernatural grace means that each child lacks the power to be God's friend; he cannot fulfil the function for which God intended him; he cannot rise above himself to love God in that supernatural way which God desires; he is, in fact, defective in God's sight. This state of deficiency is called original sin. It does not involve the notion of a personal fault—the only personal fault was that of Adam and Eve—but it does involve that want of due turning to God, which is essential in all sin. Personal sins involve a personal *act* of aversion from God; original sin arises from the act of Adam and Eve and leaves the human being in a *state* of aversion from God.

Man therefore became incapable of loving God and of reaching eternal happiness, which, in fact, was to have been the flowering and fulfilment of that love and friendship of God, that we call habitual grace. Man also became subject to concupiscence. His lower nature is no longer subject to reason. Desires spring up unbidden, and almost carry him away before he averts to their presence; passions draw him to evil and resist all control; the mind itself is clouded and blinded, and readily falls into error; the ordinary toil of life that had been man's pleasure is now his penance; even the agents of disease are no longer held in check, and pain is added to his miseries. To all that opposition which he meets from the powers of nature endangering his happiness, there is joined the still more dangerous subjection to the devil.

When one remembers the tremendous powers of mind and action that lie at the devil's disposal to wreak his immeasurable malice against the human race, one can see how pitiful was the plight of man. He had lost all power to achieve the supernatural happiness for which he had been destined. To escape eternal damnation he had to keep the law which was written in his heart. Considering his own weakness and his proneness to evil, as well as the enmity of the devil and his unrelenting efforts to drag men down to the same torments as he himself was suffering, one can see how well-nigh impossible it was for man to avoid adding his own personal sins to the sin of his first parents. Whatever chance may have been offered to the child who died before the use of reason, there was no hope for the man who reached adult age, unless God took pity upon him.

And God did take pity on him. For God, we repeat, made the world for His own glory, and His plan is to glorify Himself by His mercy. And mercy is the attitude of goodness confronted with misery. And indeed man's condition was truly miserable. It is idle to discuss here what God *could* have done to repair the situation. The human beings He had created and raised to a sharing of His own nature had rebelled against Him. The infinity of the Being offended gave a certain infinity to the offence. If God chose to exact condign, or strict, satisfaction, no work of man could satisfy Him, for God alone could render to God such due and full reparation. It is true that God might have condoned the offence; He could have restored to the children the privileges of grace lost by their parents without insisting on full satisfaction. But in fact, He did not do so. He decided to insist on full and adequate satisfaction being offered to His justice; but at the same time, He exercised His mercy by giving men a divine Redeemer who could save them from their sins.

Even before passing the sentence of exile and punishment on Adam and Eve, He promised salvation for them, in those mysterious words which He addressed to the devil: *I will put enmities between thee and the woman, and thy seed and her seed: she shall crush thy head, and thou shalt lie in wait for her heel.*[1] To what extent Adam understood the full meaning of the promise it is not easy to state; our understanding of it is helped by tradition and confirmed by the event, and we can see in it a foreshadowing of the way in which God had decided to restore the happiness of His creatures.

By their sin of pride and disobedience, Adam and Eve had deprived their children of that supernatural life that was to be the seed of their eternal happiness. God, in His infinite mercy, decided to give men a new Adam and a new Eve who by their humility and obedience would repair the spiritual ruin caused by the first man and woman, and who would thus become a new source of spiritual life for the human race. The new Adam was to be the Son of God Himself—made Man for us; the new Eve was to be the Virgin Mary. It was by Adam's sin that death had entered into the world, and it would be by merit of Christ that life should be restored to it. And just as Eve had played a real, though subordinate, part in the ruin of the human race (for if Adam had not sinned, original sin would not have been transmitted to his progeny), so also Mary was to play a real, though subordinate, part in its restoration; for although Mary is the Mediatrix of grace, which is our supernatural life, yet her part would avail nothing without the merits of her Son, upon whom all the restoration depended. In brief, all things had been ruined in Adam; it was God's plan to re-establish all things in Christ.

[1] Gen. iii, 15.

The working-out of that plan is a gradual process, involving the whole history of Christianity, and extending to every detail of the spiritual life of each individual soul. Before attempting to examine any of its parts, certain general principles, which are apparent even in its broadest outlines, should be noted, for they form a pattern which, crystal-like, is repeated in many of its details. There is first of all a very close parallel between the fall and the restoration, and it is for that reason that the last chapter was devoted to a discussion of the fall. There is an element in Adam's sin that repeats itself in all our sins; and there is a pattern in Adam's pardon that can be traced in our own. Particularly noteworthy is the way in which God deals with the results of sin, even when He pardons it. He does not take away all its consequences. On the contrary, He leaves them as they are; but He makes them a means of restoration and repair. He did not take away all the results of original sin. The loss of those great privileges, the unbridling of concupiscence, the reign of death and of disease, the weakness and ignorance of men and their liabilities to error and their tendencies to evil, the malice and machination of the devil against the human race—all which miseries Adam brought upon us—they still remain. It is true that a new spring of supernatural life has been given to us; a new means of making reparation for sin, a new source of light and strength, a redemption from the power of the devil, have been placed at our disposal. But the difficulties remain.

But these very difficulties are by God's mercy to be the very instruments of a still higher happiness. His original proposal was that we should be happy here below and, after a term of probation, should enter into an eternity of happiness with Him in heaven. This proposal for our happiness here below was rejected, but He has deigned to make the very miseries of our fallen state a means by which we can earn still greater happiness in heaven. In a word, while God's second proposal—if one may so speak—is more difficult for us, it can also be more profitable for us, for it contains more opportunities of exercising virtue, and is gives us a source of more ample strength for its exercise. *Where sin abounded, grace did more abound.*[2] The point will recur in the discussion of the effects of our own personal sins, and it will be examined in more detail. For the moment it is sufficient to draw attention to the pattern thus laid down, and to observe that the infinite Wisdom of God is such, that He would only permit His plan to be rejected if He foresaw that He would achieve a greater good by doing so.

Here one must remember the limitations of human thought and of human speech in the discussion of God and His actions. We can only speak of God in a human way, and represent Him as working after a human fashion. But is must be noted that there is no multiplicity in God's mind. He is one and essentially simple. He conceived the world and its history in one glance; in fact, in that one glance He saw all the possible worlds and all their possible histories. With the same simplicity of action, He decreed and permitted the existence of the present scheme of things, forseeing its whole history with every single detail of every individual life. He could have chosen otherwise; but for His own wise ends He chose this particular universe with its history. Not until it is all over can we expect to see the wisdom, infinite as it is, behind His design. But, if He permitted man's power of free choice to lead to evil, He did so because He saw that He could turn man's malice and mistakes to good purpose. One might say that He saw therein an opportunity for mercy.

Even though the infinite intelligence of God sums up everything in one idea, yet we have to represent the immensity of His mind by a multiplicity of thoughts, and His one decree as a long series of decrees. We speak of God's first plan, and of His second plan, and so on; and if we remember the limitations of human speech and powers of description, we shall not be misled. In fact, to get a fair idea of God's arrangements for the mis-

[2] Rom. v, 20.

deeds that every man's free-will produces, we can think of God as having an unlimited number of plans, each one of which comes into operation to provide for each sin according as it occurs in the course of time. It is only a human way of saying that God has provided for everything—literally everything. And so, in fact, He has; we must never forget that. He has even provided for our sins. But it is His provision of a remedy for original sin that must be first examined.

Only an infinite Being could make full satisfaction in the exact rigor of justice for the offence given to God by the sins of men. And so God's plan of mercy unfolded itself. God himself should come to save us. The Second Person of the Blessed Trinity, whom St. John called the Word, should assume a human nature as a first step to identifying Himself sufficiently with the human race to satisfy for its sins, and to give its members a share of the divine life. The mystery of the Incarnation was to be the beginning of God's redemption of His fallen creatures.

There was a special fitness in the fact that the redemption should be wrought by the Incarnation of the Second Person of the Blessed Trinity. The Second Person, as we have seen, is represented as the Word or Idea, by which God expresses His knowledge of Himself. Now all things that exist must first of all have existed in the mind of their Maker. In some way each creature reflects in a very limited way some aspect of the divine Being, or what, in ordinary speech, we should call some idea in the divine Mind. All these "ideas" are really only one Idea —the Word, the Second Person of the Blessed Trinity. And St. John says of this Second Person: *All things were made by Him; and without Him was made nothing that was made.* St. Thomas Aquinas says that just as the idea in a craftman's mind is the model of the thing he makes, so "The Word of God, which is His eternal concept, is the exemplar and model of every creature."[3] Now the Redemption is a new creation or one might say a recrea-

[3] *Summa,* iii, 3, 8.

tion, and it is, therefore, fitting that the Person in whom is found the original design for creation, should be the Person by whom the restoration of all creation should be effected.

Many centuries were to elapse before the momentous announcement would come to a village maiden in Nazareth, telling her that she was to be the mother of the promised Redeemer who was to be the Messias—or the *Christus: i.e.* the Anointed One—as He was known to the Jews by prophecy; but, even during those centuries, faith in Him who was to come was to be at the root of men's hope and salvation. Of those intervening years it is unnecessary to treat here. We are concerned with the Christian era, for that is the beginning of our own spiritual re-birth, and it is in that light we must examine it.

CHAPTER 3

The Redemption

THE story of our fall begins with the words of an angel—albeit himself a fallen one —to a virgin in Eden. The story of our resurrection begins with the words of an angel to a virgin in Nazareth. St. Luke tells us how the angel Gabriel stood before Mary—then a girl of some fifteen years—and saluted her: *Hail, full of grace, the Lord is with thee. Blessed art thou among women;*[1] and announced to her the part that God wished her to take in the Redemption. Mary was well acquainted with the prophecies concerning the Redeemer, and she knew well what a unique share in His sufferings was involved in the association with Him proposed to her by the angel. Her only question was how the virginal consecration she had already made of herself to God would be affected, and when the angel had informed her of the special miracle God intended to perform so that she might remain a virgin while becoming the Mother of the Redeemer, she gave the simple but profound answer: *Behold the handmaid of the Lord: be it done unto me according to thy word.*[2] And then, *the Word was made flesh and dwelt amongst us.*[3]

The parallel with the fall is very close. To the devil's *I will not serve*, is opposed Mary's *Behold the servant of the Lord*. The pride and disobedience of Eve are replaced by the humility and obedience of Mary. We shall return to this reply made by Mary, for it contains the secret of the whole spiritual life. It is, moreover, only a re-echo of what the Prophet David, and after him,

[1] Luke i, 28.   [2] Cf. Luke i, 38.   [3] Cf. John i, 14.

the Apostle St. Paul, tells us of the first sentiment of the Son of Mary on becoming man: *Sacrifice and oblation thou wouldst not: but a body thou hast fitted to me . . . then said I: Behold, I come to do thy will, O God.*[4] Here the parallel is even closer. The new Adam begins His earthly course with an act of humility and complete obedience, of which His life is but the fulfilling and consummation. In passing, let us draw attention to the words given by St. Paul: "*A body* thou hast fitted to me." The possible significance of this expression will become evident in the course of our discussion.

Of our Lord's birth, His flight into Egypt, His mysterious appearance at the Temple in Jerusalem and the eighteen subsequent years of hidden toil as a workman in Nazareth, there is no need to tell. St. Luke, under the inspiration of the Holy Ghost, is content to sum up this hidden period in the significant phrase: *And he went down with them and came to Nazareth, and was subject to them.*[5]

Here we must pause to examine the unfolding of God's plan. God Himself, with His infinite power, His infinite knowledge, and His infinite wisdom became man, and took upon Himself the sins of the whole human race. He became man to atone for the sins of mankind, to win for men the supernatural life which they had lost in Adam; to found His church by which that life was to be given to men, and to convert men by His life and doctrine so that they might receive His grace. His life on earth was planned by the divine Wisdom, even to the smallest detail. Its duration was known, and neither its development nor its end took Him by surprise. And yet during the first thirty years of the thirty-three allotted for the fulfilling of that mighty work, His whole plan of life, apart from that one mysterious visit to His Father's house in Jerusalem, is summed up by the inspired writer in the words: *He was subject to them.*

The significance of that description is incalculable. It means that the only important external feature of our

[4] Heb. x, 5–9.   [5] Luke ii, 51.

Lord's life during that period was His subjection to His Mother Mary, and to the carpenter, Joseph. His external life was that of a village workman, quite an ordinary life which as such left no mark on the world, at least, as one ordinarily understands it. Its real significance must await discussion, for it is best considered together with the value of our own actions; but the pattern is what we desire to emphasize here; namely, a life of humble submission to the Will of God, *made known by human authority*. Judged by our standards—especially by the standards of the present day—it was sheer waste. Such a judgment, however, rather condemns the standards on which it is based; for they are not merely inadequate— they are absolutely misleading.

At first sight, the next stage of our Lord's life—His public work—seems more in accordance with our ideas. For the next three years, we find Him preaching His gospel to the Jews, confirming it by miracles, and recruiting and forming a number of chosen followers among whom twelve take a prominent place. His fame spread throughout the whole country, He spoke as one having power and authority and His influence became so great, that the Pharisees and Scribes, fearing for their own position, began to plot against Him. But the Jews began to hope that He was the deliverer for whom they had waited so long. To understand their attitude we should remember that the tradition of a Redeemer to come had been confirmed and developed by a long line of prophets sent by God; but in the minds of an oppressed people, suffering under the foreign yoke of the Romans, it had taken on a more political color. Among the Jews in the time of our Lord, there was a widely spread hope of a redeemer who would come as a king to free Israel from its subjection and restore the ancient kingdom of the Jews. The religious and political aspects of this redemption could be found mingled in varying proportions in many minds. Despite our Lord's insistence upon the true nature of His kingdom, even His own chosen twelve apostles, who were so closely associated with Him, did not escape from the popular error. When our Lord began to speak of His own death as a criminal on the cross, consternation took hold of them, so much so, that Peter, who was to be the head of His followers, remonstrated with His Master and earned a sharp rebuke from the lips of Christ. The triumphal entry into Jerusalem on Palm Sunday seemed to lend color to the Jewish hopes of national deliverance; the people acclaimed Him as their king and gave Him a public reception of such enthusiasm that it only needed a definite sign from Him to start a general movement for national deliverance.

To us, it might seem that this was the opportune occasion to seize temporal power as a means to building up a spiritual empire. Such was not our Lord's plan, nor were these developments anything but an accidental result of His policy. All His work was directed quite differently. *The kingdom of God,* He preached, *is within you.*[6] In fact, when one remembers who our Lord really was, and what infinite power was at His disposal, the whole wonder of His public life is not the marvellous works He actually did, but the many and more wonderful works which He could have done and did not do. And one gets the impression that, throughout all this period, His chief desire was to press on to the final stage of His life—that the works of His public ministry formed but a small part of His plan, a part perfectly performed, but still something that He seemed to have far less at heart than the final stage,—*the baptism wherewith He was to be baptized,*[7]—and to which He hurries on, if one may say so, with the impatience of a lover.

Our standards cannot be adopted to measure this period, of which certain things are noteworthy. He wrote nothing with His pen; He shared the work of preaching with His disciples and eventually left the whole of that ministry to them; great as were the works which He performed, His disciples were to do still greater; the one pre-eminence He seemed determined to reserve for Himself was that of suffering. Looking at His work

[6] Luke xvii, 21.   [7] Cf. Luke xii, 50.

as it appeared on the day of His death, it seemed to have been a complete failure. The crowds who had acclaimed Him on the previous Sunday, are replaced on Friday by a mob who clamor for His death. The thousands who heard Him and saw His wonderful miracles, and who were helped by Him and healed by Him, seem to have disappeared. At His death on the cross we find only His Mother, one of the apostles, a few faithful women; and in a crowd, a few of His followers, whose eminence, perhaps, gave them courage to be present. He Himself is branded as an imposter, disgraced as a criminal, and put to a death that carries with it the stigma of the deepest degradation.

All this is part of a plan, but the plan is one which shatters our standards of value. On that very end of our Lord's life, which material standards condemn as a complete failure, the whole history of the human race hangs in eternal dependence. Since our Lord was God, since the Person who acted and suffered in the human nature of Christ, was divine, all His acts were of infinite value. Had God so willed, any single one of them, however small, would have been more than sufficient to satisfy for the sins of the world and to redeem all men. Yet God's love had decided otherwise. For His own wise reasons, to help men to understand the enormity of sin, to win their confidence and their love, and to show them His own immense love and desire for their happiness, God had decreed that the salvation of the world should be purchased by the Passion and Death of His Son.

The five sorrowful mysteries commemorated in the Rosary, contain a summary of those crowded hours from Thursday night until Friday afternoon: the Agony in the Garden, the Scourging at the Pillar, the Crowning with Thorns, the Carrying of the Cross, and the Crucifixion on Calvary. It was a short time as measured by movement of the sun; but if measured as moments of pain are really measured, by the intensity of agony, those few hours were longer than the whole duration of the world. For we cannot conceive what our Lord endured in those hours.

His body was designed for suffering, and the power of His divinity was used only to avoid the remedy that human weakness would otherwise have found, that of loss of consciousness, and even of life, through sheer pain. No human being ever suffered as our Lord suffered in that physical agony, and the physical agony was a mere drop in the ocean compared with the exquisite agony of His mind and heart. For the heart of the Crucified burned with a more intense love of God than the world has ever known, and the Son's heart was torn by the offences that men offer to His heavenly Father. And in that same heart there was a fire of love for men, of love for each man and for every man; and the Lover's heart was torn by the thought of the coldness of those whom He loved and the loss they were incurring by their refusal to love Him. On the previous Sunday we heard the lament that wrung tears from the eyes of God: *and thou wouldest not;* on the cross on Friday the same love wrings every drop of blood from that divine heart. Truly, we must call Him, "This Tremendous Lover."

And we must remember that His love for men is not merely a love for humanity in general. God is in love with each human individual, personally and particularly. It is essential to remember that fact. Each of us can rightly regard the whole of our Lord's heart and interest as centered on our own self, for our Lord would have undergone all His passion for any one of us, and each of us was present to His mind just as clearly and as significantly as if there were no one else to redeem. The heart of our Lord is the heart of a man who is God, and who has all God's infinity of knowledge and power and love. And yet it is a human heart with all the human heart's longing to love and be loved; and no lover has ever been treated and slighted as bitterly as has "This Tremendous Lover."

Thus the human race, which was lost at the tree in the Garden of Eden, was redeemed at the tree of the cross on Calvary. And just as Eve stood by the tree in Eden and played a cardinal part in our fall, so the new

Eve—Mary, the Mother of Christ—stood by the cross on Calvary, and played so important a part in our redemption, that theologians do not hesitate to call her the Co-Redemptrix. Of her sufferings also there is no measure. She was only a human creature, but the very grace that filled her soul gave her a capacity for suffering that we cannot understand. Only a mother can know the sufferings of a mother, only a lover can know a lover's anguish, and only the Mother of God herself can know the sufferings that racked the heart of Mary at the foot of the cross. She knew, as no one else could know, the horror of sin; she knew, as no one else could know, what agony men were causing the heart of her Son. She knew, as only the Mother of all men could know, what a loss men were inflicting on themselves. *Great as the sea is thy destruction, O Daughter of Sion.*[8] She is the Mother of Sorrows; more than that we cannot say.

As it was in this sorrowful Passion and Death that the redemption of men was achieved, the parallel to the fall in Eden becomes more and more evident. Pride and disobedience were the source of our ruin; our redemption was won by the humility and obedience of Christ. St. Paul sums all up when he writes of our Lord that He *emptied himself, taking the form of a servant. . . . he humbled himself, becoming obedient unto death, even to the death of the cross.*[9]

Historically, the next stage of the restoration commenced on the third day after the Crucifixion, when Christ rose from the dead glorious and immortal *for our justification* and became *a quickening spirit* to those who believe in Him.[10] This was the beginning of His triumph. Forty days afterwards, He ascended into heaven, having put the finishing touches to His work of founding the Church. In heaven He rules at the right-hand of God, and reigns as king of the universe for ever and ever. His work on earth was done—in one sense; and yet in another, it was only beginning.

[8] Cf. Lam. ii, 13.   [9] Phil. ii, 7–8.
[10] Cf. Rom. iv, 25, and I Cor. xv, 45.

Here we meet with that especial difficulty that besets all attempts even to outline the plan of our redemption, namely, the unique manner in which the interaction between the life of our Savior and our own life transcends not only space, but time also, defying even the external sequence of events. For example, our Lady was preserved from original sin and sanctified by the merits of Christ nearly fifty years before the Passion and Death that were the source of that preservation. Our Lord in Gethsemani and on the cross was stained with the shame of the sins that we commit today and even of those sins which those who come after us will commit until the end of time. In fact, the whole of God's plan for our sanctification consists in making us living partners in the life and death of Christ. That partnership demands an intricate succession of mutual interaction and co-operation, a relationship of mutual cause and effect repeated over and over again; and yet our Lord's part in the partnership on earth was completed nearly two thousand years ago, while our part has still to be performed.

The organization of the Church, the sacraments, the sacramental presence of Christ on our altars, and His glorious presence in heaven help us to some extent to overcome the difficulty of realizing that He still acts on us; but the part we played in the life and death of Christ remains a mystery that is not easy to penetrate. Yet our part is quite real. In the succeeding chapters we shall make some attempt to visualize the working of this partnership from different points of view; here we shall merely follow the historical sequence of events, while warning the reader that the connection between our Lord's life and our own is by no means limited by the time sequence.

Our Lord, having won for us as the new Adam the supernatural life that the old Adam had lost, made certain arrangements to transmit that new life to each of us. Direct action on each of us is of course always possible, and since sanctification is a supernatural work in the strictest sense of the term, God alone can be its principal

cause and agent. Yet in His mercy, He deigned to associate
His creatures with Him in His work so that they may
share His happiness. The most obvious part of His plan
for extending His benefits to all men is His Church. The
association of this word with a building in which acts
of worship are performed may distract us from its real
meaning, which is an organization, a congregation of
persons arranged in a hierarchy of authority, endowed
with certain powers, subject to Christ, and which transmits to each of its members the fruits of the Redemption.
St. Peter was its first visible head exercising his authority
as vice-gerent of Christ, and has been succeeded in an
endless succession by a long line of popes, each possessing
full authority in the name of Christ.

The twelve apostles were the first bishops, possessing certain privileges that were unique, and they are
succeeded by bishops who are placed by the Holy Ghost
to rule each diocese in union with the pope. They are
assisted by the Catholic priesthood in whom our Lord
has perpetuated His own priesthood. The lower orders
of the clergy are associated with them in their ministry.
Finally the Church includes all the faithful, who become
its members by the sacrament of baptism. They are
thereby made partakers of the life that Christ won for
them on Calvary; they are united to Him as the branches
are to the vine; and they are accordingly subject to the
laws regulating that supernatural life in their souls, made
by the lawful authority governing the Church. The
Church is unique among the societies known to men.
There are many other societies,—some natural, some
artificial, some covering a whole nation, some limited to
one family; there are societies of every type, and yet
the Church is different from them all. For the Church is
not merely an organization, it is a vital organism; it is,
in fact, the living Body of Christ.

With that expression we reach the heart of the whole
problem; and its explanation, or rather its discussion,
will occupy the many pages of this book. Let us here
notice two vital processes that are found in this society,

which will illustrate its unique character. The first of these is the sacramental system. This system centers around the great sacrament of the Blessed Eucharist, in which the Body and Blood of our Lord and Savior Jesus Christ are made the essential food of the life of the Christian soul, without which life he cannot have everlasting happiness. In the Blessed Sacrament there are really and truly present the Body, the Blood, the Soul and the Divinity of Christ. If this be the food of the soul, —what must be its life? Can it be anything less than God Himself, in some way living in the soul?

And so we find that in the sacrament of baptism, in which the soul receives its supernatural life, the Blessed Trinity come and take up their abode in the soul of the baptized, and enter into a vital union with that soul, in which the Holy Ghost plays such an intimate part that there is a true sense in which He may be said to be the soul of the soul. For He is the animating principle of its supernatural life, which He gives to the soul by grace. It is of course true that this does not involve what philosophers call a substantial union, such as is that of the human body and its soul, for that union produces one new substance. The technical term for the union of grace is "accidental union"; and while being made a partaker in the divine nature, the soul does not become God, nor does it in any way lose its individual personality or distinctness of substance.

Yet there is a real transformation produced in the soul, by which it becomes capable of actions completely above its human nature. As iron is plunged into fire and shares in the glowing heat and burning power of the fire even though it still remains iron, so the soul is plunged into God, and shares in a real and vital, withal limited, way in His nature. So real is the change, that the soul becomes truly a son of God. It becomes a son by adoption; but whereas human adoption merely confers legal rights and gives extrinsic assets without effecting any change in the nature of the adopted child, divine adoption actually confers a new nature upon us, and makes us children of God and heirs to His kingdom.

There is then in the sacramental system evidence of the extraordinary nature of the Church as a vital organism. The functions of her priesthood afford another illustration of it. The priest in saying Mass, takes bread into his hands, and speaking in the first person says: "This is *my* body." In virtue of these words the bread is changed into the Body of Christ. The same priest in the confessional, speaks to the penitent in the first person, saying: "*I* absolve thee from thy sins in the name of the Father and of the Son and of the Holy Ghost." And by virtue of those very words, all sins properly confessed with sorrow are forgiven. And if we remember our Lord's words we shall know that the forgiveness of sin is a work proper to God alone.

Here then is clear evidence of the living presence of Christ in His Church, and a manifestation of that vital union and intimate partnership that exists between Him and the members of what we have called His Body. One other example may be cited from the same sacramental system. Not only has our Lord perpetuated His real presence in the sacramental species of the altar, and His priesthood in the person of His ministers, but He has even found a means of perpetuating His sacrifice—that unique sacrifice of Calvary—in the sacramental sacrifice of the Mass. There is a mystery here, *the* "mystery of faith"; but we can say that the Catholic who assists at Mass, is as near to the sacrifice of our Lord on the cross, in all that concerns its supernatural essentials, as were those who stood at the foot of the cross, for the Mass is *the perfect sacrament of the Passion.*[11]

The second vital process referred to is still more mysterious. In St. John's Gospel, we read of our Lord's dying words to our Lady and to St. John as they stood at the foot of the cross. To Mary, He said: *Woman, behold thy son;* to St. John: *Behold thy mother.*[12] There is ample authority for the statement that St. John here stood for the whole of the redeemed.[13] Mary was then proclaimed the Mother of the living, the new Eve, who

[11] Cf. *Summa* ii, 73, 5, 2. [12] John xix, 26–27.
[13] Cf. Leo XIII, *Adiutricem populi.*

was to be the custodian and the dispensatrix of the life
that our Lord was pouring out for our Salvation. In some
real but mysterious way, Mary begets us in Christ and
Christ in us, and she plays such a vital part in the supernatural regeneration and growth of each one of us that
she is, in fact as well as in name, our Mother.

It is not without significance that she is mentioned in
the first announcement of our salvation in the Garden of
Eden, when God said He would place an enmity between
her seed and the seed of the devil. And the significance
is all the more deepened when we read in St. John's
prophetic work, that forms the last book of Holy Writ,
his vision of the great sign in heaven:

A woman clothed with the sun and the moon under her
feet and on her head a crown of twelve stars: And being
with child she cried travailing in birth and was in pain to
be delivered. . . . And the dragon stood before the woman
who was ready to be delivered: that when she should be
delivered, he might devour her son. . . . And the dragon was
angry against the woman: and went to make war with the
rest of her seed, who keep the commandments of God, and
have the testimony of Jesus Christ.[14]

That this vision describes the Church as well as our
Lady is clear; the very duality of its applications only
lends further reality to the extraordinary relation that
one glimpse between Mary and the Church. Both are
mothers, both are mothers of Christ. And in Mary the
Church finds its life—for she is the Mother of the Head
of the Church. Pope Pius X, applying the above text
from the Apocalypse to our Lady, asks whose birth is
in question. He replies: *Clearly* ours, *who, still detained*
in exile, have yet to be begotten in a life of perfect charity
of God and eternal happiness.[15] Can one then question
our right to regard the whole plan of redemption, which
St. Paul summed up in the phrase: *to re-establish all*
things in Christ, as the rebirth of the whole human race,
through the exercise of the maternity of Mary—who is
the Mother of the whole Christ?

[14] Apoc. xii, 1–17.   [15] *Ad diem illum* 1904.

CHAPTER 4

The Mystical Body of Christ

IN the previous chapters we have been drawing an outline of the fall of the human race, and of the work of its redemption as far as the Death and Resurrection of our Saviour and the foundation of His Church. Now we must examine, somewhat more closely, the connection between the different parts of this story, and in particular the connection by which we obtain pardon of our sins and become partakers in the merits of Christ. Once it is remembered that Christ is God, and that, although there were two distinct natures in Him, the divine and the human, yet there was but one Person who was God, and that all His human actions shared in the infinite dignity of the divine Person who performed them; then it becomes easy to understand that His Life and Death would offer to God a glory and a worship which would infinitely outweigh all or any insults or sins which the whole human race could ever commit against Him. And at first sight there is no great difficulty in seeing that God's anger could have been thus appeased so that He should be ready to restore men to His friendship. Yet a closer examination of the case reveals some difficulties.

The guilt of sin is a personal thing. One man can repair the injury done by another man; one man can use his own personal influence or credit with an offended party to induce him to overlook the offence offered him by another man; one man can pay another's debts; but how can one man take away another's guilt? How can one man actually render the offender pleasing in the eyes of the offended? How can one man actually merit in the name of another? Questions like these cause us to seek for some light on the "how" of the Redemption; that is; how is it that each of us is redeemed from our sins, made holy in the sight of God and made a partaker in Christ's merits by His Passion and Death?

Three suggestions which occur in this discussion may be cited.[1] The first would take the redemption in the literal sense of a ransom or a "buying back." This suggestion does find an application, but it must not be pressed too far, or else we would have God paying a price to the devil for our deliverance, which is unthinkable. The second suggestion is that of penal substitution. This again finds a true application in the scheme of the Redemption, but it, also, had its limitations. Pressed too far, it would lead to the notion of God persecuting God; and no matter how far it is pressed, it still leaves unsolved the difficulty of the transfer of merit and the vicarious removal of guilt. The third suggestion is the theory of satisfaction. The offence must be atoned for, and that calls for a divine agent to make due satisfaction; Christ does this super-abundantly since He is God and Man. But the theory presupposes that every sin must either be punished or have adequate atonement made for it. Now God could have forgiven and remitted sin even after inadequate satisfaction. And on this theory, the former difficulty of the transfer of personal merit and guilt remains; and there is the further difficulty that it seems, at least, fitting that satisfaction should be also in some way personal.

The solution of all these difficulties—and in fact, the foundation of the whole spiritual life—lies in some principle of solidarity between Christ and the sinner. When St. Thomas considers this difficulty just mentioned of the transfer of punishment and merit between Christ and the Christian, he solves it by saying that Christ could do all these things for us because He and we together form "one mystical person." There is, of course, no question of our forming one *physical* person, as we shall explain.

[1] Cf. Prat, *The Theology of St. Paul*, ii, 190, *et seq.*

To the question then: "How did Christ save us?" the answer is: "by making us part of Himself." And when we ask: "How are we to save ourselves?" the answer is: "by making ourselves part of Christ." Obviously such expressions need careful understanding. They could be understood in an heretical or in a pantheistic sense by taking them too literally; but they can also be interpreted in a metaphorical, or even sentimental sense that is utterly inadequate. Despite the difficulty which their proper interpretation presents, we must attempt to examine them and to reach some definite understanding of the unity that embraces both ourselves and our Redeemer, for that unity is the central point of this whole book.

We first meet a clear statement of this unity in our Lord's last address to His apostles. His words are a summing up of the whole Christian scheme of life and form a key to the understanding of all His doctrine. Speaking to His apostles at the Last Supper, bidding them farewell and preparing them for their fruitful work, He first recalls the unity existing between Himself and His Father; He then promises to send His followers another Paraclete, the Holy Ghost, who would abide with them and be in them. Significantly, He immediately reverts to the unity of men with Himself, and still stresses the unity of the Blessed Trinity:

I will not leave you orphans, I will come to you . . . you shall know, that I am in my Father, and you in me, and I in you.

Being asked how that would be, He explained:

If any one love me, he will keep my word, and my Father will love him, and we will come to him, and will make our abode with him.[2]

A little later He continues:

Abide in me, and I in you. As the branch cannot bear

[2] John xiv, 18–23.

fruit of itself, unless it abide in the vine, so neither can you unless you abide in me. I am the vine; you the branches: he that abideth in me, and I in him, the same beareth much fruit: for without me you can do nothing.[3]

Almost immediately after that He lays down the principle of unity among men:

This is my commandment that you love one another as I have loved you.[4]

Finally, in His concluding prayer to the Father He reveals the unity of what St. Augustine calls "the whole Christ":

For them do I sanctify myself, that they also may be sanctified in truth. And not for them only do I pray, but for them also who through their word shall believe in me; that they all may be one, as thou, Father, in me, and I in thee; that they also may be one in us. . . . And the glory which thou hast given to me, I have given to them; that they may be one, as we also are one: I in them, and thou in me; that they may be made perfect in one. . . . And I have made known thy name to them, and will make it known; that the love wherewith thou hast loved me, may be in them, and I in them.[5]

A life-time of prayerful meditation on these words, would not exhaust their meaning. Here we can do little more than refer the reader to the text of St. John's Gospel where these words occur in Chapters XIV to XVII, and beg him to read and re-read them, and to remember that they are our Lord's last words to His followers, spoken on that night before His death. Three points may be noted: firstly—that the unity of all the faithful is "in us," that is, in the Father and the Son; secondly—that the unity of the faithful is modelled on the unity of the Blessed Trinity, "as we also are one"; and thirdly— that our Lord sanctifies us by sanctifying Himself so

[3] John xv, 1–5.   [4] John xv, 12.   [5] John xvii, 19–26.

that, He being in us, we are "made perfect in *one*."

The next witness to this unity is the Apostle St. Paul. His conversion started with the famous vision on the road to Damascus, as he was going to persecute the Christians. *Saul, Saul,* exclaimed our Lord, *why persecutest thou me?—who said: Who art thou, Lord? And he: I am Jesus whom thou persecutest.*[6] This identification of the Redeemer with the redeemed seems to have taken possession of St. Paul's mind, for throughout his Epistles, there runs the ever-recurring theme which he sums up in the phrase: *"In Christ."*

In one place[7] he speaks of the process of regeneration as the grafting of a wild olive into a healthy stock. In another,[8] he compares the union of Christ and the Church to that of man and wife: *And they shall be two in one flesh.* But throughout all his writings he continually uses or assumes the figure of the union of a body with its living members. Christ is the Head, we are His members—the arms, the hands, the mouth, and even the heart of His Mystical Body. Texts such as the following could be multiplied. *For as the body is one and hath many members, and all the members of the body, whereas they are many, yet are one body; so also is Christ.*[9] . . . *Now you are the body of Christ.*[10] For our purpose here, it is best to try to see what was St. Paul's notion of this Mystical Body of Christ.

The human body is composed of many members, or organs, each of which has its own function yet shares the personal life and identity of the whole. If my mouth speaks, or my eyes see, or my hand strikes, it is *I* who speak or see or strike. The ancients ascribed many more functions to the head than modern knowledge would warrant. St. Paul is using the parallel as it was understood in his time, and thus when he speaks of Christ as the head of the body, he is ascribing to Him, not only the functions of government and all the superiority that belongs to the brain, but also many other functions that

[6] Acts ix, 4–5.   [7] Rom. xi, 24.   [8] Eph. v, 23–32.
[9] I Cor. xii, 12.   [10] Ibid., 27.

today are known to be performed by other organs, especially the heart; for as the body is supplied with its life-giving blood by the heart, so also Christ's Mystical Body derives its vital circulation from Him.

But a closer examination of the human organism will throw more light on this union of the Mystical Body. Speaking in everyday terms, and not in strict scientific fashion, we can say that the human body is built up of small units called cells; in fact, it originated in the union of two elements to form one cell, which grew and multiplied. There are living beings of a very low order which consist of single cells; but in the human body, the number of cells is enormous. Yet they form only one body. Why? The reason is because they are all animated by the same one principle of life, the human soul; and accordingly each cell lives, not for itself, but for the whole. These cells are united to form organs, and these organs, in turn, function not in their own interest, but in the interest of human being of whom they form part. Foreign matter, such as a leaden bullet, may be lodged in the human body, but it forms no part of it, because it does not take part in the vital processes. Sometimes it happens that cells rebel, as it were, and cease to be subordinate to the benefit of the whole organism, and we get a cancer, which may ultimately destroy the life of the whole body; but in a healthy body, all the cells are subordinated to the one principle of life. Even the chemical action of many materials in the human body is modified by their participation in the living being; once death occurs, they assert themselves, so to speak, and corruption sets in.

To what extent may this concept of a body be applied to the union of the faithful "in Christ"? As a first step to the finding of an answer to that question, let us note that the term "body" can be applied to such unions in various ways. For example, it is often applied to any group of persons who unite for some special purpose. Such unions are called "moral" bodies; their unity depends on the wills of the members who are animated by a common purpose, and one finds in such bodies various degrees of organization, involving the bonds of authority and inter-dependence as well as mutual rights and duties. Clubs, corporations, societies, religious communities; all such have a moral unity that causes them to be called a "body." Is, then, the unity of the Mystical Body of Christ such a unity?

If that question inquires whether the unity of the Mystical Body involves the will of its members and depends on it, the answer is most emphatically, "Yes"; and we shall see in our discussion of the spiritual life that our part in it involves that continual use of the will which is called love. But if the question would limit the unity of that body to such unity as is illustrated by these societies, the answer is best given in the words of our Holy Father, Pope Pius XII, in his encyclical on the Mystical Body of Christ.

> *Comparing now the Mystical Body with a moral body we must notice also between these a difference which is by no means slight, but, on the contrary, of the very highest importance. For, in a moral body, the only principle of unity is a common end, and a common aspiration of all to that end by means of social authority. But in the Mystical Body, there is an addition to this common aspiration, another internal principle, really existing and operative both in the whole structure and in each of its parts, and this principle is of such excellence that by itself it immeasurably transcends all bonds of unity by which any physical or moral body is knit together.*[11]

This principle of unity whose working we shall have to examine, is, as the Holy Father says, the Holy Ghost Himself, who, *numerically one and the same, fills and unifies the whole Church.* There is then something more than moral unity. But can one say that the unity of the Mystical Body is of the same nature as that of the cells of the human body uniting to form one single physical

[11] *Mystici Corporis.*

person? The Holy Father answers that question also in the following words:

> *Whereas in a physical body, the principle of unity forms the parts together in such a way that each of them lacks a subsistence of its own: on the contrary, in the Mystical Body the cohesive force, intimate though it is, unites the members one with another in such a way that each retains his own personality.*[12]

So therefore the Mystical Body is not one *physical person* involving the destruction of the individual personality of the members. The pope then points out a further difference:

> *In a living physical body, the sole final purpose for which each and every individual exists is the benefit of the whole organism, whereas any social structure of human beings has for its ultimate purpose, in the order of utilitarian finality, the good of each and every member, in as much as they are persons.*[13]

And the pope shows that the Church, the Mystical Body of Christ, exists for the good of the faithful, and to give glory to God and Jesus Christ whom He sent. Further, the pope condemns as erroneous the theory that *the Divine Redeemer and the members of the Church are united to form one physical person, and which consequently, while attributing divine properties to human beings, makes Christ our Lord subject to error and human frailty.* He also condemns the error of those who *would attribute the whole of the spiritual life of Christians and their advance towards virtue solely to the action of the Divine Spirit to the exclusion and neglect of the co-operation which we must provide.*

The pope, therefore, teaches that the unity of the Mystical Body of Christ is something far more than moral unity, but he rejects any idea of unity which would involve the negation of the personality of each member, and the consequent need for his personal co-operation

[12] Ibid.   [13] Ibid.

in the life of that Body. The Mystical Body of Christ, while being one mystical person, endowed with life coming from within, is not one physical person. There are two special unions which may help us to understand the unity of the Mystical Body, although its unity is not the same as either of them. In our Lord Himself, there are two natures united in one person. While we have a human nature, and a participation in the divine nature by grace, there is no question in our case of this hypostatic union, as it is called. The other union is the one which our Lord Himself cited as the model of the union between Himself and His members, namely, the unity of the Blessed Trinity. In God there are three persons, yet there is only one divine nature; so also in the Mystical Body of Christ, there are millions of persons, sharing in the divine nature, but each preserving his own human nature. But we must immediately mark the difference. In God, each of the Divine Persons *is* the Divine Nature and the Divine Substance; in the Body of Christ each of the members only shares in the divine nature in a limited way after the manner of an *accident*, not as a *substance*. Otherwise we would have pantheism. Yet despite that important difference there is a parallel.

To return now to St. Paul's doctrine of the Mystical Body of Christ; we see that it cannot be pressed so far as to exclude the individual physical personality of each member of any of its consequences. But as long as that limitation is kept in mind, we can use St. Paul's concept to throw much light on the unity of the whole Christ. In fact, it is that very opposition between the claims of personal independence and supernatural dependence that leads to the struggle which characterizes the spiritual life. For in the human organism, as we saw, the cells and the members and all the components are only completely part of the organism insofar as they are vivified and ruled by the vital principle which is the human soul. The individual parts have no "personality" of their own; they have no freedom of choice. In the Mystical Body of Christ, conditions are quite different. The Holy Ghost acts in that Body in a way which corresponds to the action of the soul in the human body (although He is *not* its substantial form). He vivifies and rules every healthy member of that Body insofar as that member is living the life of that Body. But each member retains the dominion over his own actions; he can choose in every action whether he will live the supernatural life of the Body of Christ, or live his own natural life; and his actions only belong to the supernatural organism insofar as they are in accordance with the rule of the Spirit of that organism, in other words, only insofar as they are in accordance with the will of God. Conformity, then, to the will of God, is the fundamental principle of vital union with the Body of Christ, and every act of obedience to God's will is an act of real communion with Christ. There is the secret of the whole Christian philosophy and history.

Let us be clear on the point. We are not at the moment discussing how one becomes a member of this Mystical Body; that, as we shall see, is effected by the sacrament of baptism. But we are examining what is the fundamental condition of healthy living membership. Each member retains his own personality, and the consequent dominion over his actions; he can live in every act either as a member of Christ or as a private independent individual. In fact one could even say that he can do both at the same time, at least to an imperfect degree, insofar as human actions can spring from very mixed motives. The man who, in any particular action, does the will of God for the love of God, is living in full vital union with Christ. The man who deliberately acts against the known will of God in a matter that binds under venial sin, definitely removes that action from the life of Christ, without severing the vital connection that joins him to the Head; or rather, it might be better to say that he prevents Christ from participation in that particular action, for he does not prevent his Redeemer from having to participate in paying the penalty for His member's sin. The man who deliberately acts so as to commit mortal sin, not only removes his action from the life of the Mystical Body, but he stops the vital circulation that joins him to that Body. It is true that he has still faith and hope, and unless he sins against faith he is still a member of that Body; but until charity is restored to his soul through contrition and the grace of God, he is a dead member, and like all dead members, is liable to decay, with all its consequences.

To sum up then what we have established: God's plan for our Redemption is to re-establish all things in Christ. Our Lord, by His Passion and Death, laid the foundations of a supernatural organism, of which all the faithful are members, united to Him in somewhat the same way as the members and head of the human body are united together, yet without any loss of individual personality or responsibility, such as the formation of a new physical person would involve. In this organism the Holy Ghost acts as a soul, and Christ as the Head; but because of the vital and mystical union between Christ and each member, the whole organism can be called Christ, as is evident from the writings of St. Paul and St. Augustine. Our salvation depends upon our membership of this body; and the fullness of our membership depends upon our doing the will of God; for as our Lord said: *Whosoever shall do the will of God, he is my brother, and my sister and mother.*[14] Is it any wonder then that the one counsel which Mary, the Mother of the Mystical Body of Christ, gave to men is: *Whatsoever He shall say to you, do ye;* or that our Lord Himself should say: *My meat is to do the will of him that sent me, that I may perfect his work.*[15]

There is then a vital unity embracing Christ and the faithful, which is unique in its nature. It is called mystical, not because it is not real—one might say, figuratively speaking, that it is the only reality in the world— but in order to distinguish its nature from all other corporate unities. But it has very real properties. To quote Prat:[16] "There are in this marvelous composite, first a real action of the head on each and all its mem-

[14] Mark iii, 35.   [15] John iv, 34.
[16] *The Theology of St. Paul,* ii, 285.

bers, then a reaction of its members upon one another through the communion of saints, and lastly, a real interpenetration of the Holy Spirit, who vivifies the entire body and forms in it the most perfect of bonds—charity. What distinguishes the mystical body essentially from the moral entities, incorrectly named 'bodies,' is that it is endowed with life and that its life comes from within."

The Mystical Body of Christ is thus a four-dimensional entity; it completely transcends space and time. The interaction of the head and members is not limited by separation of space or time, and—what is important to realize especially as far as time as well as space is concerned—this mutual action can take place in either direction, into the past as well as into the future. For example, Christ, as we have pointed out, suffered for our sins before we committed them; our Lady was redeemed before even the birth of the Redeemer, whose Death was the source of her Redemption. For let it be remembered that the "soul" of this Mystical Body is the Holy Ghost, who is outside all time; He *is* eternally. We exist in time; that is to say, we enjoy or possess our life bit by bit in a long series of "nows"; an eternal being possesses his life *"tota simul"*—altogether and all at once—his existence is one eternal "now." With such an eternal being giving life to the Mystical Body, it is evident that the limitations of time and space cannot be applied to it in the ordinary way.

At this point, we would suggest to the reader that a re-reading of St. Paul's Epistles with this concept of "Christ" in mind would not be fruitless; and if one goes to the Gospels realizing that our Lord often had this concept of the Mystical Body in His mind when He spoke of the Kingdom of God, or the Kingdom of Heaven, one will find much light on this mystery, and great comfort of heart in those sacred pages.

As an authoritative statement of doctrine, let us conclude this chapter by again quoting the Holy Father:

Christ is in us through His Holy Spirit, whom He im-

parts to us and through whom He acts within us so that any divine effect operated in our souls by the Holy Spirit must be said to be operated in us also by Christ. . . . It is due also to this communication of the Spirit of Christ that all gifts, virtues and miraculous powers which are found so eminently, most abundantly, and fontally in the head stream into all the members of the Church and in them are perfected daily according to the place of each in the Mystical Body of Jesus Christ, and that, consequently, the Church becomes as it were the fullness and the completion of the Redeemer, Christ in the Church being brought to a complete achievement, (or, as another translation has it, "attains a fullness in all things.") This, in brief, is the reason of St. Augustine's doctrine which we mentioned above: that Christ, the mystical head, and the Church, which like another Christ represents His person on earth, together constitute one new man joining heaven and earth, in the continuance of the saving work of the Cross; Christ, Head and Body, is the whole Christ.[17]

[17] *Mystici Corporis.*

CHAPTER 5

Partnership with Christ

MUCH more might be written that would throw helpful light on the nature of the Mystical Body of Christ, considered in its total aspect; but we must pass on to consider the mystery —for it is a mystery—from the point of view of the individual Catholic, since it is his spiritual life and partnership with Christ that is our main concern in this book. It is by baptism that one is made a member of this Mystical Body of Christ. The ancient ceremonies used in the administration of this sacrament, in which the neophyte was completely immersed in the water to come forth regenerated in a newness of life, have a very real significance. Our Lord Himself did not wait long in His public life before warning us: *Unless a man be born again of water and the Holy Ghost, he cannot enter into the kingdom of God.*[1] Baptism, then, is a rebirth, but it leaves the roots of the old life still within us, so that really it is only the beginning of a process of putting off the old man and putting on the new, which will only reach its normal and natural end with our death.

If we have lived properly—indeed, one might say, if we have died properly—throughout our life, we go straight to heaven after death. If not, then the work of our transformation and renewal must be completed in purgatory or else eternally regretted in hell as no longer possible. Its very impossibility then, in fact, *is* hell. St. John the Baptist sums up the whole process in a few words: *He must increase, I must decrease*[2] St. Paul

[1] John iii, 5.   [2] Cf. John iii, 30.

frequently speaks of "putting on Christ." In fact one cannot help noticing the almost excited eagerness of this inspired writer, carried away as he is by his vision of the magnificence of God's plan, searching for words and multiplying images in his endeavor to express some shred of the wonders of Christ. Uninspired pens may be pardoned if their efforts to express it lack clarity.

By this rebirth of baptism we are made living members of the Body of Christ, sharing in all its riches, in His merits and His sonship, so much so that an infant who dies immediately after Baptism enters heaven by the title of inheritance, not of personal merit, for he is a son of God and therefore heir to His kingdom. Being living members of Christ, it follows that Christ is in us, and also that the Holy Ghost is in us. As the Holy Father points out, St. Paul often says: *That Christ is in us and we are in Christ.* This double point of view might lead to confusion. However the confusion will disappear if we remember that God is a Spirit, and the presence of a spiritual being is not like corporeal presence. When a material body is present in a particular place, each part of it is in a part of that place, but the whole body is not completely present in each part of the place. Nor is the body present at that time in the same way in any other place. A spiritual being like the soul is, on the contrary, either completely present in a place or not there at all. The whole human soul is in the finger, and the whole human soul is in the eye; of course, it exercises different activities in each organ. The Holy Ghost is the soul of the Mystical Body, and is wholly present in each member. So also Christ is wholly present in each member.

Baptism then is the beginning of the soul's vital partnership with Christ and His Holy Spirit, who descend into the soul and take up in it their abode. They regenerate it and transform it and raise it up to a newness of life, and endow it with all the powers necessary for the performance of the actions involved in that vital partnership. To realize how extraordinary is this "new creature," the baptized soul, let us remember that our Lord insisted that its food must be His own

Flesh and Blood; and He warns the Christian that unless he eat of this Flesh and drink of this Blood, he shall not have life everlasting. In fact, the Blessed Sacrament of the Body and Blood of our Lord is the sacrament of union *par excellence,* to which baptism is only, as it were, the gateway. Let it then be clearly understood that Christ and His Spirit are not present in the soul inactively, merely as in a dwelling; Their desire is to share and to animate every single action of our lives. It is true that God, as our Creator, has the right to demand that every action be done for Him and according to His will; but even apart from that right, Christ, as our crucified Redeemer, has earned such a right by His Passion and Death. For we were partners in His crucifixion. And here we meet with a still more difficult mystery.

The writings of St. Paul leave us in no doubt that from the time of His Passion, there was a very close partnership between our Lord and ourselves. In passing, let it be remembered that it is perhaps more than a coincidence that it was only after the celebration of the First Holy Communion, at which our Lord entered into such an extraordinary union with His apostles, that He reminded them that this that is written of Him must yet be fulfilled in Him: *And with the wicked was he reckoned;* [3] and on His reaching the garden immediately afterwards, we are told *He began to fear and to be heavy,* saying *My soul is sorrowful even unto death.* [4] Then began that mysterious agony in which He seems to have felt in Himself the effect of His Father's horror for the sins of men, "with whom He was reckoned," culminating in that extraordinary anguish of dereliction on the cross, when He cried: *My God, my God, why hast thou forsaken me?* [5]

Before enlarging on this particular point, let us first quote the present Holy Father who writes:

By means of the beatific vision, which He enjoyed from the time He was received into the womb of the Mother of

[3] Luke xxii, 37.   [4] Mark xiv, 33–34.   [5] Mark xv, 34.

*God, He has forever and continuously had present to Him
all the members of His Mystical Body, and embraced them
all in His saving love. . . . In the manger, on the cross,
in the eternal glory of the Father, Christ sees and embraces
all the members of His Church, and He sees them far more
clearly and embraces them far more lovingly, than does a
mother the child of her bosom—far better than a man knows
and loves himself.*[6]

And God Himself says: *I have loved thee with an
everlasting love.*[7] And, as we have already pointed out,
our Lord's love is infinite, and, therefore, it is not
lessened by being shared, so that each of us can say with
St. Paul: *He loved me, and delivered himself for me.*[8]

If, then, you who now read this book, say that you
were in our Lord's thoughts, in His mind, in His heart,
throughout all His life—that your salvation was a motive
of all His actions —you say truth. Because our Lord
would have done it all for a single soul. In fact, you can
say that if it were necessary for your salvation, that He
would have suffered it all over and over again. It is,
however, not necessary, for He has done more than
enough to save the whole human race. And when
speaking of "saving," the word must be taken in its
broadest sense, for our Lord has, in fact, lived your life
for you. He has saved you, not merely from original
sin, but from each of your personal sins. He has saved
you not merely from your own mistakes, but also from
the mistakes of others. He has saved you not only from
your own wilfulness, but also from the malice of your
enemies; so that you can truly apply to yourself the words
of St. Paul *To them that love God, all things work
together unto good!*[9] and in doing so you must remember
St. Augustine's comment: "All things—yes—even your
sins!"[10]

One other point must be noted before considering the
special stage of this partnership which depends on the

[6] Loc. cit.   [7] Jer. xxxi, 3.
[8] Cf. Gal. ii, 20.   [9] Rom. viii, 28.
[10] Cf. Augustine: *De catech. rud.*, lib. 4, and *Summa* iii, 1, 2.

Passion and Death of Christ; namely, that peculiarity of the Mystical Body which we have called "four-dimensional." It is not subject to the limitations of time. Leaving aside for the moment the special aspect of the Passion, one can take the whole of Christ's life and put it, so to speak, alongside the life of any one Catholic, in such a way that the two are in perfect partnership and harmony. Not only is it true that there is a reciprocal association between each point of the soul's life and some point of Christ's life, but also each moment of the life of the soul is connected with *every* moment of the life of Christ, and each moment of the life of Christ is connected with *every* moment of the life of the soul. It is not our intention here to assert that this relationship is always of the same type; but what we do stress is that the time sequence of either life, and the time sequence intervening between the two lives, must be completely disregarded if one is to come at all near the proper notion of the connection between them.

Suppose we represent the two lives—that of Christ in Palestine in the first century, and that of the reader here and now—by two slips of paper or by two rulers. They can be laid side by side, and can be moved along each other, so that any point in one can be put opposite any chosen point in the other. So far the similitude is true of the two lives. But the reality goes further. Either life can be folded up—so to speak—or even condensed into a single point, and put opposite to, and in full union with, any point in the other. And this is what happens in Holy Communion. Our Lord, so to speak, "folds up" His whole life and death and sacrifice, into the Sacrament of the Eucharist, re-enacts His sacrifice sacramentally on the altar, and comes to us in Holy Communion with His whole self and all His riches as God and Man. Why? St. John Chrysostom gives us the answer. Because: "He wants to show us the ardent desire that He has for us. On which account, He pours Himself into us, intimately unites Himself to us, and mingles His Body with us, so that we may be *unum quid*—one thing, one entity—as a body joined to a head; for this is the very desire and longing of ardent lovers."[11]

The life of Christ in us begins at baptism. But something of our life in Christ seems to have begun at His Passion. There are two points in St. Paul's treatment of the subject that are full of a significance which calls for a more authentic exposition than is here possible. The first is his association of our baptism with the *death* of Christ. *Know you not,* he writes to the Romans, *that we who are baptized in Christ Jesus are baptized in his death?*[12] The second is that famous collection of unusual words which St. Paul either invented or adapted, in his efforts to show our union with Christ, and which cannot be translated into single words in English. The list would include: "To suffer with Jesus Christ; to be crucified with Him; to die with Him; to be buried with Him; to rise from the dead with Him; to live with Him; to be made alive with Him;" and many others: all of which are marked with the prefix *con* in Latin. He seems to be unable to find words that will give adequate expression to the closeness of our ineffable union with Christ and in Christ.

Prat's interpretation of this text[13] leads us to believe that there is a special mystical union with Christ, which "does not extend to the mortal life of Jesus; it originates only at the time of the Passion, when Jesus Christ inaugurates His redemptive work; but from that moment on, it is continuous and the *communicatio idiomatum* (that is, the sharing or pooling of merits and demerits, and the opening of what might be called a 'joint spiritual account') is henceforth complete." He further suggests: "That if we go back to the source of this union of identity, we see that is exists by right and potentially at the moment when the Saviour, acting in our name and for profit of guilty humanity, died for us, and causes us to die with Him, but it is realized, in fact and in deed, in

[11] St. John Chrysostom, *In John,* Hom. 46.
[12] Rom. vi, 3–7.
[13] Cf. Prat. loc. cit., ii, 257.

every one of us, when faith and baptism graft us upon the dying Christ and make us participate in His death." And the Holy Father Pius XII states that: *It was by His death that our Saviour became, in the full and complete sense of the word, the Head of the Church.*

To discuss in what sense we were sharers and partakers with Christ at that moment would be a difficult task and would only end in uncertainty. But what we have already said above about the time-defying nature of this union, is sufficient to make it clear that we can regard our actions at any moment as performed in partnership with Christ on the cross. In fact, the life of our Lord, and in particular His Passion and Death, may be regarded —if the comparison be not irreverent—after the manner of an incompleted motion picture, which has to be re-taken to allow some character to play his part in the different scenes. There is, for example, some such technique in use to allow one actor to play two parts. Our part in Christ's life and death is being played *now;* the re-running of the film starts with our baptism and ends with our death, and we have to fit in our actions in the place left vacant for us in the original taking of the film and to make our part harmonize with Christ's when He lived His part. Any thing we do that is out of its proper place or out of harmony with His plan is useless and harmful.

But that does not mean that our Lord does not adapt His work in the partnership to our needs and limitations. He is *our Saviour;* that is something that must never be forgotten. And it is as *our Saviour* that He enters into partnership with us. In fact, it is by that very partnership that He saves us. He comes to us full of perfect knowledge and unlimited love. He knows exactly what we are, and He knows exactly what our life will be. He knows all our defects and weaknesses, those that are natural to us, those that are the result of circumstances and those that are the result of our own sins. He knows all that has happened or will happen to us. He knows all that might have been done for us or by us, but which has been neglected. He knows all our mistakes and all our sins; He knows all our misfortunes and all our miseries. He knows all these things in advance, but being the perfect lover, He comes with the power of God to heal all these ills. He is perfectly prepared to repair our life completely if we do not prevent Him. *And God is able to make all grace abound in you; that ye always, having all sufficiency in all things, may abound to every good work.*[14] *Our sufficiency is from God.*[15] He is our perfect supplement.

Just as the two torn pieces of a sheet of paper fit perfectly together, so Christ fits perfectly into our life, and fills it completely. It does not matter how small is the part of the page which represents our life—or if you prefer it, our lack of life—He can and will supply all the rest of the page. He is our full complement; He is our perfect supplement. And that is true, not only of His coming in baptism, but also of His help at any time of our life, most especially in Holy Communion. In one Holy Communion we can receive the perfect complement of all our wasted past and our damaged self. *Of His fulness we have all received,* says St. John.[16] Our Lord Himself tells us: *I am come that they may have life and have it more abundantly.*[17] And St. Paul, filled with this vision of the Body of Christ, writes to the Corinthians giving thanks *for the grace that is given you in Christ Jesus, that in all things you are made rich in him . . . that nothing is wanting to you in any grace.*[18]

It is of capital importance that we should be convinced not only of the completeness of God's work for our salvation, but also of His readiness to bestow its superabundant fruits on us at any time we approach Him with suitable dispositions. There is no moment in our life in which we cannot turn to Him and find in Him not only the perfect complement of our self, no matter how much we have lost, but also the perfect restoration of all our past. For He is God, and He is our Saviour.

[14] II Cor. ix, 8. [15] II Cor. iii, 5. [16] John i, 16.
[17] Cf. John x, 10. [18] Cf. I Cor. i, 4–7.

In the beginning of the partnership at baptism, when Christ and His Holy Spirit come into our souls, the fundamental effect is the infusion of sanctifying or habitual grace. The best way, perhaps, to regard grace is as a new nature—a participation in the divine nature —which is superimposed upon our old nature. A "nature" is a principle of operation, and by this new nature, the soul becomes capable of living in a higher order and of becoming the agent of acts which are completely beyond its natural possibilities. If a plant were given a true power of sensation, or an animal a true power of reason, we would have some example of the radical transformation that is produced in the soul by grace, but still the example would be quite inadequate. Only God would have thought of such a gift as supernatural grace, and only the love of God would have given it.

Of course, for action in this new and higher sphere, something more than grace is required. And so, we are given also the infused theological virtues of faith, hope, and charity which are called theological because they deal directly with God; the infused moral virtues, which depend on prudence, justice, temperance and fortitude; and the seven gifts of the Holy Ghost. Grace, however, is the fundamental thing. What must be stressed here in connection with our partnership with Christ is that grace does *not* destroy human nature, nor does it remove all the consequences of original sin.

This point is of capital importance for a correct understanding of the spiritual life. At baptism, God restores to us, through the merits of Christ, the supernatural life that we lost through the sin of Adam; but He does not take away the weaknesses, especially that of concupiscence, which remain as a result of Adam's fall. What God actually does is to give us the means to fight against those weaknesses, and He also enables us to gain merit by doing so; but the fight depends on the use of our own free will for its continuation; God will not force our free will.

The use of this free will is, then, beset with all the

difficulties that arise out of the insubordination of our passions. We must, first of all, by continued efforts, subject our reason and our will to God, and our pride resents that subjection. We then have to subject the desires of our animal and emotional nature to our reason and our will. The concupiscence which is left in us makes that a difficult task. St. John sums up the forces opposing our proper way of life under three heads: *the concupiscence of the flesh, the concupiscence of the eyes, and the pride of life.*[19] St. Paul laments the continual rebellion that he experiences in his own body: *For I am delighted with the law of God according to the inward man, but I see another law in my members, fighting against the law of my mind, and captivating me in the law of sin that is in my members. Unhappy man that I am, who shall deliver me from the body of this death? The grace of God, by Jesus Christ, our Lord.*[20]

This deliverance by grace demands our co-operation. If, therefore, baptism is considered as a death, it is a death to one's self that only takes place gradually; the sentence of death is passed at baptism—for there we renounce the world, the flesh and the devil—but the carrying-out of that sentence is the work of a lifetime, and will end only in our grave. It is this need for dying to oneself that leads to the asceticism of the spiritual life. But if baptism is a death, it is also a resurrection. St. Paul writes to the Romans: *For we are buried together with him by baptism into death; that as Christ is risen from the dead by the glory of the Father, so also we may walk in newness of life. . . . So do you also reckon, that you are dead to sin, but alive unto God, in Christ Jesus.*[21] And he tells the Galatians: *And I live, now not I, but Christ liveth in me. And that I live now in the flesh, I live in the faith of the Son of God, who loved me, and delivered himself for me.*[22]

We may then think of Christ dying on the cross, and rising from the dead, to live again in us; for every single Christian, unless he reject Christ by mortal sin, can

[19] Cf. I John ii, 16. [20] Rom. vii, 22–25.
[21] Rom. vi, 4, 11. [22] Gal. ii, 20.

make St. Paul's words his own. But this particular resurrection that takes place in us—let us call it the mutual resurrection of Christ and our new self—is also a gradual process, which will not end until we are one with Him in heaven. The old self in us struggles hard against its death, and in every single action we are confronted with the choice: who shall live in this particular moment in me—myself or Christ? The self asserts its claim, but the choice rests with our free will, even though the grace of God comes to our aid. We can decide; we have the awful power of saying "No" to God, of denying Him life in us. It is true that we depend on His grace for the power to do good; but grace does not take away our freedom, nor can we thus escape responsibility for a refusal. The two lives are present in us; that of Christ which He wants to make ours, and that of the old Adam, our own independent self. In every single deliberate action we have to choose between them.

It might seem, then, that God's redeeming work is imperfect inasmuch as it still leaves in us many of the effects of original sin. But this very fact only shows the completeness of God's plan, and the extent of His merciful love and good-will towards us. God's plans are never incomplete; they provide for everything. But it is of great importance to notice *how* God has provided for the effects of original sin, since it reveals a pattern that is repeated many times in God's dealings with men, particularly when He forgives them their personal sins.

In forgiving sin, God reconciles the sinner to His friendship, removes the guilt and takes away any eternal punishment due to the sin. But there is also a temporal punishment, which is not always completely remitted unless one's sorrow and love are sufficiently intense. And there are a number of other consequences of sin; bad habits for example, embarrassment, losses of various kinds, and many others which vary according to the circumstances. These God does not remove, at least in connection with His pardon of the sin. But He does something else instead. As we have already said in regard to original sin, He attaches merit to the work of penance and of

overcoming the difficulties that arise out of our sins, and
to the patient bearing of their consequences; and He
also offers us His grace—that is, a share in His own
strength—for our task. The result is that we are put in
a position where we can more than compensate for what
we have lost by sin. *Where sin abounded, grace did
more abound.*[23]

The point will be discussed again in reference to
the details of our spiritual life; but let us anticipate by
saying that when God forgives sin, He does it in a manner worthy of God. He is always ready to give the
repentant sinner all the help that is necessary to atone
for his sin; but He will go further, He even offers him
an opportunity of recovering more than he lost, and of
supplying for all that he might have been or might have
done. That does not mean that the second chance, so
to speak, may not be more difficult; but its very difficulty
is a means of the exercise of God's mercy. In fact this
opportunity to share in the work of one's own restoration
is but the result of the delicate tact that characterises
our divine Lover. To St. Peter, who denied Him thrice,
He offers a threefold opportunity for the public profession
of his love. To every repentant sinner He likewise offers
an opportunity for acts of love that will supply for the
failures of the past. But even that very love by which
we are animated in carrying out our share of the partnership and in availing of the opportunities with which God
provides us to make up for past failures—that very love
is itself the gift of God. For the charity with which we
love God is poured into our hearts by the Holy Ghost;
He Himself is the subsisting Love of the Father and
the Son, and it is, as it were, the glow of His presence
and the echo of that Love that we make our own and
offer to God.

Truly indeed is God the perfect partner; the tremendous lover. And the more we understand His attitude
to us in our soul—the more do we cry out with St. Paul:
*Gladly therefore will I glory in my infirmities, that the
power of Christ may dwell in me.*[24]

---

[23] Rom. v, 20.   [24] II Cor. xii, 9.

CHAPTER 6

Membership of Christ

THE partnership with God of which we have been treating can be regarded from two points of view; we can look at it as personal union with God living in the soul; or we can regard it as the grafting or the incorporation of the soul into the Mystical Body of Christ. Let us return now to this second point of view, and examine the individual Christian's membership of this Body, and we see that three things which characterize a healthy member of the human body find their counterpart also in the membership of Christ. To be a true member of the human body, the organ or constituent in question must be animated by the life of the organism; it must be subject to its vivifying principle; and it must exercise its activity, not merely for its own benefit, but for the benefit of the whole organism and its other members. A leaden bullet in a human body is not a member, for it is not animated by the soul, nor does it act for the benefit of the surrounding tissue and organs. Certain growths in the human body, which in popular parlance may be called cancer, live indeed, but they live for themselves and are not properly subject to the vital principle of the organism; in fact they are a menace to the life of the body.

So it is in the Mystical Body of Christ. To be a living member the Christian must be in the state of grace—he must be vivified by the Holy Spirit who is the soul of that body; he must be subject to that vivifying Spirit, which means that he must love God and do His will; and He must act for the good of his fellow members, which means he must love his neighbor. Examine for a moment the dialogue in St. Luke's Gospel [1] where the lawyer asks our Lord: *Master, what must I do to possess eternal life?* Our Lord replied by asking him to quote the law, and received the answer: *Thou shalt love the Lord thy God, with thy whole heart, and with thy whole soul, and with all thy strength and with all thy mind; and thy neighbor as thyself.* Our Lord approved of the answer saying; *Thou hast answered right; this do and thou shalt live.* Could there be any more explicit declaration of the law of the life and membership of the Mystical Body of Christ?

Love of God, therefore, is the essential principle of the spiritual life; without it everything else is useless. But man is a rational being; one cannot love the unknown. So knowledge must precede love. And if that love is going to mean a complete abandonment of one's own self, a losing of one's own life, to find a new self, a new life—to find one's all, in fact, in membership of Christ, it is still more urgent to have a sure and certain knowledge of Christ and His love. But in this world, the only way one can know God supernaturally is by faith. Reason can give us a certain, but natural, knowledge of His existence and of some of His attributes; but faith alone can tell us of the wonders of His love and His plans for us. Faith alone can put us in vital contact with Him, for when we believe in God, we share His knowledge, we lean on Him, and draw our strength from Him.

But we must be clear about the sense in which we use the words "faith" and "believing," for there is much misunderstanding, and one finds many wrong notions of their true nature. The verb *to believe* is frequently used in ordinary speech to indicate an opinion, a conjecture, and implies uncertainty; in religious discussions, it sometimes refers to a form of forcing one's own assent without proper foundation, in a way that almost amounts to a sort of self-hypnotism. Both of these notions are

[1] Luke x, 25–28.

quite wrong, if applied to Catholic faith. There is nothing uncertain and there is nothing unreasonable about Catholic faith. The proper meaning of belief is to accept truth on the testimony of another. Since in ordinary cases, our informant may be in error or may mislead us, there may be room for uncertainty. But in supernatural faith, we accept truth on the testimony of God Himself, so that it leads to absolute certainty. There is no doubt about it, even though there may be difficulty. The point about faith is this; that when one *sees* truth, one accepts it because of its intrinsic evidence which compels the intellect; but when one *believes* truth, that intrinsic evidence is lacking, so that the intellect is free to refuse its assent, and an act of the will is necessary to elicit it. But in the present circumstances, this action is not unreasonable.

The Church insists that reason authorizes faith, and so far from asking us to deny our reason, She teaches that faith insists on being founded on reason. Once, however, the reasonableness of believing our authority is established, that authority may ask us to go *beyond* our reason, but never to go against it. We may not see *how* there are Three Persons in One God, but we cannot deny that it is reasonable to accept God's word *that* there are. "Faith," as Prat points out, "is not a pure intuition, a mystical tendency towards an object more suspected than known; it presupposes preaching; it is the yielding of the mind to divine testimony. Faith is opposed to sight, both as regards the object known and the manner of knowing; one is immediate and intuitive, the other takes place through an intermediate agent. Nevertheless, faith is not blind: it is ready to give a reason for itself and aspires always to more clearness." [2] All this, of course, is not to deny that, in the order of time, many born in the Catholic religion first believe; and it is only on enquiry afterwards that the rational basis of the act of faith is found.

In the Scriptures, faith is not often used in the

[2] Prat, loc. cit., ii, 236.

isolated sense of a mere intellectual assent to truth; "there is nearly always added to it a sentiment of security, confidence, abandonment, obedience, and filial love; the adhesion of the mind produces a thrill of the heart." [3] In St. Paul's writings some such complex meaning of the word is common; in particular when he uses the phrase to believe *in* God, it means not only to "believe in His existence, but, variously, to rest upon Him as on an immovable support, to take refuge in Him, as in a sure place of shelter, to tend towards Him, as to one's supreme end." [4] This usage is only a reflection of the fact that a living faith always tends to action of some sort. For our purpose, therefore, it can be better examined in connection with its manifestations. Here we shall insist merely upon its supernatural character, which, therefore, presupposes some supernatural power in the soul. This is the infused theological virtue of faith, which is the foundation of the whole of the spiritual life and which is given to us in baptism.

One might perhaps liken the Christian soul to a pilot "flying blind," taking his course and all orders by wireless. He must be equipped with a properly tuned receiving set, and must have faith in the existence and in the instructions of his mentors. The Christian soul is in a similar position. He needs a supernatural equipment to receive and follow the directions of God with certainty and confidence. His need is far greater than that of the pilot, for the Christian has even to believe in the existence of the airplane in which he is travelling! As St. Paul says: *Faith is substance of things to be hoped for, the evidence of things that appear not.* [5]

The supernatural virtue of hope is also given to us with that of faith, in baptism. Here again one meets many wrong notions of the true meaning of the word in its religious significance. The classical significance—as "an expectation, more or less vain or well-founded, of an event fortunate or unfortunate"—does not apply to Christian hope. "There is nothing vain or uncertain about hope in God, because our hope like our faith is based on God's goodness and God's omnipotence.[6] In referring to the testimony that the Holy Ghost gives of our sonship resulting from our incorporation in Christ, and our consequent right of inheritance, St. Paul tells us: *We are saved by hope; but hope that is seen is not hope.*[7] It is true that we do not yet possess or even see the joy and glory that await us in heaven. But we have a right to them, and no one can disinherit us without our consent.

The point is so important that it is worth examining the theology of hope. Hope is a theological virtue; its object is God. We hope for God—for possession of Him, and for the means to obtain it. We also hope in God, because it is upon His infinite power that we rely to bring us to Himself, and because it is upon His goodness and mercy that we count to move Him to do so, and not upon our own merits. Let us quote the theologian Billuart, commenting on St. Thomas.[8] He is discussing "the motive and reason why we hope or expect with certain confidence eternal happiness and the means to attain it." He proceeds: "That motive is the help of the divine omnipotence. For we cannot hope with a sure confidence for happiness except from Him whom we know to be able and to be willing to give it; but God as omnipotent, can give it, and as 'helping'—that is, as offering us help—is willing to give it." And he continues: "The ultimate analysis of our hope goes back to the divine omnipotence: for, to one who asks why do you hope for beatitude, the adequate answer is because God can and will give it, just as to one who asks why do you believe in the Unity and Trinity of God, the adequate answer is because God who is true, has revealed it."

St. Thomas sums up the theology of Christian hope in his usual laconic style. "Hope," he says, "reaches out to God, relying upon His help to acquire the good hoped for." And he points out that we hope for the

[6] Cf. Prat, loc. cit., ii, 333.   [7] Rom. viii, 24.
[8] Billuart, *De Spe*, i, ad 2.

infinite good which is God Himself, and that we rely on the infinite power— which alone is capable of leading to infinite good, and this power is God Himself.[9] When he comes to the question of the certitude which attaches to our hope while in this life, he considers the objection that hope comes through grace and merits, and we cannot be certain of these in this life. His answer is illuminating. "Hope," he writes, "is not based upon grace already possessed, but upon the divine omnipotence and mercy, by which even he who has not got grace, can obtain it that so he may reach eternal life. Anyone who believes in God can be certain of the omnipotence of God and of His mercy."[10]

The ultimate authority on earth is the infallible Church, and her teaching may be found in the definitions of the Council of Trent, where we read: *All should place a most firm hope in the help of God. For just as God has begun the good work, so He will perfect it, working in men both to will and to accomplish, unless they fail to co-operate with His grace.*[11] Even those who are not in the state of grace need not lose their hope, for the Council condemns those who say that one who falls after baptism is not able by the grace of Christ to rise again. But for one in grace and therefore in vital contact with the Mystical Body of Christ, there is another reason for hope, that may seem unbelievable. In discussing the effects of baptism, St. Thomas lays down the principle:

"By baptism we are incorporated into the Passion and Death of Christ as St. Paul says:[12] *If we be dead with Christ, we believe that we shall live also together with Christ.* From which it is clear, that the Passion of Christ is communicated to the baptized as a remedy, as if he himself had suffered and died."[13]

And in dealing with the objection that guilt is only

[9] Cf. ii, ii, 17, 2.   [10] ii, ii, 18, 4, ad 2.
[11] Council of Trent, Sess. iv, cap. xiii; cf. cap. vi and can. xxix.
[12] Rom. vi, 8.   [13] Cf. iii, 69, 2.

remitted by expiation, he repeats the principle that the baptized, inasmuch as he is a member of Christ, communicates in the expiation of His Passion as if he himself had undergone it.[14] The member of Christ, then, can call the infinite merits of Christ his own, and offer them to God for all his needs; and that special title to them acquired in baptism endures as long as he is not in mortal sin. What limit then is there to his hope?

We shall return again to this question in regard to the confidence that must characterize the life of a Catholic. But we insist here, that the foundation of Christian hope is not one's own merits, but the infinite merits of Christ; not one's own goodness and justice, but the infinite goodness and mercy of God. The radical power of hoping thus in God is given to us by the infused virtue of hope at baptism and is only lost by a deliberate sin of despair.

The two virtues of faith and hope are closely connected and manifest themselves in many ways in the spiritual life, where we can examine them further. There is however a still more important theological virtue given to us in baptism, and that is the virtue of charity. Here again we have to start by removing the misunderstandings that the common use of words involves. Charity nowadays generally means a sort of humanitarian compassion for the poor, and generally denotes alms-giving. This meaning of course is not altogether wrong, but it is only a shadow of the reality. The charity we speak of is that virtue by which we love God above all things for His own sake, and by which we love our neighbor for God. It is in fact the essential virtue of a living member of the Mystical Body of Christ. We have seen that the very nature of membership of a natural body demanded that the organ or member should live for the benefit of the whole organism. Now in the Mystical Body that is no less true; membership of Christ demands that we live for Him and not for ourselves. It is true that in His goodness He has made it well worth our while to do so, but true love seeks not its own benefit but the good of

[14] Ibid., ad 1.

the beloved. This supernatural love of God for His own sake is altogether above the powers of our nature, and we need a special virtue infused by God to enable us to love Him as He should be loved.

But only God can love God as He should be loved, and therefore the power of loving which He gives us is a certain created participation of His own love for Himself. God's Love for Himself is God the Holy Spirit, and the Holy Spirit comes into our hearts to pour forth charity there. But there is a delicacy about God's work in our soul that must be noted. He wants our love, but He wants more than our natural love. Our love for Him must be supernatural, yet it must be *ours*. The Love He has for Himself, although worthy of Himself, cannot be our love for Him, for then we would have to be God—which is impossible—and then, too, He would not have that special tribute that comes through our own personal love from our heart. He never forces our free will, but He has designed this most wonderful partnership in which we are associated with the Holy Spirit so that we can give Him the love of our hearts, but still give Him a love, that can be truly called divine, for it is given to us by the Divine Spirit. In fact St. Thomas does not hesitate to say that: "Charity produces an infinite effect, when it joins the soul to God and makes it holy. This shows the infinity of the divine power, which is the source of charity"; [15] and elsewhere he says charity is given to us "by the infusion of the Holy Spirit, who is the Love of the Father and the Son, and of whom created charity itself is a participation in us." [16]

Let us note here the special nature of these three fundamental virtues of the Christian life. They represent a power to perform an action which directly tends to God, and this power itself can be rightly described as a participation of God's own power. This threefold power is the first effect of our incorporation in Christ and consequent divinization of our souls by grace. While each

[15] ii, ii, 23, 2, ad 3.   [16] ii, ii, 24, 2.

of them represents a capacity to act "divinely"—in a created way of course—and implies a corresponding operation on the part of God, yet this action depends also upon our own free will—so that we are truly authors of these acts, and cannot lose these powers except by our own deliberate choice.

They represent the essential acts of the spiritual life. In fact without them there is no spiritual life. They give us a clear illustration of the fact that the Christian life is a vital partnership between God and the human soul, and they show us one result of the vivifying influence of the Holy Spirit who acts as the "soul" in the Mystical Body of Christ. The value of the acts produced in this manner must not be measured by human standards. They refer directly to God, and of themselves need not produce any visible effect. We are tempted to measure the value of our acts by the "good" they do—good for souls, good for men, good for the poor or the sick, or some such good. The error of that standard is best seen by reading St. Paul.

In the 12th Chapter of the First Epistle to the Corinthians, St. Paul discusses the various ways in which the Holy Spirit was accustomed to manifest His presence in souls; miracles, prophecy, the gift of tongues and other extraordinary phenomena were well known in those days, but they were all the work of the same Holy Spirit. St. Paul insists upon this fundamental unity and in that very connection gives a most explicit description of the unity of the Mystical Body of Christ, and portrays the mutual dependence of its members.

The necessary variety of members leads to a variety of operations, and St. Paul enumerates a numbers of different offices that were found in the Church: apostles, prophets, doctors, workers of miracles, those gifted with tongues, those with the power of healing and with other remarkable gifts which were of great service in the building up of the Church. But despite the value and the wonder of these gifts, St. Paul exhorts the Corinthians in an address that is classical:

Be zealous for better gifts. And I show you a more excellent way. He then bursts into a paean of praise for charity, which is the best gift and the most excellent way, and finishes with the assertion: *And now there remain faith, hope and charity, these three; but the greatest of these is charity.*[17] [But not only is charity the most excellent, it is also the one essential virtue and way; for he writes:] *If I speak with the tongues of men and of angels, and have not charity, I am become as a sounding brass and a tinkling cymbal. And if I should have all faith, so that I could remove mountains, and have not charity, I am nothing! And if I should distribute all my goods to feed the poor and if I should deliver my body to be burned, and have not charity, it profiteth me nothing.*[18]

Those are St. Paul's words; they are also the words of God, who is the author of all the inspired Scripture. There is no evading their meaning; it is quite clear. No matter what we do, unless we do it in the love of God, it profits us nothing. God wants our love, He will be satisfied with nothing else. That is what He principally looks for in our works. The things we do or achieve are not of primary value to God, for He can create them by a mere thought; or with just as much ease He can raise up other free agents to do what we do. But the love of our hearts is something unique, something no one else can give Him. True, He could create other hearts to love Him, but once He has created us and given us free will, the love of our particular heart is something unique and in a way irreplaceable. In any case, it is not for His own sake that He wants our love, but because He desires to make us happy with Him for ever, and He can only do that if we are in love with Him.

It might seem that that is something beyond our power or choice. One speaks in human relationship of "falling in love"; it is not, as it were, something deliberate, something that can be done at will. That peculiar acquiring of a new and special interest in another person, and the development of a new power to love that person,

[17] Cf. I Cor. xii, 31.   [18] Cf. I Cor. xiii. 1-3.

which raises the whole level of the life of a man or woman and opens the door to the highest form of human happiness, seems to be something fortuitous, an accident, a stroke of luck. Whether that be so or not, there is a very close analogy between the human and the divine, which we intend to stress in this book. But there is one important difference in regard to the love of God. There, instead of speaking of a soul falling in love, it would be nearer the truth if one spoke of love falling into the soul. For God gives us the love with which we are to love Him; more than that, He gives us the gift of wisdom, by which we acquire a taste and a relish for God and for His friendship and His ways. Both the love and the wisdom come from God; this will help us to understand the otherwise seemingly harsh treatment of the guest who, in the Gospel parable, came to the wedding-feast, without the ceremonial garment. Unless one realizes that such garments were provided by the host, one will not understand the host's resentment at the guest's refusal to avail of his kindness, and one will completely miss the parallel with the man who comes to the service of God without love in his heart. For if there is one gift that is to be had for the asking—and there are many—it is the gift of love for God.

There is only one source of true happiness in this life or in the next, and that is to love and to be loved. Knowledge that does not lead to love is worse than vain and sterile. It is of course quite true that love expresses itself in many ways, and it is true that its reality can be questioned if it does not seek expression in some way; but for all that, it is love, and love alone, that matters. St. Paul and all the saints knew that; our Lady knew that; our Lord knows that, and God Himself knows it and tells it to us in the Scripture. *I have loved thee with an everlasting love.*[19] *My son, give me thy heart.*[20] *Love is the culmination of the law.*[21]

But when we examine the Scriptures, we notice that God does not confine His commandment of love to love

[19] Jer. xxxi, 3.   [20] Prov. xxiii, 26.   [21] Rom. xiii. 10

for Himself; He insists that we must also love our neighbor, and it soon appears that He speaks as if the two loves were inseparable, and, in fact, one and the same. We read such texts as: *Thou shalt love thy neighbor for God;*[22] *All the other commandments are comprised in one word: Thou shalt love thy neighbor as thyself;*[23] and the final exhortation of our Lord to His disciples was "His own commandment" to *love one another as I have loved you.*[24] This insistence on fraternal love and its identification with divine love seems surprising at first sight, but its significance becomes obvious if we remember the principles that govern the membership of the Mystical Body.

The organs of a human body are mutually dependent and operate for the benefit of each other and thereby for the good of the whole organism. Foreign matter lodged in the organism is distinguished from that in living union with the whole, by its failure to interact beneficially with the rest of the system. It is at best a nuisance. If we then do not interact beneficially with the rest of the members of Christ's body, our title to living membership is immediately compromised. And we cannot distinguish completely between Christ and His members; we cannot love Christ without being willing to love the whole Christ—Head and members. What we do to our fellow members is done to Him—for they are His Body. We have His own word for it: *Amen, Amen, I say to you, as long as you did it to one of these my least brethren—you did it to me.*[25] It is Christ whom we serve, or injure, in the person of our neighbor.

But if our fraternal charity is to be Christian, its prime motive must be the love of Christ. That is why theologians do not distinguish essentially a double precept of charity, one for God, and one for our neighbor; they only recognize one, the love of God. And that is why St. John writes:

If any man say, I love God, and hateth his brother,

22 Cf. Luke x, 28.   23 Cf. Rom. xiii, 9.
24 John xv, 12.   25 Cf. Matt. xxv, 40.

he is a liar. For he that loveth not his brother whom he seeth, how can he love God, whom he seeth not. . . . If we love one another, God abideth in us, and his charity is perfected in us. In this we know that we abide in him and he in us: because he hath given us of his spirit.[26] *Let us love one another, for charity is of God. And every one that loveth, is born of God, and knoweth God. He that loveth not, knoweth not God, for God is charity.*[27]

Volumes could be written on these texts. One thing is clear: that to abide in God, one must love one's neighbor; fraternal charity is a necessary manifestation of love of God, which does not exist without it. In the practical part of this book we shall discuss the working of fraternal charity. Let it be noted here that charity does not compel us to *like* people, but to *love* them. And love is an act of the will wishing one well. Further what passes for fraternal charity is often not really Christian. Modern civilization is full of a humanitarianism which is not Christian charity, for its motive is not the love of God. It may be a love of man, though it is more often a love of management. Whatever be its motive, unless it be derived from the love of God, *it profiteth nothing.* It is on this point that many Catholics—even many Catholic religious—make a fatal mistake that renders much of their works for their neighbor sterile and unprofitable; for their motives are human. To them can be applied that threefold warning of our Lord: *Amen, I say unto you, they have received their reward.*[28] Still we must not be too general in our condemnation, for when a man works according to what he believes to be his duty, God will not fail to have compassion on him, and will give him the grace to rectify his outlook. But for a healthy Christian life, all a man's work must be done with God, for God, and in God; the love of God is at once its source, its end, and its principal value.

For the whole spiritual life is a love affair with God, and if that expression has associations that are out of place here, it is because of the abuse of it, not because of its proper use. As we shall see, God Himself uses human

[26] I John iv, 12, 13, 20.   [27] I John iv, 7, 8.   [28] Cf. Matt. vi, 2.

love to teach us the secrets of divine love. The love of God for us is shown forth in the Life and Passion and Death of our Lord. Our return is the influence of love for God in our own life, and that is especially shown by our fraternal charity. God not only gives us the power to love Him, He also gives us the opportunity of exercising that power. God is completely self-sufficient, and as we can add nothing to Him, our love at times seems hopeless and helpless. But God has so identified Himself with the needs of our neighbor, that what we do to others for God's sake, is done to God Himself.

The love of God, then, and the love of our neighbor are one and the same virtue. This virtue is the effect of our incorporation in Christ, but it is also the means of fulfilling the law of our life in Christ. It is God who works in us both to love and to do the works of love. These works are many; and for their performance God has given us other virtues called the moral virtues, which depend upon the four cardinal virtues of prudence, justice, temperance, and fortitude. These we need to regulate all our actions, to be honest with our neighbor, to control our lower appetites, and to overcome our weakness and fear, so that all actions which we perform may belong to the life of the Body of Christ.

In addition to these virtues, and to the seven gifts of the Holy Ghost, our life in Christ needs a continual series of helps called actual graces, by which we are moved to do good, and we are sustained in all our actions. We cannot begin a single good act without the help of God. *Without me, you can do nothing,* said our Lord.[29] But God is our Father, and He does not fail His children, and Christ is the Head of His Body and as the Church teaches: *He constantly pours forth His grace (virtutem) upon those who have been justified, as the head exercises its influence on the members and the vine on its branches; and this grace ever precedes, accompanies, and follows their good actions.*[30] There is,

[29] John xv, 5.
[30] Council of Trent, Sess. vi, cap. xvi.

so to speak, a complete nervous system in the Mystical Body, which controls the actions of all its members, and without that vital initiation and guidance, they are paralyzed. The working of actual grace is of great importance in the spiritual life, but to examine the virtues or the different graces in greater detail here, would make the treatment too theoretical, and would put us in danger of losing sight of the main outline of the Christian life, which is lived through Christ, with Christ, and in Christ, in the unity of the Holy Spirit, for the glory of the Eternal God.

CHAPTER 7

Seeking Christ through Humility and Obedience

I N order to avoid missing a clear view of the wood through making too close an examination of the trees that are found in it, we did not pursue our study of the results of our incorporation in Christ to the extent of examining them in detail, but broke off our discussion with the statement that is was a life lived through Christ, with Christ, and in Christ. One question, however, must be faced, and it is this. If God be the source and strength of our supernatural life, and its first mover and its last end—if the divine Omnipotence that can do all things, and the divine Goodness that will do all things necessary for God's glory, are so intimately at work in our souls—why is it that we are not all saints? Why is it on the contrary, that—even in the best of us— there is much of the pagan left? One possible answer to that question could be drawn from our discussion of fraternal charity in the last chapter, and indeed St. John's words could be quoted to show that lack of love for our neighbor interferes with God's action in our souls. But that is a symptom rather than the disease. The real trouble lies deeper; to get to the roots of it, let us go back to the beginning of wrong-doing.

We have seen that the first sin was that of the angels, and that it was a sin of pride, manifesting itself through disobedience. We have seen that the original sin on earth was that of our first parents, and that it also was a sin of pride manifesting itself by disobedience. We have seen, too, that when the new Adam and the new Eve, Jesus and Mary, set about their work of restoring the ruin caused by these sins, the way they followed was the way of humility manifesting itself by obedience in direct opposition to the source of the evils they were combating. And since they were models for us, their personal example lends cogency to the lesson of the original fall. The pride and disobedience of Adam and Eve still have their roots in us, and they are the chief obstacles to God's work of re-establishing all things in Christ.

When we asked ourselves the question: "How did Christ redeem *us?*" we found that the answer was: by making us part of Himself. We found too that the completeness of our incorporation in Him and of our identification with Himself depended upon the continual exercise of choice on the part of our own free will. Now whatever is the root-cause of our tendency to refuse to abandon and deny ourselves and to put on Christ, is also the source of our failure to live fully the life of Christ. But even this self-love would not be an obstacle to God's all powerful grace unless there were some reason why God should not use His power to move our hearts. Unfortunately, there is one such obstacle which is our pride. If we examine the nature of pride we shall see why it prevents God's grace from working in our souls.

Pride is an inordinate desire of one's own excellence; that is its classical definition, but perhaps, for our purpose, it will help better to take Tanquerey's definition: "Pride is an inordinate love of self, which causes us to consider ourselves explicitly or implicitly, as our first beginning and our last end."[1] Pride, then, makes us attribute the good that we find in ourselves to our own efforts, or, if we see that it does come from God, to attribute it to our own merits; it leads us to exaggerate the good we possess or have done, to imagine that we are what we are not, and to despise others in order all the more to exalt ourselves. Pride goes even further: it makes us consider our own selves as our last end; the

[1] Tanquerey, *The Spiritual Life.*

proud man lives "his own life," for his own sake. But in the Mystical Body of Christ, the supernatural life of each member with all his virtues and all his works, come from God, are operated by God's power, and are directed towards God for the sake of God. By pride we consider our good to have come from ourselves, to be done by ourselves, to be directed towards ourselves, for the sake of ourselves. The opposition is manifest.

But there is an even more fundamental opposition. God's primary motive in all His works—in creation, in redemption, and in every single act—must not be less than Himself. That is a law of His Being; He cannot cease to be God—to be supreme; He cannot subordinate Himself, in His divine nature, to a creature, without self-contradiction. It is true that His goodness has led Him to seek His glory by making us happy—by His mercy, in fact. But the glory of His mercy is His own. *I am the Lord, this is my name: I will not give my glory to another.*[2] Pride, which makes us appropriate the glory of all the good we have or do, is directly opposed to this law of God's action, and therefore puts a limit to it. God *cannot* pour out His gifts to the proud without self-contradiction as long as they are obstinate in their attitude. As God Himself tells us by the pen of St. James: *God resisteth the proud and giveth grace to the humble.*[3]

But most people are conscious of the effort involved in the doing of good, and feel conscious that many things—their good habits, and the results of their work —are the fruit of their own labors; they feel then that there is something unreasonable in the request that they should refer all these things to God as to their source and their end. Let us, however, examine the facts of the case; let us see how the creature really stands in relation to his Creator. In the first place we owe our existence to the free choice of God; He created us and He need not have done so, nor had He anything to gain by doing so. Having been created, we still need God's further intervention to keep us in existence, for our existence depends

---

[2] Cf. Isaias xlii, 8. [3] James iv, 6.

upon the continual exercise of God's power of conservation. We are like the sound of a man's voice; if he stops talking, the sound ceases to exist. If God stopped thinking about us, we would cease to exist. But our dependence does not end there. Even in the natural order, we cannot think a single thought, or perform a single action—even the purely reflex physical actions of breathing or digestion —which does not owe its origin to Him and which is not dependent upon His co-operation for its performance. It is true that having created us, it would be somewhat unreasonable for Him to deny us the further co-operation necessary for our existence, but—quite apart from our abuse of His gifts—He does not owe them to *us*; any "debt" there is in the matter is to *Himself*. And one could continue the catalogue of God's freely given gifts even in the natural order indefinitely, by considering the arrangements He has made for our fundamental needs of air, food, light and warmth, vesture, knowledge, and for innumerable others. The details of God's design for the support of our life are still beyond the telling of science.

All that would be true and striking even if we were perfect men and were perfectly subordinate to Him. But we are rebels, and despite that, He still continues to co-operate with us. Still more than that, He has even deigned to raise us to a new and superhuman order, in which we share His own nature and are to share His own happiness. And in that new order, a similar wealth and generosity of co-operation on His part are necessary; and in this case, He does not even owe it to Himself— it is quite gratuitous. In this new order there must be a new creation by grace, an endless series of the helps and impulses we call actual grace; there must be all those manifold arrangements that are necessary for the support and development of the supernatural life in our soul. All these must come from Him.

But His generosity becomes all the more wonderful when we remember that men had rejected this gift by sin, and that in order to restore it to them, God Himself became man, and suffered and died for those who sinned against Him, even for those who put Him to death! We do not realize that we owe the grace for every single act and also every single good thing in our spiritual life to God; that all had to be earned for us by the merits of our Lord and obtained for us by the intervention of our Lady, at a cost to themselves in suffering that is beyond all telling. Even the very act of our will in which we would glory comes from God; *it is God who worketh in you both to will and to accomplish.*[4] Even when a man commits sin, the only thing that is his own in the act, is the failure of his will to conform itself to God's will; all that is positive in the action depends upon the First Cause of all being and action.

It is only when God withdraws His help and leaves the proud man to his own devices, that it becomes evident what a man is worth without God. God sometimes does withdraw His usual help in order to make a man humble enough to allow His grace to sanctify him. Otherwise his pride would avert God's mercy. We have God's word for it that we have nothing that we have not received.[5] Even when we "merit" anything, God is the first principle of our action, and His rewards are only earned, first of all, because of a free promise made by God that He would reward such actions—for we have no claim against God except that which He Himself gives us—and secondly, because of Christ's merits, upon which all our own are dependent.

There is a special deformity in pride when we consider it in a member of Christ's Mystical Body. Pride makes a man live by himself for himself; but as a member of Christ, a man must live by Christ and for Christ. The proud man, then, opposes the life of the Mystical Body of Christ; he is like a cancer in that Body, and in fact, we can properly designate him as anti-Christ. For other sins evade God, so to speak, but pride opposes Him.

The first manifestation of this attitude of opposition to God is in the refusal to obey Him, and this is the

<hr>

[4] Phil. ii, 13.   [5] Cf. I Cor. iv, 7.

other evil wrought by pride. The first is, as we have shown, that because of God's nature as supreme being, our pride makes Him cease to co-operate with us; this other effect is to make us cease to co-operate with God. The full gravity of this effect—we are not now considering so much as an offence against God, as an offence against ourselves—becomes evident when we consider the Mystical Body of Christ. Obedience is obviously the law of its life. Every single act, even the slightest, done contrary to the will of God, cannot be shared by Christ, it is not part of the life of His Body, and therefore it has no real value. To partake in the life of the Body fully, the members *must* be subject to the Head—the ruling principle. The peculiar circumstances of the human soul in its membership of Christ, must always be kept in mind. Incorporation into Christ does not take away one's own personality; one has free will and retains full domain over one's own actions—one can determine what one's actions are to be. Deliberate refusal to conform to the will of God in a grave matter means mortal sin, and a consequent severing of the vital circulation that makes the soul a living member of Christ. Such disobedience is fatal. Even if the matter is not grave, the action, though not its agent, is severed from that vital circulation and the way is paved for complete severance of the agent by more serious falls in the future.

Such refusals to submit to the will of God can be traced to some form of self-love and self-seeking. We can generally distinguish two types of such self-love, corresponding to man's two-fold dual composition of body and soul; pride corresponding to the latter and sensuality to the former. These two sources, however, are not quite distinct; and it is significant that St. Gregory and St. Thomas speak of pride as the origin of all the other capital sins. Indeed, sins of the flesh do often have their beginning in pride, for even if some direct form of self-exaltation may not always be their motive, yet pride can make a man heedless of the dangerous occasions of such sins and it will prevent him from seeking God's help in prayer or in the sacraments; in short, it will make him blind to his own weakness and lead him to refuse to admit it. Very often, too, pride is such an obstacle to God's plan, that He deliberately withdraws His grace, and leaves a man to his own weakness, in such a way that the shame of the consequent sins of the flesh may lead him to humility. Finally, one cannot forget that the animal passions in man were chained and subject to the easy control of his reason until he refused to submit his higher powers to God by the sin of pride. It was then that he discovered that his own house was also in rebellion.

In fact, we have God's word for it that He *resisteth the proud, and giveth grace to the humble.*[6] The humble man, then, can easily find the grace to overcome his weakness, the proud man cannot. As we have already pointed out, pride opposes God, the other sins rather run away from Him. God can give a humble grace to overcome his passions, without having to deny His own glory. In fact man's weakness and misery are a continual prayer and appeal to God's mercy, especially where a man admits and accepts the humiliation of his position. Such men in their sins do not so much reject God; they are rather carried away from Him by the revolt of their lower passions; the government, so to speak, does not deny God's authority, but is not able to assert its own authority; whereas, in the case of the proud man, it is the government which rejects God, and very often, the more perfect is such a man's control over himself, so much the worse is his sin of pride. But for practical purposes of avoiding sin, it is well to recognize a two-fold source of disobedience, and to plan our spiritual life accordingly.

Both sources, however, are merely different forms of self-love and self-seeking. Both represent an attempt or a decision to live one's own life instead of that of Christ. We have seen how fatal is such an error. Ever since the elevation of the human being to the supernatural, our

[6] James iv, 6.

own life—however excellent—is of no avail. Our only hope of salvation is "in Christ"; all that is done outside of Him *profiteth nothing*. In fact, all such deeds and such things come to an end in the grave; and they may have to be expiated either here on earth, or else in the cleansing fires hereafter; they may even be the cause of our eternal damnation. Only what is done in Christ will rise glorious and immortal from our tomb.

Now, perhaps, we are in a position to realize what our Lord had in mind when He insisted in repeated declarations: *He that will save his life, shall lose it; and he that shall lose his life for my sake, shall find it.*[7] And if we have any doubt as to what He meant by "losing our life," let us note that these words were uttered in explanation of another significant assertion: *If any man will come after me, let him deny himself, and take up his cross, and follow me.*[8] The taking up of one's cross will be treated in connection with the perfection of our union with our Lord. Here, it is the importance of putting off our own selves and putting on Christ that is to be emphasized. All such self-denial and the acceptance of Christ, and the opposite, our own self-assertion and the rejection of Christ, depend upon our will; and that is why wilful disobedience to the will of God is the death blow to the life of Christ in us. But if we use our own will to accept the will of God, and to conform our heart to His, then we do our part to let Christ live in us and to find our life in Him.

If then the question be asked, how can one put on Christ and find salvation and holiness, the answer can be reduced to one word and that word is humility. In practice it includes two things: an attitude of mind, and the expression of that attitude in action. The attitude is humility of soul, and its practical expression is the search for God by obedience to His will. And let us note that the two are really the same thing. But, one may ask, what about all the other commandments and virtues and practices of the spiritual life? Surely faith,

[7] Matt. xvi, 25.   [8] Matt. xvi, 24.

hope, and charity are essential. Despite many such possible objections we still insist on the same statement: humility is the one thing necessary. By that we do not mean to deny the need of all the other riches of God's grace; on the contrary, it is because they are *so* essential, that we insist that humility is the one essential.

The paradox disappears if we remember that God resists the proud and *gives grace to the humble*. Our sufficiency is from God, and if we are humble, God will do the rest. That is not a mere sentimental opinion. It is based upon a very definite law of God's own being; on a principle which the scholastics formulated in the words: *Bonum est diffusivum sui*. Goodness will always tend to pour itself out. Goodness is expansive, it must give itself. It is dynamic: it is always avid to share itself and communicate itself. And God is supreme goodness itself. Therefore, if there are no obstacles to His action, God will communicate Himself to us without limit until we are full of His grace.[9] The goodness of God is like the atmosphere; it penetrates every nook and cranny that is left open to it. It is like the ocean that overwhelms everything and fills all things that are not already filled by themselves. And be it always remembered that the goodness of God is dynamic—it leads to action; it not only fills the soul but it makes the soul love and makes it manifest its love in deeds.

The chief obstacle to such an expansion and outpouring of God's grace is pride. Pride tends to usurp God's glory; it is a disposition that leads us to label and brand as our own all the things wrought in us by God's goodness; it actually tends to deny the supremacy of God. As long as such a disposition lasts in a soul, God cannot give His grace to that soul. His goodness is limited by its attitude. For pride brings the very law of God's being into operation to prevent His mercy from acting. Humil-

---

[9] In illustration of this principle, an excellent parable is found in the reply of an English gardener when asked to explain how an engine worked: "She g es by vacuum; vacuum's nothing, but it's powerful strong!"

ity, on the contrary, not only removes the obstacle, but invites God's help. As long as a man is humble, God can pour His healing grace into his soul and so remove all the other obstacles to divine union; the humble man will not rob God of the glory due to His merciful goodness. In fact, there is an eternal significance in the choice of words with which our Lord opened His first sermon: *Blessed are the poor in spirit—for theirs is the kingdom of heaven.*[10] Here is "poverty of spirit" set down by divine truth as the *title* to the kingdom of heaven. And poverty of spirit means far more than absence of love of riches; it is in fact that self-abnegation which, while it may reveal itself by material poverty, is really humility of heart, and so St. Augustine understands it. Let no one then be surprised that St. Benedict, writing for men seeking perfection, and St. Thomas, the Doctor of the whole Church, lay down humility as the first virtue for the acquisition of the kingdom of heaven, for it removes the obstacles to God's action and to God's mercy. We have God's word for it.

Let us be clear though what we mean by humility. It does *not* mean that we are to deny the good that is in us. Quite the contrary—for humility is truth. If a man who knows six languages denies his knowledge, he is not telling the truth. But if he ascribes his ability to learn languages and all his other talents, to himself or to his merits, he is also far from the truth. The most wonderful person that God ever created was His Mother, and she knew it. She even knew she was humble. In her great poem of praise to God—the *Magnificat*—she tells us that it was her humility that attracted God's attention and grace. But she ascribes all that she sees within herself to the mercy of God. *He that is mighty hath done great things to me. . . . All nations shall call me blessed.*[11]

What then is humility? Our Lady's *Magnificat* gives us the clue. Humility is a supernatural virtue by which we lovingly recognize our true value in God's eyes, and

[10] Matt. v, 3.   [11] Luke i, 49, 48.

are disposed to render Him due recognition for all the good we find in ourselves. It and its shadow, meekness, are the only virtues that our Lord pointed out in Himself for our imitation. *Learn of me because I am meek and humble of heart.*[12] His own humility is best seen in His life of obedience. We know, too, that He always insisted on giving all the credit to His Father for all the works He performed. But His humility went further; He seems to have laid His own "personality" completely, in the sense that He allowed the Holy Ghost to take complete charge of His life and was subject to Him in everything. When we remember that our Lord's human nature was the most wonderful nature God had created, we may realize how great was this humble emptying of Himself.

The development of this humility of heart in us is a matter for the practical part of this book. But having shown how this attitude of mind leads to the free inpouring of God's grace and power into our soul, let us examine the similar effect of the expression of humility by submission to the will of God.

First let us notice that there is hardly anything else which is so characteristic and insistent in our Lord's preaching and practice as this submission. When asked by the disciples for instruction on prayer, our Lord gave them a model prayer, which however, contains no other appeal for their sanctification than: *Thy will be done on earth as it is in Heaven.* And He tells them: *He that doth the will of my Father who is in heaven, he shall enter into the kingdom of heaven.*[13] *If anyone love me, he will keep my word and my Father will love him, and we will come to him, and will make our abode with him.*[14] The whole tenor of His doctrine insists on the close connection between true love of God expressed by doing the will of God, and the consequent entering into life and abiding union with Him. St. John had learned the lesson so well that he writes: *He that keepeth his word, in him in very deed the charity of God is*

[12] Matt. xi, 29.　　　[13] Matt. vii, 21.　　　[14] John xiv, 23.

perfected; and by this we know that we are in him.[15]
*He that keepeth his commandments, abideth in him,
and he in him. And in this we know that he abideth
in us, by the Spirit which he hath given us.*[16]

To the lesson of His preaching our Lord added the
example of His own practice. We know that His first
act on becoming man, was to consecrate Himself to the
doing of the will of His Father: *Behold I come to do
thy will.*[17] (Let us here draw attention to St. Paul's
comment immediately following his quotation of those
words: *In which will, we are sanctified by the oblation of the body of Jesus Christ once.*)[18] We know that
His hidden life was one long act of obedience, for *He
was subject to them.* Of His public life He Himself
tells us: *I do nothing of myself, but as the Father hath
taught me, these things I speak; and he that sent me
hath not left me alone, for I always do the things that
please him.*[19] *I came down from heaven not to do my
own will, but the will of him that sent me.*[20] And He
lets us see that He had a human will of His own which
He conformed to the will of God, for in the Agony in
the Garden, we hear Him pray: *My Father, if it be
possible, let this chalice pass from me. Nevertheless not
as I will, but as thou wilt.*[21] There is however no need
to multiply texts. St. Paul sums up the whole "mind"
of our Lord thus: *Let this mind be in you, which was
also in Christ Jesus: Who being in the form of God,
thought it not robbery to be equal with God, but emptied
himself, taking the form of a servant, being made in
the likeness of men and in habit found as a man. He
humbled himself, becoming obedient unto death, even
to the death of the cross. For which cause God also hath
exalted him, and hath given him a name which is above
all names.*[22] So that He who knew that He was God,
and could claim divine rights without injustice or "robbery," could find no better way of living on earth than

---

[15] I John ii, 5.   [16] I John iii, 24.   [17] Heb. x, 9.
[18] Heb. x, 10.   [19] John viii, 28, 29.   [20] John vi, 38.
[21] Matt. xxvi, 39.   [22] Phil. ii, 5–9.

"emptying Himself" and humbling Himself, becoming obedient to the extent of willingly losing His life on the cross according to the will of the Father.

The consequence is of capital importance. *For which cause God also hath exalted Him.*[23] In this is the whole secret of God's providence; the more we conform ourselves to His will, even though we lose our own "life" in doing so, the higher will He exalt us. The point is well worth a closer examination. Our whole fear of leaving our own will to do the will of God is based upon the desire of living "our own life" and the consequent dread of losing it by trusting ourselves to God's will. Now it is essential to remember that "God's plan is of a piece," as Juliana of Norwich puts it. We can distinguish an almost infinite number of "plans" in God's mind, but we must always remember that God has really only *one* will, and that there is complete unity in His plan, for all the plans which we distinguish are only different aspects of the one plan that He has at heart. St. Paul tells us what His plan is insofar as it concerns us: *This is the will of God, your sanctification.*[24] And there is perfect harmony and co-operation between that part of His plan and every other part. St. Paul again reminds us *To them that love God, all things work together unto good.*[25] At first sight, that appears difficult to understand. We see in the events around us, the effects of the many wills of our fellow men—indeed the effects of their sins. Surely their sins are not part of God's will! We see the number of apparently chance happenings that can have such a great effect upon men's lives; we examine the careers of great men, and realize to what an extent they were indebted to circumstances, to that mysterious thing men call luck, and we wonder whether St. Paul really means to include all things such as these in his assertions.

Yet that is certainly his intention, for the two texts we have quoted really come to the same thing. For the truth is that nothing happens here by chance; all that

[23] Phil. ii, 9.   [24] I Thess. iv, 3.   [25] Rom. viii, 28.

takes place contrary to our will, all that is done even in direct defiance of God's commandments—in short, everything that happens, issues from or depends upon the will of God, upon the Providence of God, upon the order He has chosen, upon the consent which He gives, and the laws which He establishes.[26] Even the sins of men must at least happen with what we call the "permission" of God. Having willed to make creatures endowed with free will, He foresaw their abuse of that free will, yet He consented to let it occur.

But even that abuse of free-will does not fall outside His providence. His plan has provided for every such detail. What has really happened is that the sinner has put himself outside God's plan for him; but the whole plan is still intact. So that as far as each one of us is concerned, we have only to consider two wills— our own will and God's will. His will covers all events outside those covered by our own, even our past acts. Our position in His plan at any moment depends upon our will at that moment. If we reject His will, then we put ourselves outside His plan for us; if we conform our will to His, then all things work together for our good. For, as we have said, "God's plan is of a piece" —He wills our happiness, and His plan is to lead us to happiness through Christ. His plan, in fact, is to re-establish all things fully in Christ, and every single detail that He wills co-operates to that end. The one exception is the case of the unrepentant sinner, whose sin puts him outside that plan insofar as it provides for his happiness, but who falls immediately into another plan in which God's justice rules. But the sins of others need not interfere with our trust in God's providence. We cannot improve on God's plan for our happiness. God loves us better than we love ourselves, and He has a better knowledge of our needs and of our heart than we have ourselves, and He has the will and the power to satisfy all the longings of our heart, if we only trust Him. We need never be afraid to abandon ourselves to

[26] Cf. Augustine, *In Ps. cxlviii*, 12.

God's will, for God's will is God Himself—and God is infinite goodness.

He is also a loving Father, and being a Father, He begets a Son—and the whole of His will is replete with His fatherliness and breathes the life of His Son into every soul that does the will of the Father who is in heaven. We must never forget this—God never ceases to be our Father, and He never ceases to be the Father of Christ. And the will of God represents God's plan to bring forth men in Christ, and to bring forth Christ in men.

For that reason we can be sure that by doing the will of God we are bringing forth Christ in our own soul, and entering into a still closer union with His Mystical Body. Indeed the very phrase in the Scripture that speaks of entering into life by keeping the commandments is pregnant with meaning. For that is the way we make ourselves perfect members of the Body of Christ and find our life in Him. There is here, however a still deeper mystery. There is a sense in which we can truly say that Christ has lived our life for us.

Let us remember that our Lord is the mediator between God and man, the head of creation and the universal priest. He, so to speak, received the will of God for all men, or if you prefer the "wills" of God for each man.[27] As man He certainly adores all these wills, and as our Saviour and the Saviour of God's plan, He actually accomplishes all these wills in as far as in Him lies. We have already hinted at the fundamental relationship that exists between the Son of God, who is God's "Idea" of Himself, and us creatures, each of whom is in some way or other an imitation of some part of that "Idea," realized outside God. Christ, as God the Second Person of the Blessed Trinity, contains, so to speak the original model according to which we were made, and according to which our life should be lived. To what extent He can realize that for us and instead of us, is a point which is not easy to determine, but remembering those famous

[27] Cf. Msgr. Gay quoted in chapter xiv.

texts of St. Paul referring to our life and death and to crucifixion and resurrection in Christ, it is hard to deny the possibility of some such accomplishment of God's will for us by and in Christ. The one thing He certainly can *not* do without our co-operation in some way is to make what He has done *ours*. Our consent and acceptance of God's will is necessary for that.

In any case, as we have already insisted, one must overlook the interval of time and space between us and Christ, and see His life as lived in partnership with our own. Now, our share of the partnership consists in doing or accepting His will; if we do that, He does the rest. This then is the importance of obedience to the will of God, that when perfect, such obedience identifies us with Christ. Note the qualification—when perfect; for the will of God applies to our motives and our interior acts as well as to our external achievements; in fact it is rather with the love that directs our action, than with the acts themselves that His will is concerned. When we do His will for love of Him, we are united to all His members, past, present, and even future. We have a share in every single good work that is going on in the Church, or has ever been performed in it, and our share depends not so much on our external actions as upon the love with which we embrace His will. St. Thérèse of Lisieux quotes with approval the doctrine of Tauler who said that if he loved the good done by St. Paul more than St. Paul himself did, it belonged more to him than to St. Paul. That doctrine applies to us when the motives of our love of the good done come from the love of God. It quite often happens that the real supernatural merit for many a good sermon belongs far more to some humble soul who may be doing the will of God in her own kitchen, and is thus the real source of supernatural energy, than to the eloquence and learning of the preacher.

And it is not merely to the other members of the Church that we are thus united; as we saw, doing the will of God identifies us with Christ Himself. Christ is not merely one man among millions, however outstanding. Christ is all in all. There is only one true adoration and service of God on earth and that is Christ's; there is only one true life on earth, and that is Christ's; there is only one vital good being done on earth, and that is the work of Christ. Our only hope of serving God, or of praying to God, or of living for God, is to enter into that life and work of Christ—or as St. Paul says—*to put on Christ*. And we do that by doing the will of God for the love of God.

By the way of summing up the notions we have been trying to indicate in the latter part of this chapter, let us take some of the comparisons which our Lord used, and develop them to suit our purpose. First we must warn the reader that in doing so, we do not intend to lessen in any way the reality implied by the vivid figure used by St. Paul when he speaks of the Mystical Body of Christ. But the mystery is so extraordinary, that no one comparison can give any adequate idea of it.

Our Lord compared Himself to a vine of which we were the branches; He also spoke of the seed which, being cast into the ground, had to die to itself in order to germinate and grow to fruit-bearing maturity. Let us think of Christ as a seed cast into the barren soil which we can consider to be the whole universe. The seed dies of itself and becomes a plant sending out roots in all directions. Each of these tiny roots embraces the particles of the soil, chooses out what is in harmony with its needs, absorbs and makes it part of itself. And so in the course of time all the good that is in the soil is transformed into the living tissue of the plant. Is not this the parable of the mustard tree, altered perhaps, but none the less true? For indeed the world was barren of supernatural life, until Christ's death sowed the seed of His life in it. And it is by His life that we are made truly alive. He is not only the vine, He is the *only* vine; and there is no other life that really matters except that which is found in Him

And His Father is the good husbandman. He cares

for the vine. He has control of all things and He arranges all things for its growth. But He respects the free will of the souls who are to be the food of Christ. The roots of the little plant pick out what suits them in the surrounding soil, and leave the rest. We are the soil in which Christ grows; His roots will only pick out from us what is in accordance with His Father's will— (did He not say that was His meat?),—and therefore it depends upon us to decide whether by doing the will of God we are to be absorbed by Christ and are to enter into life—or to be left by Him in the exterior darkness of our own will.

CHAPTER 8

Seeking Christ in Prayer

OUR examination of the supernatural life that is given to every soul at baptism, has reached a point where we shall have to consider in more detail what is the program to be followed by one who wishes to live that life. We saw that in baptism an intimate union is established between God and the soul of the baptized person. God gives the newly-made Christian a participation in His own nature; He pours into his soul the infused virtues of faith, hope, and charity, and makes him a member of the Mystical Body of Christ. The fundamental duty of the Christian is to love God with all his heart, and to love his neighbor for God. The general outline of the policy that such a Christian should adopt is, as we saw, an attitude of humility and the practice of conformity to the will of God, in faith, hope and charity.

We now have to consider how that policy is to be carried out, and the question immediately arises, for whom are we writing this book? To whom do its principles apply? The answer is, that all that has been written up to the present point applies to every soul who has been baptized, and our intention in applying these principles, is to apply them even to those in the lay state, just as much as to priests and religious. And if there be any particular type of lay person whom we have in mind, it is those whose condition has already been determined either by circumstances or by their choice, and especially those who are married, or who intend to get married. But we exclude no baptized person who is willing to avoid mortal sin. It does not matter what is his or her age, condition or education, or what has been his or her history; it does not matter what sins he or she may have committed in the past, or what opportunities he or she may have neglected, or what graces he or she may have refused; as long as it is a case of a baptized person, who is willing to try to avoid mortal sin, all the doctrine we have outlined can be applied to his or her case.

The reason why that is so certain is because of the name given to the Son of God in the Incarnation: *And thou shalt call his name Jesus. For he shall save his people from their sins.*[1] And the greatest reproach the Pharisees could find against our Lord, was to appeal to the already well-known characteristic: *This man receiveth sinners.*[2] Since the spiritual life is at once a partnership with Jesus, and also a search for Jesus, no one then need have any fear of being repulsed by Him; there is no one whom He will not receive. So that whether the reader is one who "kept all these things from his youth" and wishes to do better, or one who has realized that his life is one of lukewarm mediocrity, or one who perhaps has been converted from a life of serious sin, it does not matter; this book is addressed to him, and all the possibilities of the spiritual life therein discussed are open to him. All that we ask of him at the start is that he do not glory in any good he has done (or in his success in avoiding evil), that he repent of the evil he has done and of the good he has neglected, and that he be prepared to try to do better in the future, relying on the help and partnership of Jesus, His Saviour.

The obvious policy from the very start is to get into touch as soon as possible and as closely as possible with our Lord. Our Lord is God's revelation of Himself, He is God's model for men, He is God's teacher for men, He is the partner and the saviour of men, He is, in fact, *the Way, the Truth, and the Life.* Still, His appeal to each man is different; it will depend upon individual

[1] Matt. i, 21. [2] Luke xv. 2.

temperament. Those of an affective nature will be moved rather by His kindness and love; those of the austere type may tend rather to see in Him a teacher, a leader, and a king. But He has an appeal for every man, and there is no heart that He cannot completely satisfy. There are four great ways of getting in touch with Him; prayer, the sacraments, reading, and the doing of God's will. The latter, in fact, would include them all, but we are here thinking for the moment in terms of obedience to the commandments and the duties of one's state in life. There is a fifth way, which needs a special place for its consideration; it is both a highway and still a short cut; it is to go to Him through His Mother But that way is so important that we shall leave it for separate discussion.

These four ways of searching for Him are not independent. In fact, in the development of both the practice and the knowledge of the spiritual life, one must grow in circles, so to speak;—first, a small circle, which then expands and takes in new ideas or new practices, until one reaches fullness. Development on a single line may be one-sided, and will generally fail, for the different parts of the true development are inter-dependent. We need knowledge to pray, we need grace to get knowledge, and we need prayer to get grace. We cannot pray sincerely unless we are sincere in doing God's will, and we cannot do God's will unless we pray for His grace.

One other point should be noted. We speak of searching for Christ. But we have already said that the Christian life starts by intimate union with Christ. Is there not a contradiction here? Perhaps in words there appears to be one, but the reality is not so contradictory as the appearance. Our Lord's presence outside us does not interfere with His presence within us. And our Lord's presence in our soul does not interfere with His growth in our soul, nor with His coming to us from outside, as it were, to enter into a more intimate union with us. In fact we are forbidden to receive Him in Holy Communion unless He is already in our souls by grace.

Besides, we are using human words for divine things, and human words are inadequate. At different times we have to adopt different figures of speech to indicate our meaning.

One way of viewing the problem is that of St. Teresa in *The Interior Castle*, where she pictures the soul as a castle; when a man is in sin, he is *outside* the castle. God is often in our soul, and we are outside ourselves—we cannot find Him in ourselves, we must look for Him elsewhere. It often happens that we cannot enter into our own selves; we have locked ourselves out and cannot find the key. Despite the apparent confusion of words, the ordinary Catholic is quite satisfied with the ideas expressed, and he knows that they do correspond to a reality. Even when he has found God in the depths of his own soul, he can still pray to God in heaven without any sense of inconsistency. We need not then imagine that we are denying what we have already said of the divine in-dwelling, when we now speak of setting out on the search for God. For whether we consider God within us or God outside us, we have still to set out from our own selves to find Him. And even when we are in union with Him, we shall see that that union can be intensified by the sharing with Him of those very acts by which we seek Him.

The first way of seeking God to be considered here is by prayer. Prayer, we are told, is an "elevation of the soul to God." It is also described as "a familiar conversation with God," and "the soul's affectionate quest for God." In a special sense, it is "the asking of seemly things from God." In practice, we start to pray by bringing God before our mind, or more properly, by turning our mind to God. He is everywhere; and by putting aside other thoughts and adverting to His presence, we can always pray to Him. A definite effort is necessary to get rid of these other thoughts, and we need some idea of God to supplant them in our mind, or to occupy our imagination. This is one example of the connection between prayer and reading, for our reading plays a great part in building up our notion of God.

We can choose any way we find helpful of representing God to ourselves. Individual needs vary so much that nothing definite can be laid down. For some, perhaps, the mere notion of God is sufficient; others will form a very definite picture of our Lord's humanity in some of His mysteries; others again concentrate their attention upon the tabernacle, or upon a crucifix. The golden rule in this, as in all similar questions about prayer, is to pray the way one finds best. Still there are some principles that will guide us.

Prayer in one way is a very simple thing; in another, it is extremely complex. It achieves a manifold purpose, and if we keep its different ends in mind, we shall know better how to go about it. The first purpose of prayer is to discharge that duty laid upon man by the first commandment: to give God due homage. That due homage includes adoration which is an acknowledgment of God's supreme dominion over us, and of our absolute dependence upon Him; it includes thanksgiving, for we owe everything to God's goodness; and it includes a recognition of our own state as sinners with a sincere sorrow for our offences against God and a readiness to atone for them. There is of course no need to put all these things into words every time we pray, but there should be some time every day when we make a formal protest of them in some way. And there is no better way than the way shown to us by our Lord—by saying the *Our Father*. We should then, every day take up a formal attitude of prayer, preferably on our knees, and in some short form give due homage to God.

There is also another purpose in prayer, which is to obtain for ourselves certain graces that are necessary for us. Every single action of our spiritual life depends upon God for its initiation and performance; the very preservation of our life depends upon His providence, and the final success of our efforts calls for a special grace called the grace of final perseverance. Some of these graces God gives us without our asking, for our Lord is always making intercession for us, and we have a Mother in heaven who is concerned in every good that comes to us

—and the first of all graces *must* come without our request; but there are other graces, even necessary ones, that He will not give unless we ask Him to do so. It is true that He already knows our needs, but it is not to inform Him of them that He wishes us to ask, but rather to inform ourselves of our need of Him, so that we may acknowledge Him as the source of good, and that while teaching us to have confidence in Him, He may prevent us from taking Him for granted. This then is another reason why we should fix a period of formal prayer for every day. Both these needs can be satisfied by choosing some form of prayer that appeals to us, and making daily use of it. The *Our Father* should certainly be part of that form; and, since we cannot do without our Lady's assistance, the *Hail Mary* should also find an honored place therein. If we wish to use a prayer book, well and good; let us do whatever suits us best. The one thing that is important is to keep these fixed set of prayers *short*. It is better to say one *Our Father* sincerely, than to rush through a whole Rosary without thinking of God. The prayers we decide to say every day should not be long enough to become a burden to us; otherwise it is very likely that we shall often say them badly, and that sooner or later we shall dispense ourselves from saying them at all. Further, prayer is so essential to our spiritual life that we should never let it be associated with the idea of a burden. In any case it is not for "much speaking" that we shall be heard, but rather for the dispositions of our heart.

What are these dispositions? The one condition our Lord attached to the promises He made with regard to prayer was that we should pray in His name. In other words we should pray in partnership with Him, and for the benefit of His Mystical Body. United to Him, we have His infinite merits at our disposal to put before God; united to Him we can say to God: "This is Thy well-beloved Son in whom Thou art well-pleased: Hear Him!" The dispositions then for prayer are the dispositions for healthy membership of Christ; faith, hope, charity, humility, and submission to God's will. It is true that even the sinner can pray, and should pray; even he, too, must pray through Jesus Christ, relying upon His infinite merits to make his prayer heard before the throne of God; but if he has not these dispositions in actual fact, he should at least have them in desire.

Obviously a man must believe in God's existence and in His willingness to take notice of us; this is implied in the very act of turning to God. Our request springs from the hope we have of being heard. Charity must be added to our prayer, at least in desire; for if we are in the state of mortal sin, and have not some desire of being reconciled to God, we are really in rebellion against Him. Fraternal charity is also necessary for prayer, for we remember how our Lord insisted that even the man offering his gift at the altar should first go and be reconciled with the neighbor who had something against him, and come to offer his gift.[3] This may surprise us, but if we remember that fraternal charity is necessary for living membership of Christ, we shall see why such charity is necessary if we are to pray in the name of Jesus. It is only when we are united to the rest of His members by charity that we truly can pray in His name. The need for humility is illustrated in the parable of the proud Pharisee and the humble Publican; and God Himself warns us that He resists the proud and giveth His grace to the humble. That we should be willing to submit to God's will is necessary; to refuse to do so is to refuse to acknowledge Him as God; it is to separate ourselves from Christ, who Himself has given us a classical example in His prayer in Gethsemani: *My Father, if it be possible let this chalice pass from me. Nevertheless not as I will, but as thou wilt.*[4]

Dispositions such as these come first of all from God's grace, and therefore they must be sought in prayer. They are also developed by reading and reflection—which gives us another reason for avoiding long prayers, for where there is much speaking there is little thinking. If one

[3] Cf. Matt. v, 23–24.   [4] Matt. xxvi, 39.

were to start, say, with a decade of the Rosary or some prayers of equal length every morning and evening, that would seem sufficient as far as formal prayer is concerned. If there are prayers in a book with a special appeal it is better to say one or two each time, or repeat the same one for a week, than to burden ourselves with the whole collection each night. If our facility in prayer increases we can always extend our program, but it is always better to be too short than too long. We have a long road before us, and the important thing is to persevere to the end. Moreover one of the reasons why such insistence is placed upon not making prayer a burden, is that then there is much more likelihood that informal prayer will rise spontaneously to our lips during odd moments of the day; and that sort of prayer is very necessary also. In any case *the Lord loveth a cheerful giver;* and it is far better to give Him one minute cheerfully than ten minutes under duress.

There are two sorts of prayer which are of importance: one in which we use a set formula and endeavor to conform our minds to its meaning, the other in which we pray in our own words, trying to express sentiments that have already been produced in our heart. There should be something of both forms in our daily prayers. The first form is necessary because there are necessary sentiments that will not arise spontaneously; they must be acquired by use of a formula or by reading. Further, if we had to face the effort to improvise every time we tried to pray, we would soon dread praying. The second form is no less necessary because it is an excellent form of keeping in touch with our Lord, and that sums up the whole spiritual life.

It is true that we are in union with our Lord in any prayer; in fact some such dependence upon Him is a part of all prayer. But the growth of our spiritual life depends upon the development of friendship and intimacy with Him so that we can share all our actions with Him. If we always have to be on formal terms with Him, the growth may not be so easy. We should

therefore frequently turn to Him and talk to Him in our
own words about anything of mutual interest. That is a
pretty wide range of reference. Yet since our life is only
fully Christian when it is completely shared with Him,
those terms of reference are not too wide. Now such
a form of prayer can vary very much. It may use some
well-known formula which serves to unite us to Him;
many people, for example, say decades of the Rosary
as they go about the streets and places of their daily
work. It may merely consist of occasional aspirations.
These aspirations should be sincere. There are many
aspirations to which an indulgence is attached. This
may lead us to feel that we should repeat them every
time we think of saying them. On that account one
wonders whether it would not be more prudent to put
some limit to such repetition—or even whether it should
be allowed at all. Because once we feel that burden of
an indefinite obligation to repeat them, we shall soon
find that we are very slow and unwilling to think of
saying these prayers even once. "A little and often," is
a good maxim. In any case, we can be in our Lord's
company without saying anything to Him, and such
a form of union with Him is in itself an excellent prayer
and one which should not be disturbed by any attempt to
say "prayers"—unless those prayers are of obligation.
There should be complete liberty of spirit in this, as in
all matters that are not of obligation. Otherwise there will
be no true growth in the spiritual life.

There is really no occupation except sin, which is
incompatible with such spontaneous prayer. Obviously
there must be some prayers in the day, to which we give
our whole mind and lay everything else aside, but God
forbid that any one should feel bound to limit his prayers
to those said on one's knees. Perhaps the point can be
illustrated by reference to the story of the two men who
were in the habit of saying some prayers on their way
home from work. The question whether they could smoke
while doing so arose, and they decided to seek advice
from their directors. One man was severely reprimanded

for thinking of smoking while praying; the other man found a different type of director, who said that although smoking while praying was open to objection, still, one could hardly object to a man praying while he was smoking! The story is only a story, but it may draw attention to the fact that there is a difference between formal prayer and informal prayer, and that while the former demands suitable circumstances, the latter may be used anywhere. The point about smoking is, that if it is not a sin, it can certainly be shared with God, and if so, there is no reason why we should not talk to Him while enjoying one of the creatures He has made for our recreation and refreshment. The whole question of pleasure and recreation needs further discussion; here it need only be said that pleasure has its proper place in the spiritual life, and—in its proper place—is no obstacle to close union with God.

There is then a prayer for all times, and there is certainly a time for prayer that is natural and unstudied —when we speak to God in terms very similar to those in which we speak to our friends. We have to learn to be at our ease with God, and to realize that there is no need to keep on saying something to Him. It must be admitted, however, that there is a very close connection between such silent prayer, and the purity of our conscience. It is not generally possible to be at our ease with God if we have a deliberate intention of indulging in habitual sin. But repented sin is no obstacle to such friendship, nor are those sins into which we suddenly fall through frailty. The very act of sorrow for them affords an opening for a new conversation with God, and since He is our Saviour, we need never be afraid to show Him our sins and our weakness.

A number of people experience a need of saying some longer prayers during the day, for example the Rosary, the Little Office, some of the Psalms, or some such prayers. Prudence is necessary in the choice and the measure of such practices; but undoubtedly there are many cases where prudence not only allows, but actually calls for, quite long prayers of this type. In prayers like the Rosary, the constant repetition makes it impossible to follow the meaning of each word; in prayers like the Divine Office the multitude of ideas therein expressed in too swift a sequence for any mind to adapt itself to each idea and still finish the Office in a reasonable time. In such cases the mental attitude may be somewhat different. One could attend for example to God, to whom one prays, rather than to the prayers one says to God, and be quite confident that these prayers —for example, the Psalms—are pleasing to Him by reason of their origin, or of the authority who gave them to us. In the *Hail Mary*, for example, one might have a general remembrance of the fact that the opening words are those in which God, through the angel, made to Mary the most wonderful proposal that ever came to any human being. Surely, they have a meaning for Mary that is beyond our comprehension! We can be quite certain that they are very pleasing to her.

As an alternative, one may take the view that these prayers are being said in the name of the Church and that their meaning applies to the incalculable needs of her members, of which needs we may be in ignorance. Such an attitude applies especially to the Divine Office when said by those who have been officially appointed to recite it in the name of the Church. But it applies in some degree to all prayer, for we are all members of Christ, and we all pray in His name. The meaning of the words we use may express rather the needs and sentiments of some other members of Christ's Mystical Body, and our attention then will tend more to the "whole Christ," or to an obscure sense of partnership with Him, than to the particular words we utter.

In long prayers there is nearly always difficulty in preserving our attention and avoiding distraction. Voluntary distraction is of course blameworthy, especially when it means a complete turning of our mind away from God and from what we are doing. There may be partial distractions which can be included in our prayer, under the form of an act of charity, or by some necessary action; in these cases we really do not turn our hearts away from God, we only change our way of serving Him for the moment. The saints have always been noted for their readiness to break off their private prayers to serve Christ in the person of their neighbor.

Involuntary distractions are quite different. Unless they proceed from our antecedent and deliberate carelessness, such as a lack of a proper effort to fix our attention at the beginning of our prayer, there is certainly no blame attached to them. Even with the best will in the world, they cannot be avoided. Thought evokes thought, image evokes image; the very nature of our mind and imagination is such that they tend to wander. Until we advert to such wandering, there is no question of fault on our part. When we do advert to the distraction, some effort must be made to renew our attention. Sometimes one can easily get rid of the distraction; at other times, it is so persistent, that the best plan is to leave it alone and "look over its shoulder" at God. To renew our attention is not always easy, and there are times when our prayer seems to be nothing but one long series of distractions, combated it is true, but with no sign of success. It is well to remember that such a prayer can be very pleasing to God. Each attempt to restore our attention is an "elevation of the mind" to Him made under difficulty, and therefore very pleasing to Him as a prayer—whether it be successful or not as an effort to banish distraction.

It should be noted that it is not necessary to attend to every word we say. Even in ordinary speech we use polite formulae and only advert to their general significance. In prayer one can attend merely to the saying of the words correctly; or one can attend to the meaning of the words used; or finally one can attend to the purpose of the words used, or to the person to whom they are addressed. Thus one could be attentive to God, and quite forget what one was saying to Him! Such attention is very praiseworthy, and we need never be afraid to let the Person to whom we speak distract us from the words we say to Him in ordinary prayer.

The effect of distraction on our prayer is best understood by considering the three aims of prayer. Insofar as prayer is a meritorious work, distraction does not take away its merit; for the original intention and attention are the source of the whole prayer. The same is true of our prayer considered as impetration. But prayer can also be considered insofar as it has some direct effect upon ourselves or our own dispositions. Obviously distraction can interfere with this effect.

The actual method of dealing with distractions depends to some extent upon the circumstances of our prayers. In prayers of obligation, there is a definite work to be done, and distractions when they are noticed must not be let interfere with that work. Sometimes one can use the distraction to give an intention for the prayer, sometimes one may have to struggle with it the whole time of prayer and sometimes, as we have said, one can only look over its shoulder. The important thing to remember is that, unless deliberately accepted and retained, distractions do not render our prayers useless. On the contrary they often are the occasion of very meritorious service to God.

Sometimes the source of distractions is obvious; some inordinate attachment, some inordinate worry, fatigue, the natural instability of our mind, the ordinary cares of the day's work, our surroundings—the list is endless. Where they arise from some inordinate interest, the remedy is obvious. But whatever be their origin, one necessary measure for avoiding them is to recollect oneself completely at the beginning of prayer. If that is done generously, the whole prayer is given a value that no subsequent involuntary distraction can take away. If we are praying informally—that is, if we are "talking to God"—distractions can be dealt with by making them the subject of the conversation. After all, God made all things, and every creature, then, has at least that connection with Him, which may form a starting-point for further conversation.

Before leaving the question of the more formal type

of prayer, there are a few further remarks that should be made. Of the Mass as a prayer it is better to treat separately. The Divine Office is a form of prayer, which of its kind has no equal. It is, however, not practical for many of the laity. What a layman who has an attraction for such a prayer, and has sufficient leisure, might do, would be to say *one* of the Hours daily. He could either recite, say, Vespers or Compline for each day, or he could take a different part of the Office each week. The Little Office of Our Lady seems more practical for the laity, and would often suit those who find that the repeated formulae of the Rosary make that prayer rather difficult. However, we again insist on the principle: better to say a *little* and say it *well,* than to say much and first say it badly, and later give up saying it at all. But in passing, let it be remarked that the Psalms are prayers that might well appeal to many lay people. They have God for their author, and there are few prayers which can be shared so intimately with our Lord. He said them Himself during His life on earth, and He will continue saying them in us and with us, if we allow Him to do so.

Liturgical prayer, in the sense of assistance at the public recitation of the Divine Office, is not generally available for the laity. But there are many other forms of congregational prayer; and we have to be careful of our attitude in regard to these. Too many devout people are apt to look down on such prayers, and to prefer their own private efforts at devotion rather than public devotions, on the ground that they can pray better by themselves. It is true that one may have to give up a certain feeling of "devotion" in assisting at public prayers, but the gain in doing so can be very great. Sometimes the objection arises from a loss of the self-glorification we find in such private devotion; but it is quite true that one may often find it really difficult to share in such public worship with the same fervor and recollection, and with the same apparent profit, as one has in praying alone. Nevertheless, even where that is true, let it be always remembered that Christian life is an entering into Christ's life rather than the perfecting of one's own life, that Christian prayer is an entering into Christ's prayer rather than the flowering of one's own prayer, and that in the particular case under discussion, where we have to abandon our own prayer to join in the prayers of the congregation, we are really putting on Christ. Where two or three are gathered in His name, He is in the midst of them, as He has promised, and when we join in their prayer, we are really exchanging our own poor prayer for the powerful prayer of Christ. This is of course specially true of all liturgical prayer. To join in the liturgy of the Church is to put on Christ in a very special manner and to offer to God a peculiarly acceptable sacrifice of praise. In all such cases we can say to God with special significance: "This is Thy beloved Son in whom Thou art well pleased—Hear Him."

Lest it should seem that this is a pious exaggeration, we shall quote the words of St. Augustine. In connection with the passage in the Psalms which runs: *To thee have I cried from the ends of the earth.*[5] he asks: "Who is this that cries from the ends of the earth? Who is this one man who reaches to the extremities of the universe?";[6] and elsewhere he gives the answer: "He is one, but that one is unity. He is one, not one in a single place, but the cry of this one man comes from the remotest ends of the earth. But how can this one man cry out from the ends of the earth, unless he be one in all?"[7] In another place he explains further: "Christ's whole body groans in pain. Until the end of the world, when pain will pass away, this man groans and cries to God. And each of us has part in the cry of that whole body. Thou didst cry out in thy day, and thy days have passed away; another took thy place and cried out in his day. Thou here, he there, and another there. The body of Christ ceases not to cry out all the day, one member replacing the other whose voice is hushed. *Thus there is*

[5] Ps. lx, 3. [6] *In Ps. cxxii.* [7] *In Ps. liv.*

but one man who reaches unto the end of time, and those who cry out are always His members." [8]

And more emphatically: "No greater gift could God bestow on men than to give them as their Head His Word, by whom He made all things, and to unite them as members to that Head. Thus the Word became both Son of God *and* Son of Man; one God with the Father, one Man with men. Hence when we offer our petitions to God, let us not separate ourselves from the Son; and when the Body of the Son prays, let it not detach itself from its Head. Let it be He, the sole Saviour of His Body, our Lord Jesus Christ, the Son of God, who prays for us, who prays in us, and who is prayed to by us.

"He prays for us as our priest; He prays in us as our head; He is prayed to by us as our God. Let us therefore hear both our words in Him and His words in us. . . . We pray to Him in the form of God; He prays in the form of the slave. There He is the Creator; here He is the creature. He changes not; but takes the creature and transforms it into Himself, making one man, head and body, with Himself. We pray therefore to Him, and through Him, and in Him. We pray with Him, and He with us; we recite this prayer of the psalm in Him, and He recites it in us." [9]

Despite the value of community prayer, and the need for formal prayer at regular times, there is still room and even necessity for our own private personal prayer; for those intimate talks—and even intimate silences—with Jesus which are a very important part of our spiritual life. In fact, we have only mentioned the other form of prayer in order to avoid misunderstanding, and one of our reasons for insisting on brevity in such prayers is to leave the soul free to develop this personal prayer. It is important to realize that such prayer may be quite conversational in style, and even commonplace in its topics. The more formal words of the prayer books do not generally come naturally to our lips in such personal conversation, and since our object is to develop a sense

[8] *In Ps. lxxxv.*   [9] *In Ps. lxxxv.*

of companionship with Jesus and to make ourselves at home with Him, there should be nothing forced or artificial about such prayer nor anything that would render it needlessly unattractive. In fact, it might be better not to think of it as prayer at all, but to regard it, say, as one would regard those apparently meaningless comments that men sharing a piece of work make to one another, when there is an occasional pause in the work. The important thing is to get in touch with our Lord, and to keep in touch with Him; all that helps to that end is good and holy.

This view finds support in the encyclical which we have already quoted. The Holy Father, having treated of the Mystical Body of Christ and of our union with Him, still found it necessary to correct some mistaken views that might seem to be favored by this corporative doctrine. His words are worth quoting:

There are some who deny to our prayers of petition any real efficacy, or who suggest that private prayers of God are to be accounted of little value, inasmuch as it is rather the public prayers offered in the name of the Church which have real worth since they proceed from the Mystical Body of Jesus Christ. This suggestion is quite untrue. For the Divine Redeemer holds in close union with Himself not only His Church, as His beloved bride, but in her also the souls of each one of the faithful, with whom He ardently desires to have intimate converse especially after they have received Holy Communion. And although public prayer, as proceeding from Mother Church herself, excels beyond any other by reason of the dignity of the bride of Christ, nevertheless all prayers, even those said in the most private way, have their dignity and their efficacy, and are also of great benefit to the whole Mystical Body; for in that Body there can be no good and virtuous deed which does not, through the communion of saints, rebound also the welfare of all. Nor is it wrong for individuals, simply because they are members of this Body, to ask special favors for themselves, even temporal favors, subject to conformity with the will of God; they are still individual persons, and still subject to their own particular needs. As for reflection on heavenly things, not only the pronouncements of the Church but also the practice and example of the Saints are a proof of the high estimation in which it must be held by all.[10]

The Holy Father then corrects the error of those who would hold that we should not address our prayers *to the person of Jesus Christ Himself, but rather to God, or through Christ to the Heavenly Father on the ground that our Saviour in His capacity as Head of His Mystical Body is to be regarded only as the Mediator of God and men.* He points out such a view is quite wrong, and is opposed to Catholic practice and Catholic teaching. The importance of such private prayer to our Lord is so great that we shall have to return to the subject, and consider it in connection with what is called meditation and mental prayer. Mental prayer is really nothing more than the development of such intimate conversation with God. Meditation, in the proper sense of the word, indicates thinking about God and the things of God. Before we consider these exercises, it will be better to deal with something which is a very important, if not an indispensable, preparation for them, namely, reading and reflection.

[10] *Mystici Corporis.*

CHAPTER 9

Seeking Christ by Reading

THERE are no new principles in the spiritual life. The fundamental principle—to seek God and to be united to Him in Christ—never changes. The other principles are derived from that one, and are also fixed; but their application to particular circumstances, and the choice of means to the end, must take into account the varying conditions of human life. Thus it may be the case that in modern times, there is need to insist with greater emphasis on certain practices than formerly. Now if there is one thing for which modern conditions have produced a special necessity, it is the regular practice of spiritual reading. It is, of course, only a question of degree; for reading, or some other form of instruction, was always necessary. But oral instruction, the common opinion of men, the example of our neighbors, and the trend of life in general, play a smaller part in the formation and instruction of Catholics than they did formely. People do not go to hear sermons now as they used to; religion is not talked about, at least, with any accuracy; our neighbors often have ideals that are far from Catholic—if indeed they have any at all; and there is little in our general surroundings that is of direct help to incite us or to help us to find God.

In fact the general effect of our modern environment is not merely negative; it has even a positive tendency to lead us away from God. This it does not so much by being against God, but rather by leaving Him out. We live in fact in a pagan civilization. The remnants of Christian ideals that are still found in common opinion, and which still express themselves in common practice, are divorced from their dogmatic foundation of real fact and true faith—they are based mainly on sentiment—and like all branches cut off from their original stock, they are withered and warped, and often twisted quite out of recognition. As guiding ideals, they rather tend to mislead. The need for something to counteract this effect is one of the reasons for spiritual reading.

But another reason comes from the reading matter in common use to-day. Examine for a week the ordinary man's reading by which his mind is nourished, and what does one find? One long series of items which could hardly be more efficiently designed to concentrate his attention upon this world and upon the things of this world. One may question the accuracy of much that the newspapers print, but one cannot deny that what is printed is presented in a fashion that tends to grip the reader's imagination. To the news are added photographs which are often of considerable interest and artistry. Then there are the various weeklies, the magazines, the digests, and all the other publications that one finds everywhere today. They are easy to read, they can make the most of trifles, they can flatter the intelligence of the reader and make him take superficial gossip for deep thought, and, of late, they have brought condensation to a fine art. As a general rule they do not lead to thought—in fact for the most part they only increase the passivity of the reader—but when they do make one think, it is not of God and of His love, but of the things of this world, and generally of those things which are of least importance. When one considers the skill and artistry, the attraction and the sympathy, the ingenuity and the insistence, which are therein at work to concentrate our whole attention on the. passing moment, one must recognize that there is an urgent need for some personal effort to restore the balance by keeping the realities of eternity before the mind and by making oneself see the present moment in its true context.

What has been said of periodicals is no less true of

books taken generally; and there is another effect common to all such reading: it produces a distaste, not merely for the things that really matter, but also for the style and manner in which those things are presented in spiritual books. The result is that when one does by an effort force oneself to open a spiritual book, it requires a still greater effort to keep it open, and not to close it with a yawn. And, truth to tell, it is not always the reader who is to blame. So many spiritual books come from another age or are translated from another tongue, and have, therefore, a foreign and artificial air, so many are written by religious for religious and from the viewpoint of religious—so many are deliberately "edifying" and seem, therefore, unreal—so many show a lack of understanding for the difficulties of the laity and fail still more by having no sympathy with these difficulties or even with the weakness of human nature—that it is not surprising that many lay people find spiritual books so hard to read that they soon give up the practice of regular reading.

Despite all such difficulties, we insist that regular reading of a suitable sort plays a more and more important part in the life of Catholics today, and that for the educated at least, it is well nigh essential for their progress if not also for their salvation. To our mind, this practice ranks equally with mental prayer and the other exercises of devotion in importance, and in fact it is so closely connected with these other exercises, especially the essential one of mental prayer, that without it—unless one finds some substitute—there is no possibility of advancing in the spiritual life; even perseverance therein is rendered very doubtful.

Obviously one way of dealing with this problem would be to reduce the amount of secular reading. The degree to which that is necessary or desirable depends upon so many individual circumstances that it cannot be determined here. Personal experience is the best guide, at least, if prudent counsel be taken. For our part, we do not agree with those who would have lay people live like religious, out of touch with their surroundings. They are members of society, they have their place in it and their relations to it, and they have quite a legitimate interest in it. In fact the chief hope of modern society is that Catholic laymen may exercise considerable influence on it. Therefore, they have to keep in touch with it. But, as in all such matters, they must do so prudently.

What one must do is to make a firm resolution never to cease from regular reading of the right type. And what is the right type? That is a wide question, and the answer can only be general—for here especially, the variations of individual temperament must be considered. First preference must be given to that reading which makes us know Jesus Christ, His Person, His practice, and His preaching. He is the Way, the Truth and the Life. He is God's manifestation of Himself to men, and man's model for going to God. The obvious place to find Him is in the New Testament; and the Four Gospels at least should be the familiar and frequent reading of every Catholic. The best approach to Scripture reading is a personal matter and depends upon many circumstances, but the reading of the Scripture cannot be too highly recommended; it is, however, by no means as general as it should be. The Bible contains the inspired word of God, and we Catholics have the infallible interpreter of God's word in the Catholic Church. But is must be remembered that all the Bible is not easy to understand. Only the original text in the language in which it was originally written is inspired; the English translations we read are *not* inspired, and in fact they do not always succeed in making us understand the full sense of the original. That is why it is often helpful to use one of the shorter commentaries on Scripture. But very often one will find in the Bible a personal message from God that not only gives one knowledge but also strength and joy—in fact one will often hear God speaking to one's heart from those sacred pages.

There is many an excellent life of Christ, one at least of which should be read. The teaching of Christ is found in Christian doctrine and in books on the spiritual life; and the example of Christ is reproduced in the lives of His saints. The primary purpose of our reading is not so much to educate ourselves as to produce goodness of life—to help us to live in union with Christ. But education is a first step to good living, and we can say that our initial purpose in our reading should be to educate ourselves in doctrine and in spirituality up to a level which will depend upon individual circumstances, but which should be high enough to enable us to give God that reasonable and rational service that He requires of us, to give our neighbor an account of the faith that is in us, and to give ourselves motives, direction, and strength for our spiritual life. Once that level of education has been achieved, the principal purpose of our regular reading changes somewhat. Henceforth we read to keep the supernatural before our minds, to develop and maintain the sense of the reality of the things we know by faith, to keep our attention on the eternal life of our soul rather than on our temporal interests, and above all to keep alive within us the memory and the presence of our Lord, so that we may live in touch and in union with Him, talking to Him, working with Him, resting with Him, always praying to Him and in Him.

Obviously individual needs will vary so much that there can be no question of prescribing for each one here. But some things may be said which are of fairly general application, though their adoption is left to the common sense of the individual reader. It must be remembered that although the spiritual life is a life of love, it is not a life of sentiment. On the contrary, love is based on knowledge given by faith and reason. In a word, devotion is founded on dogma. Now some acquaintance with the dogmatic teaching of the Church is essential for any Catholic. Quite a number of educated Catholics try to be satisfied with what they have learned of doctrine at school; this would seem to be a mistake. A man's mind develops after he leaves school; his knowledge and experience increase, his view broadens, his judgment matures, and he meets many problems that require a doctrinal solution. To expect the grown and mature mind of the man to be satisfied with the hazy memory of what his immature mind had acquired from the limited instruction suitable to boys is, at the least, imprudent; one runs the risk of having religion rejected as inadequate. It amounts almost to asking a grown man to re-adopt the mental habits and immature outlook of the schoolboy, to renew his juvenile tastes, and to maintain that attitude throughout his life towards the things that are of the greatest importance to him. If the man has grown up in a country where the Faith is in the atmosphere, as long as he still lives in that atmosphere he *may* retain his hold upon his religion without further instruction, but it seems almost like tempting Providence to hope that he will do so. Anyhow, the desirability of further instruction is evident. The question is still more acute in the case of the professional classes and of all those whose work produces or requires a trained mind. In one field of knowledge at least, such men are familiar with a complete and scientific treatment of a subject. Their trained minds, consciously or unconsciously, tend to estimate things by the reasons lying behind them, and if their knowledge of Catholicity is not sufficiently wide or deep to show them something of its solid foundations and extraordinary logic and to enable them to see that it can hold its own as a science with their own subject, they may be led to contempt for what little they do know of religion, and may even be tempted to abandon it altogether. Certainly, they are not likely to make it the driving force of their whole life, as God wants them to do.

Even if a man's reading of Catholic theology were only enough to teach him to know how much he does not know about it, a lot would be gained. But there is no reason why any educated Catholic should not go further, and bring his knowledge of Catholic theology up to the standards of the other branches of his knowledge—in principle if not in detail. There are sufficient manuals in English to meet the needs of most people, and their publication is on the increase. It must of course be admitted that a proper understanding of Catholic theology involves some idea of the ideas of Catholic philosophy, and the mode of thought connected with it. In fact, there is a lot to be said for the view that some training in such philosophy should be given as part of the ordinary Catholic secondary education. Theological discussion involves philosophy in much the same way as physics involves mathematics. And indeed both theology and philosophy are closely connected with the highest form of human thought, a form which has disappeared from practically the whole intellectual life of today outside the Catholic schools. For the source of all the evils and errors in the intellectual life of today—the disease that makes much of its utterances, the mere wanderings of a feverish imagination—is the loss of metaphysics and of the ability for abstract thought.

Perhaps a slight digression may be forgiven, especially as it is closely concerned with the understanding of the main thesis of this book, though it will not have the same reference to every reader. The human intellect draws its food for thought from the working of the senses, and when it represents to itself the *idea* of any object, that internal sense which is called the imagination, tries to form some corresponding picture or phantasm of the same object in terms of sensation or sense experience. Try the experiment of thinking about a triangle. Despite its name, the essential definition of a triangle is a figure which has three sides. That is the *idea* which the *intellect* forms of it, and that idea is absolutely universal in its application; it represents equally every possible triangle that exists or could exist: a figure with three sides.

The imagination, however, also tries to represent a triangle, but it has to be more concrete; and if one attends closely to its representation, one finds that the triangle in the imagination is, more or less vaguely, some *particular* triangle. It has a color, it has a definite shape, a definite orientation, a definite size, a definite feel— possibly a definite taste. It *tries* to become general by being vague. The sides are a neutral grey, and the whole thing is rather "woolly,"—but as soon as one attends to it carefuly, it becomes definite. Now one of the first things one has to learn in metaphysical thought, is to think with *ideas* and not with *phantasms*. One can imagine contradictions, but one cannot *think* them. One can imagine a being who is a man and a horse, but one cannot *think* him, for he is either rational or unrational, either one thing or the other. Obviously failure to abstract compietely from the particular accidents of the phantasm may lead to error, and when one argues from phantasms instead of ideas—doing one's thinking with the imagination instead of with the intellect—confusion and obscurity are inevitable.

Metaphysics is the science of being—that is, of any thing that exists or can exist—as being, and is, therefore, at the root of all other sciences, which indeed presuppose it. It has been abandoned by the modern mind, which seems to be unable to think otherwise than with its imagination. What cannot be imagined is—according to it—impossible; what can be imagined is, therefore, capable of being and existence. From this disease of the mind, we get sentiment for principle in morals, the particular for the general in argument, metaphor in place of reality, opinion for certainty, prejudice for judgment, quantity for quality, matter for the ultimate reality, and all the whole host of false coins that are current in the intellectual commerce of today. Curiously enough, it is often the trained mind that shows the greatest tendency to errors of this sort. The mathematician tends to think in terms of symbols and graphs, or at least in terms of quantity; the scientist, when he is not a mathematician, tends to be a mechanic. The medical man in particular finds it hard to get away from the "too, too solid flesh," and is often unable to recognize the reality of a vital principle which he cannot imagine, and which he does not know how to demonstrate by reason.

Intellectual Catholics, therefore, have need of knowing something of theology and philosophy; and indeed all Catholics of any education would do well to keep their knowledge of the Church's doctrine up to a sound standard. Where theology is read by the laity, it is usually rather from the point of view of apologetic argument than from that of a dogmatic foundation for true devotion. We would rather see the reverse. Granted that such meat is not for everyone, it is still quite true that there are a considerable number of Catholics who, if not starving, are at least undernourished for want of a proper diet of Catholic doctrine.

Such reading, however, is not the most important. In the beginning, the important thing is to acquire a knowledge of the principles of the spiritual life and to keep them constantly in mind; what then becomes more and more important as one grows in the spiritual life, is to keep one's mind supplied with motives for perseverance and advancement, and to restore daily any distortion in one's perspective and sense of relative values that may arise from everyday contacts. In all this the layman is faced with quite a different problem from that of the religious, and it is well that he should remember it. Each religious order "forms" its members in the novitiate by precept, example, and practice; each order has its own traditions, its own spirit, its own standard authors, and its own system and methods of the spiritual life. In every religious house a member can always find someone who is well acquainted with that spirit, and who is also well acquainted with him and understands his outlook. Advice on suitable reading is then easy to get, and can be accepted blindly.

The layman has no such planned path before him nor definite tradition behind him. He needs advice and counsel, but he needs it from someone who is prepared to examine his personal needs, and who is not predetermined to impose upon the client the adviser's own spiritual system. There are various schools of spirituality; in principle they can differ very little; but they can differ sufficiently in minor, accidental details to have quite opposite effects upon different souls, especially in the case of beginners or those who are not well grounded in the spiritual life. To a certain extent, therefore, the responsibility for choice rests upon the layman himself, and that is why we ask him to educate himself first in the spiritual life. The study of two or three standard works will give him some idea of its principles, and he will be better able to decide what to take and what to leave in all that he reads. For it must be remembered that not all that is written applies to all who read it. One excellent way of starting this education is by attending a series of retreat conferences, where the main points of the spiritual life are summarized. But it will probably take some time for the beginner to get his bearings and to develop a prudent sense of his own personal needs and vocation. Prayer for light and guidance is indispensable, and will always be heard.

Once educated, as we have said, one reads differently; in fact it is only then that one performs the exercise which we wish to prescribe as a daily practice of the spiritual life. The choice of a book is usually determined by its effect, and each reader has his own favorites. However, one should not be afraid to go back to some of those books that did not suit on first reading, for there is a time and a mood for every book. Prejudice must be laid aside; eagerness to master the contents of a book is a serious obstacle. If necessary, one should run through a book quickly to find out what it is about, and then go back and digest it.

That one word gives the key to the whole method of spiritual reading. For spiritual reading is a food, and we must digest what we read. First of all, therefore, the matter must be digestible. To some extent that is an individual question, but good-will can work wonders even when a book at first appears insipid and useless. The next thing is that we must read slowly; at least those parts of the book that are helpful should be read reflectively, and if they stimulate immediate thought, it is far better to pause and reflect on what has been read. Not every page need be read in this way. Common sense can never be left aside at any part of the spiritual life, and this is no exception.

Books that bear on conduct should be digested by examining one's own conduct in the light of their teaching. However, there is one mistake that must be avoided. If one finds difficulty in deciding whether some particular remark applies to one's own case, or in fact, if one hesitates to believe that it has personal reference, it is a mistake to let that uncertainty or hesitation disturb one's peace. It is always permissible to keep an open mind until one has read more, or until some advice can be obtained on the point. *Peace of mind and liberty of spirit are essential for the growth of the spiritual life;* and unless there is a *clear* reprimand from one's conscience, it is always wise to put aside anything in reading which upsets our peace or liberty—even if there be a doubt which appears to have some foundation—until some occasion of wise counsel arises. If God wishes to indicate some line of action to a soul He will not be content with speaking merely once. He will repeat His request with a quiet insistence, which sooner or later will produce a clear and certain knowledge of His wishes. He never blames us for refusing to follow doubtful leads. Uneasiness of this type is nearly always either the work of the devil or of our own pride.

This exercise of spiritual reading should be a daily one. One good way of ensuring that it be so is to fix a time for it each day. That is not always possible. But at least a certain minimum of time should be decided upon, and given to it daily. Ten minutes every single day is far better than a hundred minutes every seventh day, (we are not speaking now of educational reading). Individual needs differ widely, and any attempt here to fix a duration that would suit some readers would only mislead others. Besides, there is a close connection between reading, reflection and mental prayer; and as the spiritual life varies from season to season, or from soul to soul, time may be taken from one of these exercises and given to another of them.

If five minutes' reading is enough to start a man thinking for half an hour, then he is quite entitled to put down his book, and if it helps, to go off for a walk and think out what has occurred to him. If the mere opening of a book starts one's heart speaking to God, then reading has done its work—for the moment at any rate. Nevertheless, considering the difficulty and distaste that are connected with reading, we should be slow to dispense ourselves from our regular minimum, even for the sake of reflection or of prayer, for the gain may be short-lived. If the period we appoint for daily reading is long, it may help to use two books, one of a lighter type which could be used after a page or two of the heavier work has been read. The lives of the saints will often supply such a lighter fare.

Of some of these lives of the saints it is hard to write without apparent irreverence. Sometimes one is tempted to say that half of them should be publicly burned as obstacles to holiness. That, of course, would be an exaggeration; but like all exaggerations, it expresses a truth. And the truth is that there are many accounts written of the lives of the saints, which, because of manifold distortion and of the emphasis of the accidental at the expense of the essential, are further from the reality than are the stained glass attitudes which are seen in church windows. These latter have their justification in ornament and conventional symbolism; but a biographer is expected to tell us the exact truth about his subject. Now the truth about a saint is that he had a human nature exactly the same as each of us has, but that he so co-operated with God's grace as to love God with his whole heart and his whole soul, and that this love became the constant and principal motive of all his actions. Instead of telling us the truth, these accounts often mainly consist of miracles, extraordinary mortifications, and superhuman achievements, so that if they are taken at their face value, the saints must be a race apart, supermen, into whose ranks we have no possibility of entering. Recently, there has been a movement in the right direction; but the reader is warned that the true notion of holiness or of its possibility, must not be looked for in such books about the saints, and that is one reason why a sound grasp of the true principles of the spiritual life is so essential. There are, however, many sound works which show the true saint, and while setting a very high example before us, still leave us room to hope to imitate it.

This daily exercise of spiritual reading should always be closely connected with prayer. It should be commenced with a prayer, and if we are alone, it is good to kneel for a moment. But whatever our attitude, we should ask God to speak to us, to enlighten us and to give us the grace to carry out His wishes. In fact, we should make our reading a spiritual communion with our Lord: "Jesus, give me Yourself through this book!" If possible, one should try to read "in the divine presence." God, of course, is always present, but—there is a difference! We should try to read "under His eye," so to speak. And we should not be afraid to intersperse our reading with prayerful ejaculations, comments, or questions—any of those remarks that one might make if one could share a book with a friend.

We must, of course, read in a spirit of faith. That does not mean that we are not to read critically, or that we have to accept every statement that every writer makes, or to believe that every advice or direction given applies to our own particular case. On the contrary, one should only follow such advice with caution and prudence, taking frequent counsel of some wise priest or other guide. But we must believe that God will speak to us in our reading, and when He does speak, we must be ready to listen to Him and heed His words. In fact, if one asks in what dispositions should one read, the answer is: "with faith, hope, charity, humility, and submission to God's will."

Let us make it clear that our intention here is to give more prominence to the exercise of spiritual reading than is usually done. We regard this exercise as of very special importance for the cultivation of the spiritual life, and for facility and progress in prayer, particularly in the case of the laity. Quite apart from its fruits, it is an exercise of the spiritual life in itself, and as such is meritorious. We consider that a firm resolution to read in this fashion is of capital importance for everyone who wishes to live in Christ. In fact, unless some sufficient substitute for it be provided, we would say that there is as little chance of living spiritually without reading, as there is of living corporally without eating!

This reading has for its purpose first of all to make us know what we really have to do and how it is to be done, and afterwards to make us remember and think of what we are really doing and why it is to be done. It is so easy to forget the supernatural or to keep it all for Sunday morning, that one must do something to preserve its remembrance on week-days. Reading is a most important means to that end. And to reading one should join reflection.

We have still to treat of the exercise known variously as meditation and mental prayer, but we shall find that most books on the subject suggest a method which involves reading (generally to be done the night before), reflection, and prayer. The three things are made part of the one exercise. Our own desire to make at least two —if not three—practices of them. What we mean by reflection is that part of the exercise usually called meditation, to which the name properly applies. If a methodic approach to it is necessary, a method must be adopted. But there are many minds who pass from reading to reflection quite naturally and spontaneously, or who could easily acquire the habit of doing so. Such a habit is of incalcuable value for the spiritual life. And we do not visualize this exercise as one which is to be done in the church, or on one's knees—at least of necessity. To us it seems quite sufficient that a man should, say, sit down at his own fire—smoking if it helps him—or that he should go out for a walk, and think out the ideas he has found in his book or in his experience. As far as thinking goes, there are many men and women who will achieve much more in such a way, than by trying to think on their knees in the cold of the morning before breakfast, or in the church where their normal instinct is to pray. Besides, such a practice has the happy result of making this reflection something that fits in with the ordinary day's round; there is no question of a special religious exercise to be done and finished with when one gets up off one's knees. However, men and their minds vary, and each should do what suits him best in the matter. The usual advice in these matters is certainly sound and time tried; our own suggestions are inspired by a purpose of going as far as we can to bring the interior life within the reach of the layman, and making it spread through as much as possible of his whole day.

It is obvious then that both prayer and reading, as far as we have discussed them, lead on naturally to mental prayer, and that the boundary lines are not very definite. One subject that should be brought to our mind daily is the Passion of Christ. Assistance at Mass, or making the Way of the Cross, or some such practice would do so; but if no other provision is made for it it would be well to form a practice of spending a few minutes daily in reflection on, say, some Station of the Cross, or upon some sorrowful mystery of the Rosary.

There is no reason why we should not spend part of the time going to or from work, for example, in thinking of some of the stations. There is no reason why we may not think of the mysteries of the Rosary without saying the decade. A ploughman, for example, could take one mystery to each furrow—and we all could imitate him in some way.

Whatever way we do it, we must keep the memory of Christ and His love, of our union with Him, of the things which He has done for us and the things which He wants us to do for Him, fresh in our minds. He never forgot us for a single moment on earth; He never forgets us for a single moment in heaven; should we not daily think of Him who lived and died for love of us?

CHAPTER 10

Conversation with Christ

In the last two chapters we interrupted our consideration of the effects of man's incorporation in Christ upon his soul, to consider what each one should do that he might find and develop the life of Christ in his own soul. In doing so we did not say much about our union with Christ, even though one of the first effects of that union could be to make us pray with Christ to the Father. But we are considering things rather from the point of view of a person who is trying to find his way into the treasure chamber of his own soul—from outside, as it were. Such a one is not generally very Christ-conscious, and it needs prayer and reading to help him to become so. Another reason for the interruption in our exposition was to insist upon the need for personal effort. For it would be highly dangerous to imagine that, because everything—even every act of our will—depends on Christ, our attitude need be no more than a passive one, as if nothing depended upon our own efforts also.

And because there are so many mistaken notions about some of our duties, we went into some practical details. We are trying to meet the needs of many different types of souls, some of whom may only be at the beginning of the journey, and we wanted to show that there need be nothing burdensome or impossible about starting the practice of the interior life. As a result, our treatment had to be rather ragged, and it may be helpful to summarize here our view of prayer and spiritual reading.

Firstly, because we owe God our homage as our

Creator and sovereign Lord, there must be some formal prayer said daily in a formal posture. This prayer need not be long, but is should be sincere and fervent. Naturally, those who go to daily Mass will find this duty is best discharged there. Next, there should be some further prayer, perhaps of a different sort, during the day. What this is, will to some extent vary with the individual. Some will find a need for longer vocal prayers; the Rosary, some of the Psalms, some favorite prayers in a book, the Stations of the Cross, a visit to the Blessed Sacrament— some of these will be found helpful. But what we insist upon for all is the effort to develop a habit of talking to our Lord frequently during the day, quite informally. This should be preferred to the addition of long, regular prayers, except where there is some special reason for the contrary.

We also insist upon daily spiritual reading, and we distinguish two different types of reading. The first is to educate ourselves in revealed doctrine by reading expositions of doctrine, rather than apologetical arguments. In particular, the life and teaching of our Lord should be an object of special study, together with the general principles of the spiritual life. The education achieved, the predominant purpose of one's daily reading will be to keep oneself in touch with the supernatural, to develop a habit of seeing temporal things in their eternal perspective, and to renew one's remembrance of our Lord, of His love, and of His requirements in one's own regard. The need for this exercise we have stressed and here stress again, because it is so often overlooked or presupposed by those who write in terms of the religious life where such reading is already provided for. In addition, we urge the need for reflection, and suggest that it need not always be done so formally as some methods of meditation might seem to suggest.

Let us now approach this question of meditation and mental prayer. Let us give expression to a personal opinion and say that there are many times when we earnestly wish that both these words, "meditation" and "mental," could be completely removed from the whole literature of spirituality! There are two important meanings of the word prayer. One is the narrow sense of the asking of seemly things from God; this is the prayer of petition. The other is a broader one: the elevation of the mind and heart to God. No prayer in which the mind does not in some way share is prayer at all. No prayer ceases to be mental prayer because words are used to express one's thoughts or desires. Meditation in the strict sense of the word is *not* prayer, it may be accompanied by prayer; but in itself it is rather a preparation for prayer. It leads to prayer when acts or affections are produced; but these acts need not be expressed in words, although they may be if one finds it helpful. Meditation in the sense of thinking about God, or the things of God, is an essential element of the spiritual life which must never be omitted. It is what we have called reflection. The word meditation has unfortunately been applied to that exercise in many religious houses, at which the religious devote themselves to mental prayer, which we would rather call private prayer. Because it is called meditation, many feel that they must think about God and not talk to Him; even because it is called mental prayer, many come to the same conclusion. That is sheer nonsense. Whenever a man is talking to God in a rational way, he is praying. Whenever a man is looking at God and loving Him or adoring Him, even though no word pass his lips or form itself at all—he is praying. The essence of such prayer is the interior action of the soul; whether its acts find external expression in words or not, does not make any essential change in it.

It is interesting to note St. Teresa's mind on this point. She discusses it in her *Way of Perfection*, which is the best book to start with in studying her teaching, and one which we heartily recommend. Because, however, of the difficulty of getting a faithful translation we quote from William Walsh's *St. Teresa of Avila*.[1]

---

[1] *St. Teresa of Avila*, p. 286. The italics are Prof. Walsh's translation of St. Teresa. This will be found in chapter 25 of D'Alton's translation; cf. also chapters 22–24.

"St. Teresa bridges over the gap between mental prayer and vocal prayer, which has puzzled so many beginners, by saying in effect, that when the terms are properly understood, they are one and the same thing. When vocal prayer is properly·said—with understanding of what we are doing and with complete sincerity . . . it becomes mental prayer. What is mental prayer, then? It is *to think and to understand what we are saying, and with whom we speak, and who we are who dare to talk with so great a Lord. To think this and other similar things, of how little we have served Him and how much we ought to serve Him, is mental prayer; do not think it is some Arabic jargon, or be afraid of the name. To recite the 'Pater Noster' or what you will is vocal prayer, but see what bad music it will be without the former— even the words won't go together sometimes!"* [2]

Elsewhere she writes: "Know that with regard to our prayer being mental or not, the difference does not consist in keeping the mouth shut; for if uttering a prayer vocally, I do attentively consider and perceive that I am speaking with God, being more intent on this thought than on the words which I pronounce, then I use both mental prayer and vocal prayer together."

Leaving aside all such words with their association context of truth and error, let us say that some period of private intercourse with God forms an essential exercise for anyone who would live a spiritual life. In all religious houses a certain time is set apart for that exercise; its name does not matter. The layman, who wishes to make any progress in the spiritual life, will have to do the same. But his case is different. There is no routine or no government to see that he perseveres in this exercise; therefore, at the start at least, he should so arrange time and place, that he is not likely to omit the exercise when he begins to find it difficult to "pray." If therefore we are content to ask, say, ten or fifteen minutes daily, let no reader of St. Peter of Alcantara be scandalized. Ten minutes of genuine prayer every day will

[2] *Way of Perfection,* chap. xii.

certainly affect a man's life. So will half an hour's prayer daily—if it is kept up! But—will it be kept up? We would rather make sure of a minimum and let it grow with one's growth in spirituality, than quench the smoldering flax by too much fuel.

It is necessary, then, to make a *decision* to pray "personally" every day. The place and the hour must be chosen to suit the reader. Most authors prefer the morning; why—is not so obvious. To our mind, the evening time—especially if one can visit a church—will suit many people better. But, choose the time that suits you best and keep to it! One thing we insist upon. You must make a grim, ruthless resolve, that never, never, never, on any account whatsoever, will you give up the practice of *attempting* to pray thus daily, no matter how fruitless your attempt may seem. Until you make that resolve, your progress in the spiritual life will never be anything more than that of a cripple. No matter how often you take up the spiritual life, you will sooner or later be faced with the choice of giving it up, or making such a resolution about daily prayer. That is why we only ask you for the minimum.

The place may be the church, it may be a quiet room. You may stand, or you may sit, but it is preferable to start your prayers on your knees. If you can pray better walking, well and good. The essential thing is to talk to God; whatever helps you to do that is good. To talk to God, you have first to call Him to mind. So you must start by an act of faith in God—"O my God, I believe in You, I believe You are listening to me." Then to show that you know that He is God: "I adore You as my Lord and God"—and then to show that you remember His mercy: "I hope in You as my Father; I trust in You as my Saviour; and finally, because—well—reasons are left to yourself:—"I love You, or rather I don't love You enough; make me love You more." That is only a tentative sample. One word is enough if it puts us in touch with God. If we have anything more to say to Him, let us say it. The beginner, however, will generally find that he has very little to say, and so he will have to start thinking or reflecting. But he can at least admit his inability and accept it, and here again we have our five virtues of faith, hope, charity, humility and abandonment to the will of God.

This is where the process called meditation is of great assistance, and where one will reap the profit of the reading that has been so stressed. One should approach this exercise of prayer with a definite subject as a matter for reflection, chosen to suit one's needs. The choice of subjects is wide; they will often suggest themselves during reading. The various scenes of the Passion of our Lord, the incidents of His life, the fourteen Stations of the Cross, the mysteries of the Rosary, the four last things, sin, various virtues we need, or bad habits we wish to change; all these would be suitable subjects. If the subject has to do with our Lord, let us represent the incident under consideration to ourselves and think of it as really present. We must never forget that God is in our soul, and we can speak to Him there even under the appearance of any of the mysteries of His human life. Excessive detail of setting in the representation is to be avoided. The story of the good nun who was using the Last Supper as a subject for prayer is classical. She finished her "prayer" quite upset. Try as she would, she could not succeed in placing our Lord out of the draught! Such solicitude is unreasonable and merits the reproof given to Martha. All that is wanted is a sufficient picture to fix our thoughts and suggest some acts to us.

In the case where we choose something of a more abstract type, say the virtue of hope, our procedure is rather by way of discussion and self-examination. "What reason have I for hope? Do I hope in God, or do I hope in myself? What has God not done for me? Do I worry? Do I really trust Him?" and so on. These considerations will suggest acts or "remarks" to be made to God. "I am sorry for being such a fool as not to trust You, who died for me." "The reason I am so prone to worry is because I am trusting in myself rather than in You," and so on.

Now these "acts," or "affections" as they are called, are the important, and in fact, the real part of prayer. The whole purpose of considerations is to lead up to these acts. The word "affections," which is generally applied to these acts, has a meaning in this context quite different from its ordinary connotation in English. It does *not* imply feeling, emotion, or tenderness. Affections in prayer are essentially acts of the will, by which it moves towards God, and elicits other acts of the different virtues, such as faith, hope, love, sorrow, humility, submission, gratitude, or praise. Sometimes these acts can be made without great difficulty. More often however—especially in the initial stages of the spiritual life—they cannot be produced without consideration and effort. That is why the word meditation is so often used to describe the exercise which leads to such acts; and some such preparation is obviously necessary.

On consulting any of the numerous books on meditation, or books of meditations, it will be found that there is a method of procedure which is generally recommended, and often considered indispensable. The principle of the method may be outlined as follows: a subject for prayer is chosen and prepared the evening before, probably with the aid of a book. It is divided into two or three "points" for consideration, and each point is to lead to certain conclusions, acts, petitions and resolutions. These—to some extent at all events—are also arranged in advance. When the time for prayer comes, the exercise is commenced by a definite effort to advert to the presence of God, and to banish all distracting thoughts. A short prayer for help is made, and in some cases certain "preludes" are used to fix the faculties; for example, one forms a vivid picture of the incident which is the subject of the prayer. Then one applies oneself to the consideration of the first point. Some writers go into detail and suggest various questions which will help one to make these considerations, and to realize the lessons of what is under consideration. This manner of working is often a great help.

From the reflections of the first point, one passes on to self-examination, and certain acts or affections usually suggest themselves. These should be made, formulating them quite simply, repeating them if one feels drawn to do so. Petitions will generally arise from this reflection, and matter for some resolutions will be found. Proceeding in this way through the divisions of the subject, one finally thanks God for His goodness and light and commits to His aid the resolutions that have been made.

We cannot here treat the subject at sufficient length to give adequate practical instruction on the use of such methods, and must refer the reader to any of those innumerable works on the subject. But some discretion is necessary in the use of such books and in the use of the method they prescribe. Some simple method is desirable for nearly all beginners.[3] The more complicated methods may help, but if they do not, they should not be employed. Method is a means to an end; and in this case it is the end which justifies the method, and the method is only justified insofar as it leads to the end, to which is must always yield. Methodic meditation for its own sake is not, strictly speaking, prayer.

But it will probably be found that those books which prescribe a detailed method of meditation are aiming at something else as well as at prayer. Their purpose is to produce convictions and to apply those convictions to everyday life. Such a result is obviously essential to a proper spiritual life, and if the means usually used to produce it in this exercise are omitted, it must be provided for elsewhere. That is why we insist that these three things—reading, reflection and prayer, must be considered together.

It seems as if the program frequently drawn up for daily meditation is intended to combine these three in the one exercise. We prefer to separate them; partly, at least. We would make reading and prayer two sepa-

---

[3] We would recommend to the beginner a little work by Fr. Wilberforce, O.P., *An Easy Method of Mental Prayer.*

rate exercises, by no means unconnected of course; and reflection should be provided for in one or the other, if it is not done at some other time of the day. Therefore, if we urge that mental prayer is an exercise in which one should aim primarily at *praying* and only use considerations insofar as they are necessary to produce prayer, it must always be understood that we also insist that reading should supply the other fruits of methodical meditation. And if we suggest that the methodical consideration usually prescribed for mental prayer be reduced to a minimum, we expect that it should be replaced by the exercise of spiritual reading and reflection. In fact, the books usually written as "meditations" are the very books that we think should be included in the list for spiritual reading. They must, of course, be read properly, not as one reads a newspaper or a novel, but as a woman reads a catalog, or as a man reads, say, the specification of a new car or an insurance prospectus: *with careful consideration.* However, this separation of the process into two exercises is by no means intended to be a complete one. Indeed, we hope that in time even spiritual reading will become a prayer; and, even from the beginning, we would suggest that one try to reflect not so much by talking to oneself but rather by talking to Jesus, about the subject of one's thoughts.

But it is impossible to be definite on the point. So much depends upon the individual concerned; his mentality, his spiritual development, his reading, his habits of thought, his temperament—all his circumstances have to be considered. One man's meat, in this matter as in all others, is often another man's poison. If we are asked for a personal opinion on the point we would say that the whole arrangement of these three practices—reading, reflection, and prayer—is a personal matter that should be decided for each individual case by the advice of some competent spiritual counsellor. The person chosen as adviser should be someone who has the necessary knowledge and experience of the spiritual life, who knows and understands one's own circumstances and peculiarities, and who has a sufficiently open mind not to insist upon imposing a ready-made system without any consideration for the needs of the laity in general and of this layman in particular. It is not easy to get in contact with such an adviser, and the point should be the subject of earnest prayer to God. Books are a great help, but sooner or later personal advice may be necessary. However, it must always be remembered that the spiritual life develops, and hence it becomes necessary at intervals to revise one's arrangements. Therefore, advice once accepted need not bind us permanently. In fact, with regard to accepting and following advice, the laity are not quite in the same position as religious who can unhesitatingly follow the directions of their superior. There is a certain personal responsibility on the layman even in following advice. He is, so to speak, his own superior, and while prudent superiors do not decide things without advice, the responsibility for the decision is their own. The layman has to choose his own adviser and to use considerable prudence in accepting his advice. It is necessary to draw attention to this point, for one not unfrequently meets people who are in serious difficulties through trying to follow blindly advice which is obviously unsuited to their individual circumstances and which was probably the result of a misunderstanding.

The point becomes of further importance when it is remembered that prayer changes as one advances; and the advice of one season is not suitable to the next. Fresh counsel must be sought as one develops. As knowledge increases and convictions grow stronger, the affections in prayer are produced more freely and with less need for considerations. They tend to occupy an ever increasing part of the prayer, while considerations are reduced to a minimum and may even become quite unnecessary. Obviously, the methodical program must be altered to suit this development. A further change also occurs inasmuch as one act comes to include quite a number of others, and even one word begins to express a meaning that formerly needed a few sentences. This simplification of prayer may be quite a normal psychological development, and should not be interfered with by any attempt to follow out a fixed program of separate acts. Even it may go so far as to remove all need or desire for words, and one simply looks at God and loves Him. This must never be regarded as waste of time. It is the prayer of Mary, not that of Martha. In prayer, it is the movements of the heart that matter. Words are good insofar as they help the movements of the heart. But words for the sake of words, or repetition for the mere sake of repetition, should be avoided. There is no need to keep talking all the time.

In fact, it may be harmful to do so. Prayer is a conversation with God, and if we call it a heart to heart conversation we are giving the adjective a new depth of meaning. For in prayer heart speaks to heart as nowhere else. But God has His part in this conversation and often He wishes us to listen to Him. Sometimes the effort on our part to keep on saying something is the result of a bad conscience; we do not want Him to remind us of some infidelity or some obvious inconsistency which we are unwilling to change. In fact, the normal result of progress in virtue and devotion to God's will is to lead us to that type of prayer where words are insufficient. Silence alone is eloquent, and a smile—even a smile of the heart—can speak volumes. This simplicity of prayer, at least in a protracted form, generally presupposes a fair degree of advance in the spiritual life and a considerable purity of conscience. Of the connection between prayer and the spiritual life we have written at great length elsewhere and we would refer the reader to that book.[4] It is not a subject that can be safely summarized, although we shall have to return to the point in these pages.

For the moment, however, we are dealing with beginners, and there are some points we would like to stress. From the very beginning the beginner should try to bring

[4] Fr. Eugene Boylan, O.C.R., *Difficulties in Mental Prayer.*

our Lord as much as possible into his prayer. Even in making considerations, he should do so by discussing the point with our Lord. We would suggest that the prayer be commenced with a simple spiritual communion, which would focus one's attention upon Christ present in the soul, and the prayer could be made as if one had just received our Lord in Holy Communion. A few words to our Lady will often make it much easier to find her Son; and for those to whom the grace is given, our Lady's presence in their prayer will often be a great help. These, however, are personal questions and at the risk of being quite impractical we refuse to impose any system. One thing we wish to repeat. It must never be thought that the application of the word "mental" to prayer means that the notion of talking to God is excluded. It merely means that in talking to Him, we should mean what we say. Our words should come from our heart and mind, and must be quite sincere. Even if there are no words at all there must be sincerity. And if we are making use of some well known formula for prayer, provided we make it sincerely our own, it is still mental prayer.

This talking to God, with or without words, should not be confined to the time of prayer. That cannot be repeated too often. At various moments of the day we should make "remarks" to our Lord—petitions, thanks, admiration, comments on His providence, aspirations; anything that will keep us in contact with Him. These aspirations should either be in our own words, or in some set formula which we have made our own, so that we mean it every time we use it. Further, one should try to cultivate a habit of recollection, a constant memory of the presence of God. This involves a certain guard on one's thoughts to the extent, at least, of keeping God's law in our imaginings as well as in our deeds. This sort of interior mortification is of great assistance to spiritual progress.

Those who find it hard to do anything at the time of prayer, either in consideration or affections, may get help from the use of a book. They could take some prayer and read it slowly, stopping frequently to let the sentiments expressed sink in and become their own. Or they could read a few lines of some suitable work, and pause to think over what has been read and try to make some comment upon it to our Lord.[5] Each one has to find the way that suits him best. There are times when no way will suit; every thing is dry, dull, and insipid, even positively distasteful. All one can do is kneel there, quite helpless. That can be a most effective prayer, and may draw down great graces from God. If a man is doing all he can reasonably do, God expects no more, and He is quite satisfied with such service. There is never any need to follow a method slavishly to the extent of insisting upon completing all the points, etc. In fact, when acts or "affections" come and continue, one should not interrupt them to complete a predetermined program. If daily spiritual reading is made as we insist it should be, there need never be any anxiety about omitting considerations at prayer. On the other hand, if affections do not come,—it is good to remember that the heart often says things that cannot be put into words, and that even during consideration the heart may be praying quite fervently.

There is one particular type of reflection that should be made every day,—namely, self-examination. At the end of the day, a short glance over the day's work will reveal in what one has offended God. Having noted any sins or infidelities, one should repent of them, and decide upon suitable measures to prevent them in the future, at least to prevent their becoming habitual. There is another type of self-examination that is a most effective means of advance. In it one examines oneself upon some one particular point, some particular weakness that one wishes to overcome. A daily glance at one's performance in its regard—for example, at a habit of talking about oneself, or indulging in sloth—will soon have an

[5] A very suitable book is *The Sufferings of Our Lord Jesus Christ*, by Fr. Thomas of Jesus, O.S.A.

effect upon one's behavior. Some writers advise a detailed numerical examination of the number of falls, and a comparison with previous performances. This may be helpful; but it will not always be necessary or prudent to go into numbers. In fact, it might be misleading to do so.

The subject of this particular examination, as it is called, should not be changed too frequently, and each point should be retained until some result has been achieved. The choice of subject for this examination is a matter for prudence. Obviously, the more important failings should be dealt with first, especially those key failings that are at the root of many others. But there are times when the best way to capture a "strong point" is to by-pass it for the moment, and build up a new front from which to attack it with greater strength. It may be necessary to develop first some positive virtue or practice to deal with the situation. For example, by concentrating on developing the habit of daily Mass, one might find strength to overcome some deeply rooted habit. There is, of course, no use in worrying over trifles and letting serious faults go unchecked. That is straining a gnat and swallowing a camel. But, in the beginning especially, it would be a good plan to choose something that is not too difficult, and which admits a reasonable hope of successful warfare. By doing so, a certain degree of confidence in the method is developed; whereas, to tackle a strongly rooted habit first of all, might easily lead to failure and consequent discouragement. Prudence is an essential quality of all virtuous acts.

This particular examen is only a special part of what we have called reflection. The three practices of reading, reflection and prayer, are closely connected and interdependent. They are the fundamental part of a man's own effort at his spiritual development, and the beginning of the road that leads to journey's end—the finding of Christ. There is one particular purpose that should be aimed at in using them. It arises out of the very common habit of dividing our life into watertight compartments.

Some keep their religion for Sunday and let business and pleasure rule the rest of the week. Others do indeed devote a certain time daily to some exercises of piety, but the rest of the day is regulated by quite different principles. Men and women tend to follow the code of their associates, and in business and in pleasure this is often more pagan than Christian. What has been written in the earlier part of this book makes it quite clear that religion applies to every moment of our life. Christ wants to share every single action which we perform and what He cannot share is well nigh worthless. To enable Him to share everything, all this division and inconsistency must be removed from our life and everything brought under a uniform ideal. That a suitable ideal is supplied by the aim to do God's will in all things, will be shown in one of the following chapters.

But frequent reflection and self-examination are necessary as a means to break down these divisions. It may be granted that the problem for the laity is not an easy one to solve. The layman has to work and play on equal terms with his fellow men and still spiritualize his habitual outlook. His problems are not to be solved by a rigid application of the regime of the religious life to the lay state. They are peculiar to that state, and need very sympathetic handling. And, we may add, the solution of this general problem of making Catholicity a vital force in the everyday life of the laity is one of the most urgent needs of the day. It would hardly be an exaggeration to say that the fate of Christendom depends upon it. A considerable degree of prudent adaptability is called for to solve the problem. Our own view would be that only the necessary minimum should be insisted upon, and further development left to the spontaneous good will of the people concerned. If an atmosphere of encouragement and sympathetic consideration is created, we feel sure the necessary development will take place. And if a soul is put in regular, daily contact with our Lord, His charm will soon have its influence.

There are many things that are settled for a religious

by obedience, which have to be left to the personal judgment and prudence of the layman. Our own idea would be to get him to develop the power of solving his own problems and applying sound principles to the regulation of his day. Advice and counsel, of course, are invaluable and necessary, but the decision should be his own. After all, every baptized person in the state of grace has the seven gifts of the Holy Ghost. They are meant for use. And the sacramental graces, as we shall see, are always at the disposal of any earnest soul. If encouraged along these lines, it would seem that one is more likely to develop that sound instinct which will go far to supernaturalize all the actions of the day.

That is another reason we are so anxious to put the beginner in touch with our Lord as soon as possible in prayer, and urge him to try to develop a sense of continual partnership and friendship with Jesus in all the works of the day. For Christianity is not a set of rules; it is a Person—the Person we call Christ. And it is in Christ that all things are to be re-established and reunited and reconciled to the Father.[6]   And since Christ came on earth to do the will of the Father, He can always be found where that will is being done; and the ordinary round of the day's work is part of that will, so that this personal friendship and continual search for Christ is an excellent way to restore the unity of one's life and to supernaturalize all one's work. In fact, it will be found that if one does one's part by reading, reflection and prayer, as we have indicated, the ordinary things and events of the day begin to speak to one of God and keep one in continual mind of Him. Before, however, considering submission to God's will as a means of union with Him, let us first discuss another important means which He has provided—the sacramental system.

[6] Cf. Col. i, 19–20; Eph. i, 9–10.

CHAPTER 11

Christ in His Sacraments

I N the earlier chapters of this book we saw that we are made members of the Mystical Body of Christ by the sacrament of baptism, and in the last three chapters we have been considering certain means by which we can develop the life that is ours as a result of this incorporation. As in the human body there are special channels which supply the organs and the members with what they need and maintain in them the vital circulation of the whole organism, so also in the Mystical Body of Christ, there are special channels by which we are supplied with the graces necessary for our functions and are maintained in vital union with Christ, our head. These are the seven sacraments. A sacrament is a sensible sign permanently instituted by Christ to give grace. They are, as it were, seven principal arteries of the Mystical Body by which the power of the life-giving Passion of Christ is applied to our souls according to our needs.

Each sacrament needs a human minister; but his qualifications vary according to the sacrament. Only a bishop can ordain, and, except in special cases, confirm; only a priest can consecrate the Sacrament of the Altar, absolve sinners or anoint the dying; the two parties getting married are the ministers of the sacrament of matrimony; but because of the importance of baptism, any lay person can administer it in case of necessity. But in every sacrament the principal minister is Christ, the secondary and human minister only acts in His name. Christ still lives in His Church—He has promised to

be with her all days even to the end of the world—
and nowhere is His living power more evident than in
the administration of the sacraments, nowhere can He
be found in such an effective way as by approaching
them. There He speaks to us, there He forgives us, there
He strengthens us, there He sanctifies us, there He gives
us the kiss of reconciliation and of friendship, there He
gives us His own merits and His own power, there He
gives us Himself. We have already spoken of Him as a
seed that is cast into the soil of the universe, thrusting
out roots in all directions to seize upon the very earth
and change it into itself. Nowhere is that figure more
forcibly realized than in the sacraments. For the sacraments seize upon us, digest us and make us part of Christ.
They are the roots of the vine of which we are to be the
branches.

This is so true of the sacrament of baptism that St.
Thomas can write: "Baptism incorporates us into the
Passion and Death of Christ . . . whence it follows that
the Passion of Christ is communicated to each baptized
person as a remedy, *just as if each one had himself suffered and died. . . .* For the Passion of Christ is sufficient
satisfaction for all the sins of all men." And again:
"Inasmuch as he becomes a member of Christ, the baptized person shares in the penal value of Christ's Passion,
as though he had himself endured the penalty."[1] And
more generally he states: "Since Christ's Passion preceded our sins as a kind of universal cause of the remission of sins, it needs to be applied to each one for the
cleansing of his personal sins. Now this is done by baptism and penance and the other sacraments which derive
their power from the Passion of Christ."[2]

Here we have an authoritative statement of the working of the sacraments: they apply to each of us the
Passion and Death of Christ. There are two principal
ways in which grace can grow in our souls; two ways,
in other words, in which we can become more closely
united to Christ and enter more fully into the life of

[1] *Summa* iii, 69–2, and ad 1.   [2] *Summa* iii, 69. 1, ad 4.

His Mystical Body. These are: by merit and by the sacraments. We have already considered prayer and meditative reading as two methods of seeking God. We considered them first because they dispose us for the use of other methods. Both are meritorious, and prayer can also obtain grace for us by impetration. This we could call merit in a very broad sense. Merit we have not yet discussed. To all good works done in charity God has attached a promise of a reward. This reward includes both an increase of grace, and an increase of eternal happiness in heaven. But although God, and He alone, can produce grace in our souls, He has made His action so dependent on ours that where there is question of merit, we are the cause, in a sense, of our growth in grace; and although the increase comes from Him, it depends upon our own actions, our own powers, and our own dispositions. The scholastic theologians used the phrase *ex opere operantis* to distinguish this manner of action where the result depends upon the agent, from another where the result depends upon the thing done and not upon the agent, and which they designated by the phrase *ex opere operato*.

This latter is quite a different manner of action and is the way in which the sacraments give grace. The grace depends upon the intrinsic value of the sacrament itself and not upon the dispositions of holiness of the minister. In the sacraments, God, through Christ, is the cause of the grace produced not merely in the sense that He is the author of the giving of every grace, but in the further sense that the sacrament itself in some way replaces ourselves as the agent, and by a power derived from Christ, does for us in a more direct way what we do for ourselves indirectly in the case of merit. In fact, so far as any question of merit enters in, it is the infinite merits of Christ that are concerned in the sacraments and not our own finite merits.

The *power* of the sacraments to produce grace, once the conditions for validity are realized, is entirely independent of the dispositions and merits of the human minister; the *effect* of the sacrament is influenced by the dispositions of the recipient just as the amount of water taken from a well is influenced by the size of the vessel used. The result is that in ordinary cases, there is no comparison between the effects produced by the sacraments, and the effects produced by the merits of our own good works. To illustrate the point by an extreme example, let us take the case of a man in the state of mortal sin who is sorry for his sin with *attrition* only, his motive being, say, the loss of heaven. No matter what other dispositions that man may have or how intense his sorrow may be, he cannot *merit* the state of grace; his soul is dead. If, however, the same man goes to confession with this attrition and validly receives the sacrament of penance, his sins are forgiven, he is restored to the state of grace, his soul becomes alive again. The reason is, to put it summarily, that in one case he is depending upon his own merits, in the other, he is availing himself of the merits of Christ. It is true that the merits of Christ can be applied to us by faith, but even so, our own merits may limit the application.

The sacraments, then, perpetuate and diffuse the life-giving power of Christ in His Church which is His Body. Unlike the organs of the human body, which are in permanent connection with the arteries and channels of supply, we, the members of the Mystical Body, are free; it is by our own choice that we approach the sacraments and join ourselves by them to Christ. Each of the sacraments can give us an increase of life of grace, but each has in addition, a special grace of its own. It puts at our disposal the strength and merits of Christ for a special purpose. In baptism we are cleansed from original sin and born in Christ. The sacrament of confirmation also gives us an increase of habitual grace, as this sharing of the divine nature is called, but it adds a special help. It corresponds to a "coming of age" in civil life—to an entering into manhood—and it puts at our disposal a divine source of strength to live up to our faith in our dealings with others. We are strengthened to take our place in society as *Catholics,* as members of Christ—for that is what a Catholic is—and to profess our faith openly, even to the extent of suffering and dying for it if there be need.

When that doctrine came first to our notice at school, a quarter of a century ago, few of us visualized the prospect of ever having to put their truth to the test. Yet, it can be safely said that since then, more Catholics have suffered and died for their faith than at any period of history; and there is no reason to believe that the days of such things are over. The grace, then, of confirmation is a most practical one for each of us, even in its extreme form of giving us the supernatural fortitude to suffer and die for the faith. This grace is the source of that extraordinary strength and courage which one sees in the martyrs. Woe betide the Catholic who in the hour of trial should rely upon his own natural courage and determination. Far better for him to rely upon his own weakness and put his trust in God's strength—to glory in his own infirmities and invoke the strength of Christ, which is his by the sacrament of confirmation.

But there is no need to wait for such an extreme situation before using this grace of confirmation. Every lay man and woman in modern society has a daily need for divine help to live up to the faith. The difficulty of doing so is becoming greater every day. But this power that we have of professing our faith by confirmation is something akin to the priest's power of consecrating bread and wine. One is not conscious of it; it must be believed in, and it must be used with faith and confidence.

One way in which that belief and confidence should become manifest, is in courage with which we ought to face all occasions where there is any need to live up to our Catholicity in word or in act, and to face ridicule, scorn, loss, or even injury, by doing so. Once the prudence or the necessity of the action is clear, there should be no more hesitation—no more wondering where the strength is going to come from. For that strength is already ours by the sacrament of confirmation, and all

God asks of us is that we admit its divine origin, by an appeal—even by a mute appeal—to Him; He will be with us in the hour of need. Such occasions are numerous nowadays.

One such occasion is when one has to face the superior smiles that are directed to our "old fashioned" notions of Catholic morality, and the strain becomes all the greater when the quiet tide of tacit assumption is slowly but surely carrying the majority away from true Catholic teaching. On such occasions one cannot help feeling unreasonable, provincial, and even childish. But there are times when one has to be a fool for Christ's sake. There is also a more general need for special help which arises from the fact that we have to "die daily," to die to ourselves and to our own life because of our faith. On all such occasions, we must remember that we are living members of Christ's Mystical Body, and that in becoming such we have renounced ourselves, and "the world, the flesh, and the devil," and that we are confirmed and strengthened by the promise of God's grace to meet all such difficulties; we should remember that we have to live up to our membership of Christ— *noblesse oblige*—and instead of being self-conscious by feeling, we should become Christ-conscious by faith. But it is well to remember that although we share in Christ's strength, we must also share in His prudence, and that supernatural prudence and common sense must govern our conduct in such matters.

Among the other Sacraments which are only received once or rarely, matrimony is of such importance that we shall consider it apart, since for many lay people it can be the starting point of a very spiritual life. The sacrament of holy orders primarily concerns the clergy, but, inasmuch as it constitutes certain men as mediators between God and mankind, it has an effect that concerns the laity, especially when there is a question of discovering God's will, and it is in that connection that is concerns us. The sacrament of extreme unction has a special connection with that of penance, which is a means of approaching Christ that we must now consider.

The sacrament of penance was instituted by Christ to forgive sins committed after baptism. Baptism removes all sin that is on the soul, and all the punishment due to it; everything on the debit side of one's past life is blotted out. But is cannot be used as a remedy for sins committed afterwards, since it cannot be repeated. These sins must be remitted either through our own sorrow or normally through the sacrament of penance. Where there is question of mortal sins, they can only be remitted by sorrow when that sorrow is that which is called perfect contrition, arising out of the love of God rather than the love of ourselves, and which must also include at least an implicit desire of going to confession. In confession, the sorrow which is called attrition is sufficient; such would be the sorrow which has for its motive the fear of hell or the loss of heaven. When a sinner who has such a sorrow for all his mortal sins is validly absolved in confession, all his mortal sins are forgiven; the eternal punishment which they have earned is remitted and he is restored to the friendship of God. God again·takes up His dwelling in his soul and he becomes once more a living member of Christ's Mystical Body, participating again by grace in the divine nature.

It is true that not all the effects of his sin are removed. Even though the *eternal* punishment has been remitted, there is still a *temporal* penalty to be paid. This can be done by works of satisfaction in this life; if not paid here, it will have to be suffered in purgatory. The "penance" which the priest imposes after the confession, has a very special efficacy for making satisfaction for our sins because of its connection with the sacrament. All our good works, all that we willingly suffer, can be used to make satisfaction, and we can even invoke the merits of Christ, those of His Mother and of the saints in our behalf. The merits of Christ are always at our disposal, if we know how to make use of them by faith, hope, charity, humility and submission. But in the Mass, we can find our Lord's own satisfaction for our sins in a most accessible form. It is important to realize that there is a great difference between making satisfaction for our sins in purgatory and doing so here on earth. In purgatory, the sufferings are much greater, and we cannot merit by them. Here on earth we can make satisfaction with far less suffering, and every act we perform for that end can be meritorious; so that even in satisfying for our sins, we can grow in love of God and earn a closer union with Him in heaven.

In the sacrament of penance we obtain a special grace to help us to recover from the effects of our sins and a new strength to fight against our weakness. This aspect of confession is often forgotten, especially by those who have only venial sins to confess. Just because they are "only" venial sins, there is sometimes a tendency not to worry about them. By co-operating with the grace of the sacrament, we can acquire a new horror of these sins, a new delicacy of conscience, and a more correct notion of our own weakness. To quote the present Holy Father:

> For a constant and speedy advancement in the path of virtue we highly recommend the pious practice of frequent confession . . . for by this means we grow in a true knowledge of ourselves and in Christian humility, bad habits are uprooted, spiritual negligence and apathy are prevented, the conscience is purified and the will strengthened, salutary spiritual direction is obtained, and grace is increased by the efficacy of the Sacrament itself.[3]

It should be noted that the context of this quotation is concerned with the confession of *venial* sins.

About such confession there is one point that is important. Sorrow for our sins is an essential condition for a valid reception of the sacrament. This sorrow must extend to all the mortal sins of which we have been guilty; if there are no mortal sins, we must be truly sorry for at least some of the venial sins confessed. Other-

[3] *Mystici Corporis.*

wise the sacrament is invalid. Now sorrow implies a sincere purpose and decision to avoid sin in the future, and it is important to make sure that we have such a purpose in regard to at least some of the venial sins confessed when there are no mortal sins. To make certain that there is proper matter for absolution it is always advisable to include some sins of the past for which we are certainly sorry and which we are determined to avoid in future. Such a practice saves our confession from being invalid should it consist only of routine venial sins for which we have not such a sufficient resolution of amendment.

The question of sorrow is one which is not always properly understood. The sorrow necessary for confession is an act of the will by which through the help of God's grace we turn away from our sins, resolving to avoid them in future, and turn towards God. The motive must be supernatural; the fear of hell, the loss of heaven, or the love of God are such motives. Since the sorrow is an act of the will, *it need not be felt.* There are some who have such a lively sorrow for their sins that they can shed tears over them; others have such a vivid feeling of eternal loss that they feel a fear that is greater than any other fear. These are exceptional cases. Most souls, even very holy souls, would *feel* more sorrow at some painful loss, for example, the death of a parent, than they would *feel* for their sins. That, however, does not lessen the value of their sorrow for sin in the least. Feelings have nothing to do with it; the real measure and test of the depth of sorrow is the *will* and the *decision* to avoid sin in the future. In fact, that is the real meaning of "doing penance"; for the old word for penance meant "change of heart."

This "change of heart" is one of the best ways of finding the kingdom of God which, as He Himself tells us, is within us. When a friend has offended us, all his external protestations of sorrow and his attempts to restore friendly relations are quite inadequate if his heart has not changed. Even his firm resolve not to repeat the offence does not suffice if its motive is a mere selfish regret of personal loss quite unconnected with ourself. If he regret the loss of our *mutual friendship,* even for what it meant to him, then, of course, friendship can be restored. But to reach its fullest value such renewed friendship must be based on a regret for having offended *us.*

It is true that the power of the sacrament makes the case somewhat different when there is a question of sorrow for sin. Imperfect contrition is quite sufficient for the reception of the sacrament. But when we approach the sacrament of penance we should remember that the friendship we have injured by our sins is the greatest of all our friendships. More than that, we should remember that it is against our greatest friend and lover that we have sinned. More than that still, we should try to see that, even apart from His friendship towards ourselves, we have treated Him in His own self badly and shamefully by our sin, for He is so deserving of all our love. In other words, it is well to try to be sorry for our sins because they have offended *Him,* even if we start by being sorry because they have injured ourselves.

Still though our sorrow may not reach the height of perfect contrition, we must not fail to have complete confidence in the generosity of God's pardon. Provided that we have the minimum sorrow for the validity of the sacrament, the absolution has its due effect upon our souls; and the grace of God, with the infused virtues of faith, hope and charity—especially that of charity which has been lost by mortal sin—are poured into our soul. This restored virtue of charity gives us the power of loving God again with a supernatural love, and we should strive to awaken the love after confession if we have not been able to do so before it.

It is important to remember that it is for our sins considered as offences against God that we have to be sorry; there may have been some natural satisfaction or even good result attached to them we cannot regret as such. Even the Church sings of the "happy fault" of Adam which was the cause of such a wonderful Redemption. It is the offence against God that is in question, and for which we must be truly sorry. It should also be noted that sincere sorrow is quite compatible with a well-founded fear of falling again. When a bad habit has been formed, such a fear can easily arise. All that is necessary for absolution is that one *decide* here and now not to repeat the sin and to avoid the danger of falling into it. The fact that weakness afterwards overcomes us, does not change the value of the confession. Some people have a very obstinate sort of pride which makes them very unwilling to admit the guilt of their actions. They feel they would be lowering themselves. The truth is quite the opposite. When a man insists on the rectitude of an action which was really wrong, he is merely showing his own lack of ideals and the lowness of his moral standards. When, on the contrary, he admits that he has done wrong and says he is sorry, he shows that he has raised himself to a new level of ideals and to a higher moral standard. Even in the natural order, he has raised himself by admitting his error.

It is of capital importance that we never, never let our past sins—however filthy or treacherous they may have been—come between us and God, or make us in any way doubtful of His love and afraid to approach Him in absolute and intimate confidence. God does not do things by halves. When He forgives sins, He forgives completely. Their guilt is blotted out in its entirety, and He will not reproach us with them again. But His generosity goes even further. When a soul falls into mortal sin all the merits of its past life are lost. If, however, the soul repents and obtains pardon, these merits revive again; such is God's generosity and love.

The parable of the Prodigal Son is the picture which our Lord Himself gave us of how God forgives sins. The prodigal had claimed his inheritance and had lost everything in riotous living. Reduced to want and degradation, he was moved by sheer hunger to say: *I will arise and go to my father, and say to him: Father, I have sinned against heaven and before thee: I am not worthy to be called thy son: make me as one of thy hired servants.* And the parable tells how *when he was a great way off, his father saw him and he was moved with compassion, and running to him, fell upon his neck, and kissed him.* The parable goes on to relate that although the son begged to be allowed to become one of the servants, his father received him with all honor, putting on him *the first robe,* and making a great feast to celebrate his son's return, *because my son was dead and is come to life again: was lost and is found.*[4] This is the official picture of God's reception of the repentant sinner and no product of our own imagination should be allowed to supplant it.

The point is of great importance. There is always a great temptation to discouragement and distrust even after our sins have been forgiven. We feel that God still holds our sins against us, that His providence will be less favorable to us in future, that He no longer trusts us not to offend Him again, that He will be reserved and sparing in His graces. We feel, too, that no matter how great our progress in the future, the ultimate result will always be spoiled by that unfortunate past. The phantom of what might have been had we always been faithful mocks our efforts, lessens our hopes, and disheartens us. There is a certain height, we imagine, which formerly we might have reached, but which is now impossible.

All that, natural though it may be, is quite wrong. It is based upon a wrong notion of God and is the result of a failure to understand His power and goodness. It does not matter whether it is the case of a fervent soul who has suddenly given way to temptation, whether it be some sinner who after a life of sin turns to the whole hearted service of God, or whether it be some one who takes up the spiritual life after many years of careless-ness; God can always give us the means to make up for lost time. *To them that love God, all things work together*

[4] Cf. Luke xv, 11–32.

unto good, writes St. Paul,[5] and St. Augustine would include "all things" even their sins.[6] It follows then that God *can* use all things for the good of those who love Him. Even if we conceive of His plan as setting a certain height of holiness for each man, we should also remember that He can lead us to that height from any point we reach in our wanderings. If we lose our way and leave the path He has marked out for us, He can still bring us to the goal by another route. But it is not unreasonable to suppose that this alternative way will be more difficult; its very difficulty, however, is an assurance of the height to which it can lead us, for it affords us a new opportunity of gaining merit and showing our love.

To avoid presumption it must be remembered that this notion cannot be used as an excuse for committing sin because we feel sure in advance that God can restore everything we are going to throw away. The text says: "to them *that love God.*" Once a man is in mortal sin he does not love God, and therefore he has placed himself outside this plan. And, moreover, he cannot get back by his own efforts unless God take pity on him. He has rejected grace; he cannot love God supernaturally or repent of his sin, without God's grace; and God is in no way bound to give it to him. So much by way of warning against presumption before sinning. But after forgiveness, one should never let the thought of extra difficulty interfere with one's confidence. The very difficulties, so often themselves a direct result of our sins —bad habits, for example—are really God's providential means of giving us an opportunity of earning merit that we would otherwise have earned, in order to make up for our losses. And if there be difficulties, there is also God's grace to overcome them, which is given to us in a special way by the sacrament of penance, and which is always available in the Blessed Eucharist. There is a principle that must always be remembered. One should never consider difficulties and obstacles without also

[5] Rom. viii, 28.
[6] St. Augustine, *De catech. rud.* lib. 4; cf. *Summa* iii, 1–2.

considering ways and means. Now where God's will is concerned, God's grace is always at our disposal, and if one may suggest a slogan for the spiritual life, especially for the repentant sinner, it is: *I can do all things in him who strengtheneth me.*[7] For do we not read: *And he said to me: my grace is sufficient for thee: for power is made perfect in infirmity. Gladly therefore, will I glory in my infirmities, that the power of Christ may dwell in me. . . . For when I am weak, then am I powerful?*[8]

We would go so far as to say that there are saints in heaven who would not have reached their present glory, had they not fallen into sin. To quote Cardinal Billot: "The penitent can recover something greater; insofar as one who gave himself to heroic works after his sin, is more loved by God, than one who, though never stained by mortal sin, is remiss in the exercise of virtues."[9] Our Lord's own words are full of meaning: *I say to you that even so there shall be joy in heaven upon one sinner that doth penance, more than upon ninety-nine just who need not penance.*[10] We must, therefore, never lower our hopes or our aim. If it makes it easier for us, we may think of our new destiny, as the change in color of a flower. There are white roses and red roses. Shall we say that one is more pleasing than the other? Whatever way we look at it; whatever we have done, we have God for our Saviour, and to His saving power and saving mercy there is literally no limit.

If there is one thing in which our Lord "specializes," it is in saving sinners. *I am not come,* He said, *to call the just, but sinners.*[11] He is *the Lamb of God . . . who taketh away the sins of the world.*[12] St. John tells us: *If we walk in the light . . . the Blood of Jesus Christ cleanseth us from all sin,* and *if we confess our sins, He is faithful and just, to forgive us our sins and cleanse us from all iniquity.*[13] The whole of Scripture re-echoes

---

[7] Phil. iv, 13.   [8] II Cor. xii, 9, 10.
[9] Billot, *de Poen.* q. 89; cf. *Summa* ii, 89, 2, and St. Gregory, *Hom. De centum ovibus.*
[10] Luke xv, 7.   [11] Matt. ix, 13.
[12] John i, 29.   [13] I John i, 7 and 10

God's power and willingness to remove all our sins and repair our ruin. *Behold, I make all things new . . . I am Alpha and Omega; the beginning and the end. To him that thirsteth, I will give of the fountain of the water of life, freely.*[14] But perhaps the most appealing testimony of all is found in St. Matthew's description of the angel's message to St. Joseph concerning our Lady: *And she shall bring forth a son and thou shalt call his name Jesus. For he shall save his people from their sins.*[15] Our Lord's name then, signifying Saviour, is more than a name; it is characteristic office, the work appointed for Him by God. His very name constitutes the sinner's claim upon His goodness, His power and His mercy. To understand the spirit in which He fulfils His function, it will be helpful to recall the words He addressed to St. Mechtilde, who was lamenting her sins and her lack of good works, and deploring the negligence with which she had squandered the gifts of God. Our Lord comforted her, saying: "Even if thou wert perfectly faithful to Me thou shouldst infinitely prefer that My love should repair thy negligence rather than thou shouldst do it, so that My love may have all the honor and glory."

If we accept our misery and the humiliation of having sinned, and banish our wounded pride—there is nothing God will not do for us. We, like the Church, are His bride, and He has delivered Himself up for us that He may sanctify us, and present us to Himself, *not having a spot or wrinkle, or any such thing, but that we should be holy and without blemish.*[16] In the sacrament of penance, the Passion of Christ, with its unlimited efficacy and power, is applied to us to heal us of our sins. We are restored to our life in Christ. We have His life and power at our disposal. Even if He sent us trials as a "punishment" for our sins, they are not so much a punishment, as a medicine to stir us up to fervent contrition and to afford us an occasion of regaining all we have lost. His mercy is over all His works, and if there is one way of touching God's heart that can be recommended above all to the sinner, it is to cast oneself

[14] Apoc. xxi, 5, 6.   [15] Matt. i, 21.   [16] Cf. Eph. v, 25–27.

with all one's misery on the mercy of God, who is our Father and our Saviour, in absolute confidence and abandonment to His will. Our Lord Himself has shown us how He will *run* to receive us and restore to us our lost heritage. Many sins were forgiven to Mary Magdalen because she hath loved much. If we love Him as she did, our sins will be forgiven us; and we can be more pleasing to God by a life of ardent love after our sin than by the torpid security of our previous innocence. Truly does He say to us: *"Go in peace,"* for when our sins are forgiven we are once more in Christ, who is the peace that passeth all understanding.

CHAPTER 12

Christ, Our Food and Our Life

ALL love demands union; the more ardent the love, the more complete the union it seeks. The love of our Lord for us is no exception. As St. John Chrysostom tells us, our Lord instituted the Blessed Eucharist so that we might become one entity with Himself, united to Him as the head is united to the body, as food is united to one that consumes it, "for this is the desire of the ardent lovers." We spoke in the last chapter of the Church as the bride of Christ. St. Paul cites the marriage union as a symbol and shadow of the still more intimate union of Christ with His Church: *they shall be two in one flesh:*[1] and St. John tells us of the repeated prayer for union that our Lord uttered at the Last Supper when He instituted the Sacrament of the Blessed Eucharist, which very sacrament is His means of effecting that union.

It is difficult to write either soberly or distinctly of the Blessed Eucharist. Perhaps our best plan is to quote the Council of Trent as follows: *Our Saviour, when about to depart out of this world to the Father, instituted this sacrament, in which He poured forth, as it were, the riches of His divine love towards men, making a remembrance of His wonderful works; and He commanded us in the participation thereof, to venerate His memory and to show forth His death until He come to judge the world. And He willed also that this sacrament should be received as the spiritual food of souls, whereby may*

[1] I Cor. vi, 16.

be fed and strengthened those who live with His life, who said: 'He that eateth me, the same also shall live by me,'[2] and as a antidote, whereby we may be freed from daily faults, and be preserved from mortal sins. He willed furthermore that it should be a pledge of our glory to come, and of everlasting happiness, and thus be a symbol of that one body, whereof He is the Head, and to which He would fain have us as members be united by the closest bonds of faith, hope, and charity, 'that we might all speak the same things, and there might be no schisms amongst us.'[3]

In this sacrament, then, under the appearance of bread, our Lord and Saviour gives us His Flesh and Blood, for the food of our souls. It was not enough for Him that He should become one of ourselves by adopting a human nature like our own. It was not enough that He should share the hardships of a life like our own —that He should suffer and die and atone for our sins, in our name. He loved us, and He would not rest until He should be completely united to us. And in His love He devised this most extraordinary method of union, in which He Himself becomes our food! Truly a tremendous lover!

The first thing to realize about the Blessed Sacrament is that it really contains the Body and the Blood, the Soul and Divinity of Christ. At Mass, the priest takes bread into his hands and repeats the words of our Lord: *This is My Body.* As a result of these words, the *substance* of the bread is converted into the Body of Christ, while the *accidents*—that is, the size, the shape, the color, the taste, the physical and chemical properties, etc.—of the bread remain. As far as the words of consecration go, they affect the presence only of the Body. But because our Lord is risen from the dead and dieth now no more, His Blood and His Soul are also present. And because the human nature of Christ is forever united to the Second Person of the Blessed Trinity, His divinity is also present in the host. The priest then takes the chalice of wine, and utters the words: *This is the chalice*

[2] John vi. 58.   [3] Council of Trent, Sess. xiii, cap ii.

of My Blood, of the new and eternal testament; the mystery of faith; which shall be shed for you, and for many, to the remission of sins. And as a result of these words, the *substance* of the wine is changed into the Blood of Christ, while the *accidents* of the wine remain. And for the same reasons as apply to the host, there is also present in the chalice, the Body, the Soul, and the Divinity of our Lord.

Jesus Christ, then, is really, truly and substantially present in the sacramental species of bread, and also in the species of wine. There is one difference in the manner of His presence on the altar, and that of the priest's presence at the altar. The priest makes contact with the ground by the surface and size and weight of his *own* body; our Lord makes contact with the altar, by the surface and size and weight of the *bread*. The priest is localized by his own accidents; our Lord is localized by the accidents of the bread. These indicate and reveal His presence, but He Himself is invisible. There is no other example in nature of this sort of presence, and so no word can be borrowed from experience for it. The technical usage is to say that our Lord is *sacramentally* present. This involves real, true, and substantial presence, but it implies a difference of manner from ordinary presence. We labor the point only because it may help us to some understanding of the meaning of the Mass.

This is the wonderful food which our Lord had promised His disciples, some of whom found it such a "hard saying" that they walked no more with Him. His words are pregnant with meaning: *Amen, Amen, I say unto you: Except you eat of the flesh of the son of Man, and drink of his blood, you shall not have life in you. He that eateth my flesh and drinketh my blood, hath everlasting life, and I will raise him up in the last day. For my flesh is meat indeed, and my blood is drink indeed. He that eateth my flesh and drinketh my blood, abideth in me and I in him. As the living Father hath sent me, and I live by the Father, so he that eateth me, the same also shall live by me.*[4]

[4] John vi, 54-58.

Here we have our Lord's description of the effects of Holy Communion: we shall abide in Him, and He in us; we shall live by Him as He liveth by the Father. To understand the results of the reception of this sacrament, we can regard them as produced in three ways: by union with Christ, by spiritual nutrition, by its special signification of the Passion of Christ.

Let us consider just St. Paul's words (as translated by Prat from the Greek): *The chalice of benediction which·we bless, is it not the communion of the blood of Christ? And the bread which we break, is it not the communion of the body of Christ? For there is only one bread, and we all make one body since we all partake of that bread.*[5] St. John Chrysostom's comment on these words is: "Paul does not say *participation,* but *communion,* because he wishes to express a closer union. For, in receiving Holy Communion, we not only participate in Christ, we unite with Him. In fact, as this body is united with Christ, so by this bread we are united into Christ. . . . But why do I speak of Communion? Paul says we are identically this body. For what is this bread?—The Body of Christ. And what do we become by receiving this bread? The Body of Christ: not many bodies but one only."[6]

We have quoted these texts from the Council and from the Fathers, who weighed their words with theological precision, and had the assistance of the Holy Spirit in choosing them, lest our own attempt to express the intimacy of this union would seem merely metaphorical, an empty figure of speech. Let us be clear what the union in question is. It is *not* the fact that the sacramental species containing the living Body of Christ with His divinity are united to our body by the act of receiving the host. This is indeed a wonderful privilege, and while it lasts, we should not fail to make use of the unique opportunity to speak to our Lord and our divine lover to thank Him, to assure Him of our need and love for Him, to beg from Him the grace to love Him more

[5] I Cor. **x**, 16–17; cf. Prat, ii, 350.   [6] Cf. Prat, loc. cit.

and to live according to His will, and to entreat of Him
to re-make us and mould us to His heart's desire. If
there is any special time for making love to Jesus, certainly it is after receiving Holy Communion as long as
this presence remains.

But this presence is only temporary; it ceases as soon
as the natural processes of digestion change the species
of bread. Once the qualities of bread disappear, the Real
Presence is at an end. The presence of the Sacred Host
in our bodies is only a means to something much greater,
namely the union of our soul with the divinity of Christ
—the incorporation of our whole being into His Mystical
Body in which we are united to His in a new way, as
to our Head. The whole of the earlier part of this book
is a description of the union which is more fully established by the reception of Holy Communion. There we
attributed it to baptism, but baptism is only the gate
to Holy Communion and only gives us the germ of the
divine life. Further, baptism presumes at least an implicit intention—vicarious, of course, for an infant—of
receiving the Sacrament of the Eucharist, of which in
fact some effect is received because of this desire.[7] To
quote Prat: "It seems that without the Eucharist which
is 'the sacrament of piety, the [efficacious] sign of unity
and the bond of charity,' according to the famous expression of St. Augustine, the Mystical Body would not
have all the perfection which is its due. Christians would
neither be united with Christ nor with one another by
that ineffable union which Holy Communion produces,
and which the Lord meant for His Church when He
instituted the Eucharist. If our incorporation into Christ
by faith and baptism is sufficient for salvation, communion with Christ is indispensable for the social perfection of the Mystical Body of Christ and even, normally, for the individual perfection of the Christian. The
consequence is evident to everyone who remembers that
the Eucharistic food, unlike ordinary nourishment, has the
power of transforming us into it."[8]

[7] Cf. *Summa* iii, 73, 3.   [8] Prat, loc. cit.

Let us think again for a moment of our Lord's own words: *He that eateth my flesh, and drinketh my blood abideth in me, and I in him,*[9] and let us remember the desire of the lover that they express. For when one loves, one goes forth as it were from oneself and enters into the beloved, and holds the will and the good of the beloved as one's own; when one loves, one identifies oneself with the beloved, and wills and acts for the sake of the beloved as for one's own sake, making the beloved another self. The tragedy of all human love, even in its highest forms, is that this complete identification is impossible. But with God all things are possible and the loving Heart of Jesus has designed this ineffable manner of achieving this union and convincing us of its intimacy by means of Holy Communion. With St. Paul we can cry out: *I live, now not I: but Christ liveth in me.*[10]

And who is it to whom we are thus united? Who is it that comes into our body under the sacramental species? Jesus Christ, the Son of God, the Second Person of the Blessed Trinity; He of whom St. John says: *All things were made by Him;* the maker of all things, and the model of all things. Every maker works according to an idea, an exemplar, a model. There is some thought in his mind to which he gives external existence in a concrete thing. The artist, the architect, the composer, the craftsman, the producer and the poet all work in their own way to give external existence to their thought. So did God. When He created the world, and gave all the inhabitants of the universe their existence and arranged their history, He worked according to an idea. There is an idea in God's mind corresponding to each one of us, and to what we should or could have been, for in arranging our history, He allowed us to co-operate by the use of our own free will, and, so to speak, to alter His plan for our life. But all things whatsoever pre-exist in the mind of God.

Now God has only really one idea, for such is His perfection that His one idea embraces everything. And

[9] John vi, 57.   [10] Gal. ii, 20.

God's idea—or "Word" as the Greeks call it—is the expression of God's knowledge of His own essence. And God in creating, sees how that one idea can be imitated externally in a limited way, in countless different forms, so that each creature in some limited way partly represents the idea of God and corresponds to it. Now this one idea of God is such a perfect idea—for God's power of knowledge is infinite and perfect—that it is God, the Word of God, the Second Person of the Blessed Trinity. And this Word of God comes to us in Holy Communion and makes us one with Himself!

Words fail us here, for all human words are useless; but if in desperation we may pick out one phrase, which rather than any other may be a fitting salute to the divine Guest of our souls, is it not: "My God and my all"? If we could only get some shred of an idea of the depth of truth that is in those two words: *My all.* He is *all*—for He is God; His is *mine*—for He has made me one with Himself. What is there left for us to want? Why lose a moment's thought over our own deficiency? Why be discouraged even if our life has been one of continual sin?—*He is MY ALL! Gladly will I glory in my infirmities that the power of Christ may dwell in me. Nothing is wanting to me in any grace. The Lord, my God, dwelleth with me, and I want for nothing.*[11]

Truly, indeed, can one Communion make a saint. There is nothing in our selves or in our past that one Communion cannot more than repair—if we have but enough faith! Listen to St. Thomas:

". . . This sacrament contains in itself Christ crucified [*Christum passum*]. Whence whatever is the effect of the Passion of our Lord all that is likewise the effect of this sacrament."[12]

That is why we made so bold as to say above that even

[11] Cf. II Cor. xii, 9; I Cor. i, 7; Deut. ii, 7.
[12] *In Joan. vi,* lect. 6, n. 7.

a lifetime of sins should not discourage us. Because whatever our sins have done to *us,* the Holy Communion can repair; and whatever our sins have done to *God,* the Mass—which is part of the Eucharist—can restore. We are indeed sorry for having offended Him, and our sorrow will grow as we realize His love, but our hope and our confidence will also grow as we see how willing that love is to use His infinite power to restore us in Himself.

There must be no limit to our confidence in the power of this divine lover. He is our Creator, and the spiritual life is a re-creation. Our sins and our short-comings have interfered with that re-creation, but here in Holy Communion we have our Creator, our Prototype, coming to unite us to Himself, full of a merciful love and an ardent desire that we *may have life and have it more abundantly.* There is nothing He cannot do—for He is God, and there is nothing He will not do—for He is our Saviour, to make us men after His own Heart's desire, if we but put no obstacle in His way. He is completely at our disposal!

One of the greatest moments possible in the life of a man is when, in complete self-abandonment, some one whom he loves surrenders himself completely to him for his own happiness. In Holy Communion God completely gives Himself to us—one might almost say, surrenders Himself to us—for our own good and happiness. It is no mere gesture. Before He comes to us in Holy Communion, our Lord has lived and died for us in hardship and humiliation, and has suffered for us a Passion that is unequalled in the history of pain. And He comes to us in Holy Communion to give us the fruit of all this. His abandonment and His devotion to our needs and to our happiness it not a momentary thing; it endured for thirty-three years on earth, and He still is always interceding for us in heaven. The idea beggars description and the fact challenges belief. Only the grace of God can make us realize the love of God for us in this sacrament.

In His love, He makes Himself the food of our souls. Unlike ordinary food, however, which produces its effects by being changed into our substance, this divine food changes us into itself. It is the beginning of heaven, where we shall be united to Him for ever. Even here, we shall never cease to be ourselves—we shall never lose our own personal individuality—but we shall be renewed and remade in the likeness of God Himself. That renewal begins even here below in the reception of this sacrament. The Council of Florence tells us that:

> *Every effect which material food and drink produce in regard to corporal life—by sustaining it, by increasing it, by repairing it, and by refreshing it* [delectando], *this sacrament produces in regard to our spiritual life. . . . By it, we are withdrawn from evil, strengthened in good, and we progress with an increase of virtues and graces.*[13]

The Blessed Eucharist sustains the life of our soul by strengthening it against sin, for it gives us a permanent grace which enables us to overcome our self-love, and to live more and more for the love of God. In the same way it strengthens us against temptation, and it is a matter of daily experience that there is hardly any more effective remedy against the attacks of temptation than the devout and frequent reception of Holy Communion. It increases the life of our soul, for not only are grace and the virtues increased, but they are even excited to action. It is this increase of grace in our soul that constitutes the true growth in spiritual life. We have, of course, to use that grace and not let it be dormant, but the love of Christ shown to us in this sacrament "presseth us" and urges us on to fervor and love. Like ordinary food, the Blessed Eucharist repairs our losses. There is a continual weakening of our spiritual strength and fervor through daily venial sins and imperfections. Holy Communion can remove these; it can even lead to the remission of the punishment due to them, but for the full-

[13] DB, 698.

ness of this effect, we must co-operate by our own dispositions. The other effect mentioned by the Council, of producing delight and refreshment, is one of which we are not always conscious. It can be hidden by spiritual torpor, or bodily illness, or it may be postponed by God for His own wise and loving purposes. There are times of aridity when all feeling of fervor and devotion is dead; but true devotion consists in the alacrity of the will and the normal tendency of this sacrament is to increase the promptitude with which we conform our will to the will of God.

All the sacraments have an intrinsic efficacy by which they produce their principal effects independently of the devotion of the recipient, provided, of course, that the dispositions necessary for valid reception are present. To receive Holy Communion lawfully, one must not be conscious of mortal sin; for it is a sacrament of the living and therefore, mortal sin should be removed by confession before going to Holy Communion. But if a person in good faith, believing his sins to have been forgiven or mistakenly judging that he is in the state of grace, approaches this sacrament with imperfect contrition for any mortal sin he may have committed, then this sacrament will forgive any sin upon his soul even though it be mortal, although it does not remove the obligation of confessing such mortal sins later. This, however, is not the normal purpose of this sacrament, for like all food, it presupposes life.

And just as corporal food only produces its full effects when properly digested, so this eucharistic food may be frustrated from producing the fullness of its effects by lack of proper dispositions in the soul of the recipient. Faith, hope, charity, humility and submission to the will of God are the fundamental dispositions required. Torpor of the will, negligence, distraction, or affection for some venial sin, are the usual failings which interfere with the effects of this sacrament. Hence the need for a proper preparation before receiving it. The ideal thing is to receive it at the proper time during Mass, and to remain for about fifteen minutes afterwards making a proper thanksgiving. Under conditions of modern life this is not always possible, and, on week days many of the laity have to receive Holy Communion before Mass. Care, then, is necessary to ensure that one is suitably disposed at the moment of reception. The best preparation is, of course, a good life: and a sincere sense of one's need of God will lead to the proper disposition. But, as far as possible, some time should be spent in prayer and recollection before reception in order to avoid routine and to excite one's fervor. We can do no more here than note the need and remind the reader that many graces may be lost if one is not properly disposed when receiving.

That Holy Communion is the proper daily food of the soul is obvious; and those who can approach the altar daily should do so. But that is not always possible, and it is well to remember that we have the authority of St. Thomas for the statement that the effects of this sacrament can be obtained by a sincere desire;[14] but our desire is not sincere if we do not avail of the opportunity of reception. Those who are prevented from receiving sacramentally should appeal confidently to God, whose grace-giving action is not limited to the sacraments, and in a real sense of their need, with full confidence in His power and goodness, beg Him to give them those graces which He normally would give them in Holy Communion. Such a prayer can draw down innumerable graces, and should be the daily practice of those who cannot approach the altar.

The immediate effect of this sacrament is to unite us to Christ, but it also unites us to all His members, for we are all one body. It unites us to the Blessed Virgin, to all the saints, to all the souls in purgatory, to all living members of the Church. It unites us in a special way to our relations and our friends, and still more especially, it unites husband and wife. In former times, this sacrament was celebrated at a supper to which all were invited

14 *Summa* iii, 73, 1; 80, 1 and 2.

in order that they might signify the union of charity that was theirs. We have previously noticed that it is the same virtue of charity by which we love God and love our neighbor; and it is only natural that this sacrament in increasing our charity should promote our union with one another.

All the sacraments owe their power to the Passion of Christ, but the Blessed Eucharist is the "perfect sacrament of the Passion," for it contains Christ and the whole power of His Passion.[15] This sacrament, therefore, is a pledge of our future glory, because it was by His Passion that Christ opened for us the gates of heaven. Through its relation with the Passion it also arms us and strengthens us against the attacks of the devil. St. John Chrysostom exhorts us to remember that, "leaving this sacred table we are like lions, breathing flames, and are made a terror to the demons." The connection, however, of the Blessed Eucharist with the Passion is best considered in connection with the Mass.

If we may sum up the effects of Holy Communion in a few words, we would say it produces a "transforming union with Christ." It unites us to Him, as we have seen; and although He is our food in this sacrament and normally food is changed into body of those that eat it, yet here it is we who are changed into Him. This divine food was foreshadowed in the Old Testament by the manna, which each one found to be a complete nourishment, and exactly suited to his own taste and needs. So it is in this Blessed Sacrament. In this food we find the exact complement of ourselves. The priest at Mass breaks the large host into three pieces. Any two of these three will completely and perfectly fit in with the other one to make the perfect circle of the host. We can take that as a figure of the union with our Lord in this sacrament. By our sins and infidelity we have broken ourselves off from the perfection He intended for us; we are incomplete and disfigured. In this sacrament we can find our full complement and restoration; Christ fits in perfectly

[15] Cf. *Summa* iii, 83, 5, ad 2.

with all our needs—with all the gaps in our self and in our life, whether they are due to our own fault or not. It does not matter how many or how great were our sins or our weaknesses. He can restore *everything* in Himself. We must never doubt that, and we must never forget it. He is our omnipotent Saviour, and He does all things well!

We are here at the heart of the mystery of the Mystical Body. Obviously the sacrament, in which the Body and Blood of Christ become our food, is the principal artery that joins us to His Mystical Body. Its efficacy depends first of all on our use of it, for unlike the human body where the organs are in permanent connection with the blood supply, we are free, and must use our power of choice to attach ourselves by faith and by the sacraments to the vital circulation of Christ's Mystical Body. Even when we do join ourselves to His stream of divine life, we shall still have to use our power of choice and decide to live by it and for Him, and not by ourselves and for ourselves. But the Blessed Sacrament is more than an artery. In a sense it is the whole Body—inasmuch as it unites us to our Head and to all His members—for it actually gives us Christ Himself, and changes us into Him. There is no limit to what we may hope for from this change. In it we can find the realization of all our wildest dreams. The pagan poet who sang:

Ah Love, could'st thou and I with fate conspire
  To smash this sorry scheme of things entire,
Would we not shatter it to bits—and then
  Remould it nearer the heart's desire?

would have found the literal fulfilment of his wish in the Blessed Eucharist. It is indeed a conspiracy with love, to shatter all that is "sorry" in our self, and remould it to the desire of the Sacred Heart of Jesus. *And it is a conspiracy that will succeed,* if we but let our tremendous lover have His way. But—the eternal lament still echoes from those sacred lips—the eternal tears still glisten in the eyes of our divine lover—the gentle reproach still whispers in our ears: *Thou wouldest not!* Here, in these words, is the tragedy of the Heart of Jesus. He comes to us, daily if we will, in complete self-surrender. He gives Himself to us completely, He puts all His divine power at our disposal. He offers us complete union with Himself; and—"We will not!" We want to be ourself—we want to live our own life; we will not live by Him, as He lives by the Father.

Here, also, is our own tragedy. For there is no moment, no depth of sin or of failure, no loss or no disaster, in which we cannot still find all that we might have been, all that we would like to have been, all that God wants us to be—in a word—in which we cannot find literally *all* in the Sacrament of the Altar. And yet we are so self-sufficient, that we will not abandon our selves and put all our trust in Him. The saints go to Holy Communion in complete poverty of spirit. It is not a question of supplying for their deficiencies, of completing themselves— it is a question of replacing their nothing-ness by the fullness of Christ. Their past life—good and bad—their sins and merits, count as nothing in their eyes; their whole hope, their whole desire, their whole self, is found in the Blessed Sacrament. Like St. Paul they exclaim: *One thing I do: forgetting the things that are behind, and stretching forth myself to those that are before, I press towards the mark, to the prize of the supernal vocation of God in Christ Jesus! . . . We look for the Saviour our Lord Jesus Christ, who will reform the body of our lowness, made like to the body of his glory, according to the operation whereby also he is able to subdue all things unto himself.*[16] Why? Because: *If then any man be in Christ, he is a new creature; the old things are passed away, behold all things are made new.*[17]

We cannot believe our good fortune; we cannot realize the love and the bounty of God. We do not know the gift of God; we do not realize that God can give us all the desires of our heart. We still cling to our own selves and our own strength, and put our hope in our

[16] Phil. iii, 13–21.   [17] Cf. II Cor. v, 17.

selves. If we would be truly happy, and find all that our heart longs for let us go to Communion in faith, hope, charity, humility, and complete abandonment to the will of Him who comes as our food and our tremendous lover. For we cannot do better than to adopt the device of St. Columban: *Christi simus, non nostri*—Let us belong to Christ, and not to ourselves.

CHAPTER 13

Christ, Our Sacrifice and Our Supplement

THE reception of Holy Communion is only one part of the mystery of the Blessed Eucharist. In the Blessed Eucharist, the Canon Law tells us, under the species of bread and wine, Christ the Lord Himself is contained, is offered, and is received. This offering of Christ is the sacrifice which we call the Mass, and the reception of Holy Communion is really a partaking of the fruits of the Mass and of all that for which it stands. The Mass is the central act of the Catholic Church. Everything else is centered on it. "It is the Mass that matters." To get some idea of the extraordinary importance of the Mass, we must first consider the notion of sacrifice.

Of all the moral virtues the most excellent is that of religion, the virtue which leads us to give God the supreme honor due to Him as our first beginning and our last end. We owe Him our existence; without His conservation, we could not continue to exist; without His co-operation we could not perform a single action; without Him we can never find happiness. We are completely dependent upon Him, and we owe it to Him and to ourselves to acknowledge that dependence. Obviously, any worthy expression of such a homage must come from a heart which truly adores God. If the internal acknowledgment is wanting, the external expression is a lie. Our dependence on God is so complete that no mere prayer or praise can suffice for its expression. Words are not enough; actions are necessary. Even in ordinary life men use gestures and give presents to add meaning to their words, and the worship of God calls for some kindred method of giving external and forceful testimony to our interior worship. The supreme act of this worship is ritual sacrifice.

Sacrifice is made by offering to God some perceptible thing which is disposed of in such a way as to signify our recognition of God's supreme dominion over us and of our complete dependence upon Him. It is also offered to thank God for His benefits, to obtain His help and protection, and—where there is question of sin—to make reparation for the offence given to Him by sin. The person performing the offering must be an accredited minister recognized by God for this office. In the Old Law God laid down the rules for sacrifice, and the offering was generally something which could signify life—a living animal, or food, or drink, for example. As a rule, this offering was either slain or destroyed in such a way as to signify our recognition of God's supreme rights over our life and being. There is no need here to enter into details of this destruction, about which there is at the moment some discussion.

The important thing was that a sacrifice was an accepted way of saying something. To the external sacrifice there must correspond an interior sacrifice, by which one offers oneself to God, and of which the external sacrifice is a sign. David put that interior disposition into words: *All things are thine: and we have given thee what we have received of thy hand.*[1] Amongst the Jews the external offering had two purposes. One was to keep them from idolatry, and the other was to foreshadow the mystery of the Redemption by Christ. Of themselves, these Jewish sacrifices had no real value except insofar as God was willing to accept them. They were imperfect, and were but a shadow of the perfect sacrifice in the New Law. As expressions of the dependence of a finite creature upon an infinite Creator, they were inadequate

[1] I Paral. xxix, 14.

enough; but when the creature had added to his former obligations that of making reparation for sin, their insufficiency becomes even more marked. For sin, though the act of a finite creature, takes on a certain infinity from the infinity of the Creator offended, and nothing man can do alone can repair that injury adequately.

The perfect sacrifice of the New Law gives full homage to God and makes full reparation for man's sins; it was the supreme act for which Christ came upon earth. Even in His Mother's womb, at the very first moment of His human existence, His first act was to dedicate Himself to that end. St. Paul tells us of it:

Wherefore when he cometh into the world, he saith: "Sacrifice and oblation thou wouldst not: but a body thou hast fitted to me: holocausts for sin did not please thee. Then said I, behold I come; in the head of the book it is written of me: that I should do thy will, O God. . . ." In which will, we are sanctified by the oblation of the body of Jesus Christ once.[2]

We have previously noticed our Lord's earnest concentration on His Passion. *I have a baptism wherewith I am to be baptized; and how am I straightened until it be accomplished?*[3] He regarded it as the crowning work of His life. The story of His Passion and Death needs no telling here. We know how He was betrayed, and how while tortured with the anguish of the unrequited love that burned in His Heart for men, and oppressed by their sins, He was arrested and dragged before the different tribunals. Then He was scourged—far beyond the measure of the Roman Law—crowned with thorns, and tortured in Pilate's prison. Condemned to death. He was given His cross to carry to Calvary. There He was nailed to the cross, and died after three hours of indescribable agony of body, which was nothing in comparison with the anguish of His Heart and Soul.

His acceptance of His Death made it a sacrifice in

[2] Heb. x, 5–10.   [3] Luke xii, 50.

which He was at once the victim and the priest. By that one sacrifice He merited our salvation; He offered God a satisfaction greater than that needed for all the sins of the world in all its history; He reconciled us to God; He redeemed us from the slavery of sin and our subjection to the devil, and He opened for us the gates of heaven. By it He merited for His own human nature the highest glory and the kingship of all the universe. For once, God received perfect worship from the inhabitants of this earth—perfect interior worship and perfect exterior worship. A perfect sacrifice was offered to Him. The victim was His own son, whom He had given for the redemption of the world, and in whom He was "well pleased." Truly, could Christ as our high priest say to the Father in the words of David: *We have given thee what we have received of thy hand,* for Christ Himself was God's greatest gift to the world.

All the worship we owe God was given to Him in that one sacrifice; all the satisfaction we owe God was given to Him there also. All that we need from God, was merited for us there; and all the thanks we should give God are given there. Nothing remains but to make that sacrifice our own. And it is in making that possible, that our Lord's loving ingenuity is most wonderfully employed.

The night before He died, when one of His chosen friends was betraying Him for thirty pieces of silver, He instituted the Blessed Eucharist as a sacramental memorial of His Passion and Death.

Taking bread, he gave thanks, and broke; and gave to them, saying: "This is my body which is given for you. Do this for a commemoration of me." In like manner the chalice also . . . saying: "This is the chalice, the new testament in my blood, which shall be shed for you." [4] And St. Paul adds: *"For as often as you shall eat this bread, and drink the chalice you shall show the death of the Lord, until he come."* [5]

The Council of Trent teaches that our Lord did this:

[4] Luke xxii, 19.   [5] I Cor. xi, 26.

That He might leave to His own beloved spouse, the Church, a visible sacrifice, such as the nature of man requires, whereby that bloody sacrifice, to be accomplished once on the cross, might be represented and the memory thereof remain even unto the end of the world, and by which its saving power might be applied to the remission of those sins which we daily commit. . . . And forasmuch in this divine sacrifice which is celebrated in the Mass, the same Christ who once offered Himself in a bloody manner on the altar of the cross, is contained and immolated in an unbloody manner, the Holy Synod teaches that this sacrifice [of the Mass] is truly propitiatory, and that by means thereof this is effected that we obtain mercy and find grace in seasonable aid if we draw near to God contrite and penitent, with a sincere heart and an upright faith, with fear and reverence. For the Lord, appeased by the oblation thereof (of the Mass), granting grace and the gift of penitence, forgives even heinous crimes and sins. For the Victim is one and the same, and the One who now offers by the ministry of the priests is the very same one who then offered Himself on the cross, the manner alone of the offering being different. The fruits of that oblation—namely, that bloody one—are received most plentifully by this unbloody one.[6]

That is the Church's teaching on this extraordinary masterpiece of God's love. In the sacramental system, He has devised a plan by which both Himself and His Passion and Death are ever really present for the members of His Church. It is, of course, a tremendous mystery, a mystery of faith. But to help us to appreciate what is happening, let us consider the relation between Christ as man and the host.

Our Lord lived and died in Palestine centuries ago, and still He is really, truly and substantially present in every place and at every time bread is consecrated. Under its appearance, He receives a new sacramental location in time and space. The word sacramental does not take away from the reality; it merely indicates that it is a unique presence—a real one, but manifested and effected by a sacramental sign.

We can apply the same idea to the sacrifice of Calvary

[6] DB, 938, 940.

and the sacrifice of the Mass. The sacrifice of Calvary took place once at Jerusalem, centuries ago. Yet every time a priest consecrates the bread and the wine at Mass, his action gives the sacrifice of Calvary a new "location" in time and space, here and now at this altar; it is there really, but *sacramentally*, that is, in a sign. The sign seems to be the fact that the words of consecration, as far as their direct signification is concerned, bring about the apparent separation between the Body of Christ and His Blood, for the words only directly produce what they signify: "This (the bread) is My Body"; "This (the chalice) is the chalice of My Blood." The priest at Mass speaks those words in the person of Christ, and it is by the power of Christ that they produce their effect.

Every time then we assist at Mass we are as near to our Lord's sacrifice as we are to His Body and Blood. The exact way in which this is accomplished is a matter of discussion and need not concern us here. All that does concern us is that at Mass we have the sacrifice of Calvary really but sacramentally before us. The Eucharistic Sacrifice of the Mass contains, and shows that is contains, all the spiritual realities of the Cross. St. Thomas puts it this way:

We do not say that Christ is daily crucified and killed [in the Mass], because both the acts of the Jews and the punishment of Christ are transitory. *Yet those things which carry with them Christ's relation to God the Father are said to be done daily* [in the Mass]: *these are, to offer, to sacrifice, and the like.* On that account the victim is perpetual, and was offered once by Christ in this manner that it might be daily offered by His members.[7]

The things which carry with them Christ's relation to God the Father surely include supreme worship and superabundant satisfaction for sin, supreme love and supreme obedience, in fact the whole interior and exterior sacrifice of Christ—everything we would give to God, —and all these things are renewed daily in the Mass, *and are ours for the taking!*

[7] 4 *Sent.* vii. in lit. (*Italics ours*).

That is the important thing about the Mass. It is a handing over to us of what Christ has done in our name —a sacramental renewal of His sacrifice so that its fruits may be applied to us—and we may make it our own for worship and reparation to God. It is, in fact, the vital circulation of the Mystical Body, by which the Head shares with His members the work which is His greatest achievement and their first duty. To state the facts in their most authoritative form, let us quote our Holy Father, Pius XII:

In the Eucharistic Sacrifice . . . the sacred ministers represent not only our Saviour but also the whole Mystical Body and each of its members: in that sacrifice the faithful are associated in common prayer and supplication: and, through the hands of the priest whose voice alone renders the Immaculate Lamb present on the altar, they themselves offer to the eternal Father this most pleasing victim of praise and propitiation for the needs of the whole Church. And as the divine Redeemer, when He was dying on the Cross, offered Himself as the Head of the whole human race to the Eternal Father, so in this "clean oblation" [the Mass] He offers to the Heavenly Father not only Himself as Head of the Church, but in Himself also His mystical members, for He encloses them all—even the weak and frail among them—most lovingly in His Heart.[8]

These are the official pronouncements of the Church; they contain a wealth of doctrine which would need more than one book for its exposition and a lifetime of enlightened meditation for its full apprehension. Perhaps the best thing to do here is to tabulate the main points, as briefly as possible.

(1) On Calvary, our Lord offered Himself in sacrifice to God.

(2) This sacrifice gave God full and perfect worship.

(3) It was a complete satisfaction for our sins.

(4) It merited every grace that we might need.

(5) Our Lord instituted the sacramental and sensible rite of the Mass,

[8] *Mystici Corporis.*

(6) In which He offered Himself to God the Father,

(7) And ordered His apostles and priests to repeat the same offering;

(8) That the salvific power of the sacrifice of the Cross might be applied to our needs.

(9) In the Mass the victim is the same Christ.

(10) And the offerer is also the same Christ, who once offered Himself on Calvary;

(11) Who now offers by the ministry of His priests.

(12) The Mass, therefore, is trully propitiatory,

(13) And, if we are rightly disposed, can be a source of grace and timely aid for us.

(14) The Mass appeases God, and obtains the forgiveness of even the most enormous sins.

(15) The fruits of the cross are received most plentifully through the Mass.

(16) In the Mass the minister represents not only Christ,

(17) But also the whole Mystical Body and each one of us, its members.

(18) Through the priest we offer to God, Christ the victim,

(19) In praise and propitiation for the needs of the whole Church.

(20) As on the cross, Christ offered Himself as the Head of the whole human race,

(21) So in the Mass He offers Himself not only as Head of the Church.

(22) But in Himself He encloses each of us His members.

(23) For He encloses us all—even the weakest of us—

(24) Most lovingly in His Heart.

BEHOLD THIS TREMENDOUS LOVER!

In the Mass, then, each of us can say: Christ is offering Himself as a perfect sacrifice to God; I, too, am offering Him; He is offering me in Himself; *am I also offering myself with Him?*

To try to make things a little clearer, let us consider

the question again. Our Lord's whole life was one long act of adoration and complete submission to God's will. His "interior" sacrifice was continual from the first moment of His life. At His death, He offered the sacrifice of the cross as the exterior sacrifice expressing this interior sacrifice. In this case the victim *was* of value —of infinite value—in the eyes of God and was a complete satisfaction for the sins of all time. Before His death our Lord had instituted the sacrament of the Eucharist by which the Mass would be a sacramental renewal, re-presentation, re-offering, of this same one sacrifice which He once offered on the cross, just as the host would be the sacramental renewal of His presence on earth. In this sacramental sacrifice of the Mass, we have all the "things that carry with them Christ's relation to the Father": His exterior sacrifice, His interior sacrifice, His supreme worship, His supreme obedience, His supreme love, His superabundant satisfaction for our sins.

By our assistance at Mass we can make that sacrifice our own. It has an intrinsic value because it is the same sacrifice as that of Calvary and, therefore, as a propitiation for our sins, it need have no limits. But it is also an external sacrificial sign and expression of worship and submission to God—to which something should correspond on our part by way of an "interior sacrifice." Here is the practical crux of the whole matter. Normally, our interior dispositions determine what our external expression of them shall be. Here the external expression is given to us and we have to make our interior dispositions correspond to it. The external sacrifice on Calvary was the perfect expression of that interior sacrifice that was our Lord's whole life of submission to the will of God. That external sacrifice is given to us in the Mass, and we have to make our life one similar interior sacrifice, if the Mass is to have that full and perfect meaning for us and from us to God, which it should have. There is the plan of the whole Christian life—to live up to what we say in the action of the Mass.

The vocation becomes more urgent when we realize the full signification of our reception of Holy Communion. The Mass does not exist to give us Holy Communion; on the contrary, Holy Communion exists to make us participators in the Mass. Let us hear St. Thomas:

> Whoever offers a sacrifice ought to become a partaker in it, because the external sacrifice which is offered is a sign of the interior sacrifice by which one offers oneself to God. Hence by the fact that he partakes in the sacrifice the offerer shows that he really shares in the interior sacrifice.[9]

The context makes it clear that the participation mentioned refers to receiving Holy Communion. But the context also refers to the priest, and it might be objected that we are applying the quotation too widely. Granting the special reference to priests, the general principle still holds good. To communicate is to identify oneself with the sacrifice. St. Paul himself writes: *Are not they that eat of the sacrifices, partakers of the altar?*[10] And St. Thomas merely applies this principle to the particular and—be it granted—special, case of the priest. But does not St. Peter exhort all to be a *holy priesthood, to offer up spiritual sacrifices acceptable to God by Jesus Christ?* Does he not insist, in his first epistle to the church of which he was the pope and head: *You are a chosen generation, a kingly priesthood.*[11] This application of the designation "priesthood" to the laity must, of course, be understood properly. They are not priests in anything like the strict sense of the term. But the Church teaches that in the three sacraments of baptism, confirmation, and holy orders, a certain "character" is indelibly impressed upon the soul of the recipient. Theologians tell us that this character marks us off and empowers us for divine worship. And St. Thomas speaks of the "character" as "a certain participation in the priesthood of Christ."[12] As a result of this "character" every baptized

[9] *Summa* iii, 83, 4.   [10] I Cor. x, 18.
[11] Cf. I Peter ii, 5, 9.   [12] Cf. *Summa* iii, 63, 3.

person can receive the other sacraments and has an official status in all the divine worship performed by the Church, but especially in the sacrifice of the Mass. As the Holy Father tells us, each of us offers, and each of us is offered, in the Mass. One could deduce many duties and privileges of the Catholic from this "character," but space is not available here. Let us be content to note that Christ so loves us as to be determined to share even His priesthood with us. We are a "kingly priesthood" and—be it never forgotten—*noblesse oblige!*

In support of this participation of all in the priesthood, let us quote the late Holy Father Pius XI:

Though the ample redemption of Christ more than abundantly satisfied for all our offences,[13] *nevertheless, by reason of that marvelous disposition of divine wisdom by which we may complete those "things that are wanting of the sufferings of Christ in our own flesh, for His body, which is the Church,"*[14] *we are able, in fact, we should, add to the acts of praise and satisfaction which "Christ in the name of sinners has presented to God," our own acts of praise and satisfaction. However, we must always remember that the expiatory value of our acts depends solely on the bloody sacrifice of Christ, which is renewed with interruption on our altars in an unbloody manner. . . . For this reason we must join together, in the august sacrifice of the Blessed Eucharist, the act of immolation made by the priest, with that of the faithful, so that they, too, may offer themselves up as "a living sacrifice, holy, and pleasing unto God!"*[15] *Therefore, St. Cyprian dared to affirm that "the sacrifice of our Lord is not complete as far as our sanctification is concerned unless our offerings and sacrifices correspond to His Passion."*[16] *. . . The apostle admonished us that . . . the "life of Jesus be made manifest in our bodies,"*[17] *and, having become partakers in His holy and eternal priesthood, we should offer up "gifts and sacrifices for sins."*[18] *For not only those, who have been appointed by Jesus Christ, the High Priest, as the ministers of such sacrifices to offer to God "a clean oblation in every place from the rising of the sun even to the going down," are partakers in the mysteries*

---

[13] Cf. Col. ii, 13.   [14] Cf. Col. i, 24.   [15] Rom. xii, 1.
[16] Ep. 63; n. 381.   [17] II Cor. iv, 10.   [18] Heb. v, 1.

of this priesthood and in the duty of offering sacrifices and satisfaction to God, but also those Christians called, and rightly so, by the Prince of the Apostles "a chosen generation, a kingly priesthood"[19] who are to offer "sacrifices for sin" not only for themselves but for all mankind, and this in much the same way as every priest and "high priest taken from among men is ordained for men in the things that appertain to God."[20]

The treasures of the Mass are so inexhaustible that it is difficult to leave the subject. But it should be obvious that the Mass is *the* meeting place of Jesus and ourselves *par excellence*. And it is clear that one cannot determine any limit to the fruitful effects of even one Mass. As St. Thomas sums up the whole question:

This sacrament [the Blessed Eucharist] is both a sacrifice and a sacrament. It is a sacrifice inasmuch as it is offered to God: it is a sacrament in so far as it is received by men. It has the effects of sacrifice to him who offers it or in those for whom it is offered.[21] The effect which the Passion of Christ produced for the world, this sacrament produces in man.[22] It is nothing else than the sacrifice which Christ Himself offered[23] [and, in one lapidary formula:] The Blessed Eucharist is the perfect sacrament of the Passion.[24]

There should be no need then to labor the advantages and the need of frequent attendance at Mass for anyone who would live a Christian life. Daily Mass, where practicable, should be the normal program. It is not always possible; it may have to be omitted because of household or other duties which are God's will—and private devotions must *always* yield to duties imposed by God's will; yet it should not therefore be forgotten. The share in Christ's priesthood which belongs indelibly to every Catholic by baptism, makes each of us a sharer in every Mass that is said in the world, and remembering

[19] I Peter ii, 9.
[20] Heb. v, 1; *Miserentissimus Redemptor*.
[21] iii, 79, 5.   [22] iii, 79, 1.
[23] iii, 22, 3, ad 2.   [24] iii, 83, 5, ad 2.

this, we can always avail of that constant chain of Masses which never ceases on the earth.

What then should be our dispositions when we assist at Mass? They are no different from the dispositions that are fundamental in the life of every Christian, in every member of the Mystical Body of Christ: faith, hope, charity, humility and submission to the will of God. Nothing less is sufficient in a Christian; nothing more is required in a saint. If we are conscious of a deficiency in our dispositions as Christians, let us appreciate the dispositions of the Saint of Saints, the all-holy Victim, of whom we are members. The Mass is a complete reparation and supplement for all our shortcomings. It is also a sacramental sacrifice, which says something to God for us; in making it our own, we must mean what we say, that is, we must mean what it says. To quote Pius XI:

In the degree to which our oblation and sacrifice will the more perfectly correspond to the sacrifice of our Lord, that is to say, to the extent that we have immolated love of self and our passions and crucified our flesh in that mystical crucifixion of which the apostle writes, so much the more plentiful fruit of propitiation and of expiation will we gain for ourselves and for others.[25]

Let us repeat it again. Christ lived a life of complete and humble abandonment to the will of His Father. His whole life was one of interior sacrifice of Himself to God. He gave ritual expression to this interior sacrifice by the external sacrifice of the cross. He has given us this external sacrifice by the Mass and in the Mass, for our very own, to express our interior sacrifice to God. This interior sacrifice of ours must then be like His: a sincere, humble and complete abandonment to the will of our Father in heaven, not only at the moment of the Mass— but in every moment of our lives. Love is only repaid by love. Jesus gives Himself to us completely in the Blessed Eucharist. In the Mass, we ought to give ourselves completely to Him.

[25] *Miserentissimus Redemptor.*

CHAPTER 14

The Will of God as the Food of Christ

O F the four ways of seeking for Christ that we mentioned, three have already been considered, namely prayer, reading and the sacraments. The fourth way we suggested was by conformity to the will of God. The connection between this way and the sacrifice of the Mass is fairly evident, but before considering it in any detail, we would again draw attention to one fact that must never be forgotten. God's plan is to restore all things in Christ, and without Christ, all things are sterile and powerless. There is no other way of reaching our final end except through Him. The point is so important that we may consider it for a moment.

The human race was intended by God for a superhuman destiny—a supernatural one. Adam and Eve were raised to a supernatural state by grace, and were intended to transmit that state to their children, but by their sin lost that grace, both for themselves and for their children; the whole human race accordingly fell back to a merely human condition, surrounded with difficulties which would intefere with its reaching even a merely human end, but it was absolutely powerless to achieve its superhuman or supernatural end. For example, men were intended to be the friends of God, sharing in His nature like sons. They lost that share of His nature. The result can be illustrated by considering what would happen if some beloved friend or, worse still, some favorite child, were not merely to lose the use of his reason, but by losing his rational nature radically and completely, were to descend to the level of the brute animals. The result defies even imagination, but we can realize that such a being would have no longer any hope of finding happiness as a friend of ours. Something like that happened when we fell from grace .

Another way of visualizing the result of the Fall would be to regard the whole human race as barren soil, utterly devoid of life of any sort, and completely incapable of producing any life, until some form of seed were given to it. Whatever life eventually develops must come from that seed. Christ is that seed, as we have already said. We mortals are in the position of the friend or child that has lost not merely the use of reason, but the very faculty itself, and has become an animal. Both comparisons are to some extent inaccurate, but this much may be said; that the living plant is no more different from the dead earth, nor the rational man more different from the brute beast, than is the supernatural different from the natural. A dog has a better chance of proving Euclid's fifth proposition, or of writing a symphony, than a man without grace has of performing a supernatural act. The supernatural is utterly beyond his powers, and yet, for the Christian, his whole happiness depends upon his achieving a supernatural end.

Once the supernatural is admitted to be the one thing necessary, the natural must cede to it. Natural standards or purposes must be laid aside, and things must be judged and arranged from the supernatural point of view. Further, although we have been speaking in the last four chapters of the soul as seeking for Christ, yet is must be remembered that that search is impossible without the grace of Christ. It is a supernatural search, and must have a supernatural seeker; our search must be supernaturalized by grace, either actual or habitual, and in the present dispensation, all grace comes to us through the Passion and Death of Christ. *Without me you can do nothing.*[1] Even in our search for Jesus, we must have His aid. That is why the starting point of the

[1] John xv, 5.

spiritual life in baptism must be union with Christ. But we have already explained that our quest for Christ is a quest for closer union with Him, an endeavor to develop the life of Christ that is in us, by drawing His life from the rest of His Mystical Body of which we are the members and He is the head and the source of all its life.

The last chapter showed us how Christ has left us His sacrifice to be an expression of our own interior sacrifice to God. To make His sacrifice completely ours we have to conform our dispositions to His. In other words, on entering into Christ we have to say, as He did on entering into the world: *Behold, I come to do thy will, O God.*[2] And having said that in our heart, we have to say it in all our life. Then can we call His sacrifice, summing up all His Life and His Death, our own.

The need for this conformity to the will of God becomes clear also from another point of view. If we consider ourselves as members of the Mystical Body a little reflection will make it clear that this conformity to the will of God is the fundamental law of living membership of Christ. Let us consider again the constitution of the human body. It is made up of members, organs, and cells, all performing their own functions and each with its own special activity. Yet they all form a perfect unit. The reason for this unity is that they are all animated— in the literal meaning of the word—by one vital principle, which is the human soul. This vital principle modifies their activities and co-ordinates the function of each, so that each works for the benefit of the whole, and each in turn is sustained by the whole organism. After death, this one vital principle departs, for death is the separation of the soul from the body. Immediately, each part of the body becomes its own natural self, so to speak, and functions according to its own nature, no longer directed or co-ordinated by the same soul. The result is that the various chemical substances in the human body interact in their natural manner, destroy

[2] Heb. x, 9.

the organs and the tissues, and produce decomposition. But even in its formation, the human body resembles the Mystical Body. If we examine the beginning of the human organism, we find that it starts from a single cell, into which God infuses a human soul as a vital principle. This cell then multiplies, using the food prepared for it by the maternal organism, and in the course of development differentiation occurs, certain groups of cells being formed for particular purposes. Under the influence of the one vital principle, the cell develops into the highly organized compound that we know as the human body.

If we realize that the Holy Ghost is the Soul of the Mystical Body of Christ, we can realize how complete submission to His will is *vital* for our life in Christ. We are the members, or, if you will, the cells, of the Mystical Body, and this Body is only fully developed and healthy when all the members and the cells are fully vivified by the Holy Spirit and completely subjected to Him. Now, one important difference between the human body and the Mystical Body is that in the human body none of the parts has any will of its own. Apart from special cases of certain growths, the soul exercises its influence on each part, with full dominion and control. In the Mystical Body, each member is a person; he has a free will of his own, he has full dominion over his actions. He has the power of choice. He can either subject himself to the Holy Ghost by doing the will of God, and insofar as he does that, he is living the life of Christ, and will be identified with Him; or he can reject the will of God and live by his own will, in which case he is outside Christ, at least outside His life, and he may even be anti-Christ. We have already considered this view and there is no need to develop it further here. The lesson is obvious: No one can do his own will and be a perfect member of Christ—and without Christ he can do nothing.

The will of God then is the law of the Christian life. By doing it we find Christ; by doing it we are united to

Christ. What then is the will of God for us? The answer to that question up to a point is fairly clear; but in its fullness, the answer is not too easy. With regard to ourselves, we have to distinguish in our own mind two "wills" in God, two divisions of things willed by God, or rather two relations of events to God's will. There are certain things God wishes to happen and even commands. These are what we may call God's "signified will." There are, however, many things which happen contrary to God's signified will—notably sin. Yet nothing happens without at least God's permission, in the sense that He does not prevent it. These things, contrary to the signified will, happen by what is called God's will of good-pleasure. If we use the term permission, it does not mean that God dispenses from His laws and allows them to be broken, exempting those who break them from fault. Even though God "permits" sin to happen, He still forbids it. But He respects the free will of His creatures and does not deprive them of their liberty of choice.

About the first will—the signified will of God—there is no great difficulty, at least up to a certain point. The commandments of God and of His Church, the lawful orders of those in lawful authority, the duties of our state, the evangelical counsels and the inspirations of the Holy Ghost are means by which God makes known to us His will in our regard. The exact details of His will in an individual case may not be easy to determine. In fact, sometimes it would seem that He wills that His will be unknown. But, at least by prayer and counsel, one can always decide upon the immediate future in such a way as to please God. How that is to be done we shall shortly consider.

But God's will of good-pleasure, or His "permissions," is a much wider thing, and it is something in which it is at times very difficult to see His hand at all. Yet we must remember that even in creating free will and allowing creatures to use it, God did not abdicate His supreme dominion over all things. He rules the heavens and the earth. Nothing takes place that He has not foreseen, provided for, and "permitted." This applies even to sin, which He hates and detests. Yet because He decided to create man with free will, He does not interfere with his abuse of it, *but He does will the consequences of that abuse.* Perhaps the best way to picture the whole process is to visualize God, not merely creating the beginning of the world and leaving it, so to speak, to work out its own destiny, but rather choosing this particular world with its complete history right down to the very end, after examining every single action of every single creature in full detail and in all its consequences, comparing this possible history and sequence with all other possible ones, and finally deciding to create *this* particular scheme of things in which *this* particular event, and all its consequences occur.

From this point of view every single thing that happens to us carries in some way the mark of the choice of God. Logically we must extend that even to our sins, inasmuch as God chooses a universe in which He permits it to happen that certain sins are committed. It is true, the will responsible for this particular sin is this particular created will which decides to sin, and thereby offends God and incurs the guilt of sin. Nevertheless, if it afterwards identify itself wth God's will be repentance and by accepting the divinely willed consequences of its sin, it can apply to itself St. Paul's principle, *To them that love God, all things work together for good.*[3]

Before, however, we examine the question from a practical point of view to determine our individual conduct, let us first try to realize what is the general plan underlying God's ruling of the universe.

Christ is the center of God's plan. All things are for Him, and by Him, and all things are to be re-established in Him. All things were created in Him, but men by sin, insofar as in them lay, departed from Him. God's purpose however did not change. He wills to re-establish all things in Christ.

We speak of God's plans and God's "wills," but in

[3] Rom. viii, 28.

God there is really no multiplicity, except that connected with the Blessed Trinity. Human speech, however, can only use human terms in speaking of God's operations, although in God there is only one idea and one will. He begets His Son by knowing Himself, and the mutual Love of the Father and Son is the Third Person, the Holy Ghost. What God does in this world is only an external shadow or imitation of what He is doing in Himself. In Himself He is begetting His Son, in this world He is also forming His Son's Mystical Body. In Himself He is loving His Son by the Holy Spirit, and in this world He is loving His Son by the Holy Spirit. There are three Persons, but only one divine will.

We have spoken of the Holy Spirit as the vital principle—the soul—of the Mystical Body of Christ, and hence deduced the need for submitting ourselves completely to His guidance—to His will, for His will is the will of God. There need be no confusion if we now regard the process as subject to the influence of external events, and insist upon the need for submitting ourselves completely to the will of the Father, as shown in His commandments and in His providence—for His will is the same will, and will of God. And if in our love for the Son as our Head we wish to submit to *His* will, and in a loving embrace to identify our will with His, still there is no confusion; for the Son, too, is God, and His divine will is the will of God.

In Jesus Christ, however, since He is man as well as God, there are two powers of willing, the human as well as the divine. The whole plan of our Lord's life was the submission of His human will completely and absolutely in an ecstasy of abandonment to the will of God, as manifested by the "commandment" He had from His Father, by the "inspirations" He had from the Holy Spirit, and even by the manifestation of the will of God as shown in the course of events, notably in the sins of those who crucified Him. *He humbled himself, becoming obedient unto death, even to the death of the cross.*[4]

[4] Phil. ii, 8.

That is the complete summary of our Lord's life. We have referred to it before, we do not apologize for referring to it again. He vowed His obedience in His Mother's womb; He submitted as an infant and as a child to those whom God appointed for His guardians. *He went down with them, and came to Nazareth, and was subject to them.*[5] Until He was thirty years of age He subjected Himself to the will of God as manifested in the words of Mary and Joseph. In His public life, He never did anything but the things that were pleasing to the Father, and He always accepted the many limitations that Providence put to His work. In His Passion and Death, He suffered injustice, injury and insult from evil men, who were sinning against God; yet He never failed to see in all that was done to Him, the will of God. His last act on the cross was to abandon Himself completely into the hands of the Father. . . . He was obedient even to the death of the cross.

For which cause God hath exalted Him, and given him a name which is above all names.[6] Not only did God raise Him from the dead, but His whole plan is to raise up the whole of mankind through Him from the death of sin. Men had lost the supernatural life, and they could only find it in Christ. Now the whole of God's will—the whole of His government of the universe, and His government extends to the smallest detail—has one purpose, to re-establish all things in Christ. Therefore, if our wills are conformed to the will of God, the whole of our history, with every single thing that happens to us, is part of a plan—a plan which is being carried out by the omnipotent power of God—to unite us to Christ and sanctify us in Him.

Thus, Christian spirituality and Christian morality is not a negative thing—a mere series of prohibitions: "Thou shalt not . . ."; it is essentially positive and dynamic, an incorporating and a building up of each of us in Christ. And the whole scheme as far as any one person in the state of grace is concerned, depends only

[5] Luke ii, 51.   [6] Cf. Phil. ii, 9.

on two wills: the will of God and his own will. It does not matter what other men will, what they do to him; if a man only cleave to God by his own will, God will sanctify him.

Who then shall separate us from the love of Christ? Shall tribulation? or distress? or famine? or nakedness? or danger? or persecution? or the sword? . . . But in all these things we have overcome because of him that hath loved us. For I am sure that neither death, nor life, nor angels, nor principalities nor powers, nor things present, nor things to come, nor might, nor height, nor depth, nor any other creature shall be able to separate us from the love of God, which is in Christ Jesus, our Lord.[7]

By doing the will of God then we are formed into Christ, we are "digested" by Him, we are received into Him and transformed into Him, as the food is taken by the roots and transformed into the vine. When we do the will of God, Christ, our High Priest, takes us into His hands, and blesses us, and says: "This is My Body," and offers us up to His Father in Himself, and receives us into communion with Himself. The perfect union with Christ is to do the will of God for the love of God. There is nothing higher than that. Therein lies all holiness and all happiness; therein lies all that we may ever become, all that we ever dreamed of being; for it renews us in Christ and unites us to Him who is our God and our all!

Let us quote Monsignor Gay for what follows, lest our own words should be taken for the exuberance of wishful thinking: "God operates so that this will unites those to God who are united to it, and it tends to unite all men to one another. . . . Between the Holy Trinity and us there is an immense hierarchy. This will (the will of God), born in uncreated splendor, traverses all these created splendors, of which this hierarchy is composed. First of all, Jesus receives it. He is the necessary media-tor between God and man, the supreme head of creation,

[7] Cf. Rom. viii, 35–39.

the universal priest. As He transmits to the Father the obedience of the children, He transmits first of all to the children the wills of the Father; and before He transmits them we are sure He adores them. I will venture to assert that He has actually accomplished them; for, besides having lived here below, for all His members, He accomplished in principle, and, as it were, in substance, all the wills of God that were to concern them personally, through successive ages. Thus, we may see, that even at present, there is not a single will of God which He does not accomplish in a transcendent and heavenly manner by His perfect acquiescence in it, in the name even of that member who will perhaps never acquiesce in it himself, but who, if he acquiesced would only do so by the movement of his Head and Chief, and under His influence.

"Then what Jesus does, there is no doubt that Mary does also: if He is a mediator, she is a mediatrix, their life in heaven is not only similar, it is one. . . . There is nothing in the designs of God so particular and so individual as not to be attached to the universal plan, and which does not help to accomplish the great mystery of Christ, which is the consummation of all things in God. . . . The will of God, which is that I should be sick today, which is that I should be contradicted, humbled, forgotten, which arranges for me this unexpected event, which brings about for me this difficulty, which causes me to stumble against this stone, which delivers me to this temptation—such is its origin and its history! Born of God, as Jesus is born of Him, and truly at the same time as Jesus, since all in God is eternal, it is a fruit of which the Divinity itself is the essence. If I eat this fruit I shall be deified; for if Jesus, God by birth, has merited that His divinity, veiled and reserved for a time, should burst forth in His Body, and then should inundate His Church, it is because during all the days of His militant life He always fed upon the will of His Father.[8] But further, this deifying fruit, this will

[8] Cf. John iv, 34.

of God, which preserves me, comes to me laden, and, as it were, impregnated with the filial obedience of my Saviour, and of my sweet Mother, with piety of the good angels, and with the adoration of the saints."[9]

The truth of the matter is this: that every act of the spiritual life is performed in partnership with Jesus, and there is no comparison between His share and ours; what we contribute is but a tiny drop of water in the chalice full of the rich wine of His immeasurable love of God. Yet that little drop of our own is of supreme importance. For even though it be true to say He has done everything for us, yet there is one thing He cannot do without our co-operation; He cannot make what He has done *ours*, unless we also do our own share. We do our share by doing the will of God. It does not matter how trivial the action done is; if it be done according to the will of God, it is done in union with Jesus, and then all His is ours. By putting ourselves thus in union with Him, we are united not only with Him, in all the actions of His own life (beside which all else become negligible), but we are also united with every member of Christ in that all is being done in any part of the world at the moment, or was done at any time in the past. Since this union of will with God is only the result of the union of charity, we may quote St. Thomas in support of this doctrine, for he writes:

Just as in the living body the operation of one member promotes the welfare of the whole body, so it is in the spiritual [or Mystical] Body, which is the Church. Since all the faithful are one body, the good of each one is communicated to the others. . . . Whence it follows that whosoever possesses charity shares in all the good that is done in the whole world.[10]

We are, in fact, united to our Lady in all her actions; we are united to each of the saints in all their actions;

[9] Gay, *Christian Life and Virtues*, vol. iii. On Abandonment. The whole conference is well worth reading.

[10] *Expositio super Symbolo Apostolorum*, a. 10.

we are united to every priest, saying Mass, preaching the Faith, or saving souls; we are united with every prayer and good work of any member of the Church. And we can even appropriate the merit of these good works if we, for the love of God, love them more than those who do them. Looked at, even in this way, the fruits of our partnership seem unbelievable, but in fact even all the good works of the whole Church, present and past, do not at all compare in value with a single action of our Lord's own personal life: and our Lord's longing is to make over to us the value of every act of His Life and Passion, so that it may all be our very own. It seems unbelievable, yet such is the love of God.

And we have the sign and symbol and pledge of that in the Blessed Eucharist. As we explained, the Sacrifice of the Mass contains and represents the Sacrifice of the Cross, which was the external expression of the interior sacrifice made by Jesus Christ in a life of complete abandonment to the will of God.

The very words our Lord used show us His intention of handing over to us all His riches.

This chalice is the new testament in my blood.[11] And a 'testament' is a pact or agreement, for the disposal of our inheritance to be received. The Blessed Eucharist contains 'those things which carry with them Christ's relation to God the Father' and all those things are at our disposal in the Mass.[12]

Even by baptism, which incorporates us into Christ, we are made rich with His riches. For St. Thomas tells us that the works of Christ belong not only to Himself but also to all His members, with the very same relation which the actions of a just man have to the individual agent.

Christ by His Passion merited not alone for Himself; but He also merited salvation for all His members.[13] The Passion of Christ is communicated to every baptized person

[11] I Cor. xi, 25. [12] Cf. St. Thomas, 4 *Sent.* xii, in lit.
[13] Cf. *Summa* iii, 48, 1.

as if he himself had suffered and died. . . . The result of the pain of the Passion of Christ is communicated to the baptized person as if he himself had undergone the suffering.[14]

And the sacrament of baptism is only the gateway to the Blessed Eucharist. In the Blessed Eucharist we have Christ's sacrifice for our own and we receive His very self, who is the author of all grace! It is therefore no mere dream to speak of entering into the fruit of all Christ's merits. It is for that very purpose that He makes us part of Himself in His Mystical Body. And we are never more completely part of Himself than when we are doing the will of God.

The will of God then, in its twofold aspect, the signified will and the will manifested by the course of events under His providence, contains all that is necessary for our complete sanctification and for our perfect union with Christ. St. Teresa, who knew from personal experience the value of all the forms of union with God—even ecstatic union—insists the union of the will is the most perfect.

The sole concern of him who has but entered into the way of prayer—keep it in mind, it is very important—must be to strive courageously to conform his will to that of God. . . . Herein lies, whole and entire, the highest perfection to which we can attain. The more perfect the accord is, the more do we receive from the Lord and the greater is our progress.[15]

Our Lord preached no other doctrine. *If thou wilt enter into life, keep the commandments.*[16] *He that doth the will of my father who is in heaven, he shall enter into the kingdom of heaven.*[17] And the Holy Spirit promises us, by the mouth of St. John: *He that doth the will of God abideth for ever.*[18] As St. Teresa says, "It is very important to understand all this." Many people

[14] *Summa* iii, 69, 2 and 2, 1.
[15] St. Teresa, *Interior Castle*, Second Mansion.
[16] Matt. xix, 17.　　[17] Matt. vii, 21.　　[18] I John ii, 17.

regard perfection as something to be achieved by extra-ordinary works, by outstanding achievements, by miracles, by ecstasies, by immense sufferings. Our Lord's notion of perfection is quite different, He merely asks us to do what He did Himself: to submit ourselves entirely to the will of the Father, and He will do the rest. . . . *Spera in eo, et ipse faciet.*[19] . . . *Being confident of this very thing, that he, who hath begun a good work in you, will perfect it unto the day of Christ Jesus.*[20]

[19] Ps. xxxvi, 5.   [20] Phil. i, 6.

CHAPTER 15

Union with Christ through Abandonment

THE rule of life, then, for the Catholic who would live the fullness of his life is to seek Christ and to be united to Him, by daily prayer, by daily reading and reflection, by the frequent use of the sacraments, especially of the Blessed Eucharist, and by doing the will of God. No higher program is necessary to reach sanctity. Anyone of whom it could be said at the end of his life—"he did the will of God" —is perfect.

And we must be clear about this; there is no other way of being perfect. All the exercises of religion we have mentioned—prayer, reading, the sacraments, daily Communion, the Mass—however holy in themselves, are only means to an end. Their use and practice, however frequent and fervent, do not constitute holiness. They are a great help to holiness, but holiness itself is something quite different. Holiness is something which affects every moment of our life, something which is rooted in the depths of our being. It is a permanent union with God, a constant abiding in Christ by lovingly doing His will, always and in all things.

This alone will make our life fruitful. We see the saints praised for their great works; we are told of their great talents, their organizing ability, their keenness of intellect, their excellence of judgment, their literary skill, and their extensive learning. They are famous for their ingenuity, their originality, their initiative, their miracles, their apostolic success, their power over souls. In a word, they are presented to us as great men and women. And we are tempted to think that the possession or the achievement of such greatness, if it is not holiness itself, is at least an essential part of it. The truth is quite otherwise. In point of fact, while some of the saints had some of these things, yet none of these things is sanctity. For sanctity, as revealed to us by our Lord's teaching and example, is to live in union with Him by faith, by hope, by love, by humility, and by complete abandonment to His will. It is important then to consider the doing of the will of God from the point of view of daily practice.

The primary revelation of the will of God is in His commandments, in the commandments of His Church, and in all those just laws and genuine duties which bind us to action. *All power is from God.* Where lawful authority lawfully orders, there faith hears the voice of God. The first step in carrying out God's will is to avoid mortal sin. Where there is a habit of mortal sin which one does not intend to give up, there is no spiritual life. Such a soul is dead. If a man is in that state, he has urgent need of making a good confession and deciding to fight manfully against his bad habits. The fight may not be easy; he may, perhaps, even fall again; but he must be resolutely determined that even if he falls down again, he will not stay down, and he must follow out that determination grimly. Mortal sin must be regarded as the greatest possible evil—one to be avoided at all or any cost. On that point there can be no compromise.

The next stage of progress is that of one who has normally only venial sins to confess. Here the plan should be to attack any habit there may be of committing some particular venial sin. A daily examination of conscience is an excellent way of getting rid of such habits. And if only one such habit were broken in a year, the advance would be considerable. For the whole general health of the soul would have improved greatly as a result of the continual effort to overcome even one habit. Other habits would be found to have weakened. It is always the first battle that is the most difficult. In winning it, one has gone more than half-way to winning the next one.

The next stage would be where deliberate venial sins are unusual, and, when they do occur, are rather the result of momentary weakness, than of a set policy of not avoiding particular faults because "they are only venial sins." The determination never to offend God deliberately, forms itself as a result of reading and reflection and daily contact with God in prayer. This determination will do much to give one a positive rule of action for each day. But if one is in earnest about seeking Christ and living the life of Christ, one will wish for some indication of God's will which will cover the whole day.

This is the difficult point in the layman's life. A religious has a vow of obedience, and his day's work is appointed for him by a superior. He has absolute certainty that the work appointed for him is God's will, and all he has to do is to carry it out with as much purity of motive and of intention as he can. That is one reason why as a *state,* the religious state is the more perfect. For that reason when the desire to seek God and to live for Him alone comes to a man in his youth, the question of entering religion often presents itself. This is not the place to discuss religious vocations. Where there is doubt about one's vocation in an individual case, counsel must be sought. But there are many men whose circumstances are such that their state in life is already settled. There are many also, who are quite unsuited for the religious state. For example, there are those for whom celibacy would be imprudent, those for whom the common life would be an unbearable burden, those for whom the continual need to seek permission from superiors would be fearful strain. There are those—and they are many— whose obligations tie them to the world. In fact, the majority of men are to live in the lay state and God has His own ways of confirming them in their vocation.

What we wish to point out here, is that despite the

fact that the religious state as a *state* is the more perfect, yet for a particular individual it may be the better thing to remain in the lay state. And it must not be thought that by doing so he renounces any vocation to perfection. All are called to perfection. Other things being equal— and they often are far from equal—the way to perfection is likely to be easier in religion, but even so, perfection is far from being impossible in the world. And at the moment, the crying need is for holiness among the laity. To be quite clear as to our terms of reference, let us say that we regard the married state as the nomal one for the laity, and that it is the married man and woman whom we have particularly in mind throughout this book; we are not thinking in terms of lay recluses or hermits.

As has already been made clear, some part of the layman's day is to be given to prayer, to reading and to certain spiritual exercises, the most important of which is daily Mass and Holy Communion, where that is possible; if that is impossible one should try to make a visit to the Blessed Sacrament. However, even before these practices comes the duty of one's state of life. Every man has to earn his bread. He may do that in various ways, but it is God's will, generally speaking, that he should do it in some way. In doing so, he usually serves some social need, and since what he does to others, he does to Christ—in serving society he serves Christ. In the normal case, he has a family dependent upon him, and his first duty is to them. It often happens that a man's occupation and circumstances are such that his vocation in life is quite clear. In such a case he has a clear indication of what is God's will for him.

Sometimes the case is not so clear. Then a man may have to seek guidance by prayer and counsel. The reply may not be immediate, but where one is ready to do God's will, God generally makes His wishes clear. If He does not, then it is His will that one should be in doubt, and He wishes one to choose as best one can. This one should do with an easy mind. In the case of those whose work is done under authority, all lawful instructions carry with them the sanction of God's will. In the professions or in those employments where a man is his own master, the lead is not so clear, but there are generally duties and responsibilities that will indicate what God requires.

The chief difficulty arises from the fact that a man has a duty to himself, a duty to his family, a duty to his employer or client, and a duty to the society in which he lives. He does not find it easy to apportion his time and interest between these different objects. If he gives himself wholly to his profession, his family may be neglected. If he devotes himself to his family, his social obligations and works of charity may suffer. If he spends his time at spiritual exercises, all else may be neglected. Obviously, a hard and fast solution of this problem cannot be given here. Prudence, prayer, and counsel will find a solution for such a case. There are, however, certain guiding principles. A man's family comes first, *even before his private devotions.* We shall discuss this point in connection with marriage, but the principle must be stated here: duty first, private devotion afterwards. And a man's duty to his family comes before his duty to his clients or to his career. Still, although the family has a prior claim, it has not an exclusive claim, for a man has obligations towards those to whom he owes his own existence and development, to his own kindred and to the society in which he grew up. But all his obligations are ultimately to God and cannot therefore really be in mutual conflict.

The solution of such problems varies with the individual case, and is not always easy. But the root of the solution lies in the cultivation of an interior life by prayer and reading and friendship with God. A man will thus acquire a supernatural outlook and standard by which he will be enabled to see where the will of God for him lies. A certain flexibility of application is necessary to meet the continual changes that characterize his circumstances. There is an obedience of charity that will frequently call for modification of his program, for the love of one's neighbor and the readiness to help him is one of the distinguishing marks of the true Christian.

It may help the development of such an outlook, to consider here the principles which determine the super-natural value of our actions. St. Thomas sums the mat-ter up thus: "The merit of eternal life pertains primarily to charity, and secondarily to the other virtues insofar as their acts are ordered by charity."[1] In other words, the most important part of each action is the love that animates it. To be supernaturally meritorious, an action must be done freely during life on earth, by an agent in the state of grace; the action must be supernaturally good, and one which God has promised to reward. But the important thing is the love of God that leads to the action. This love will show itself in the degree of union with our Lord and the purity of intention with which the action is performed. The action should be done for God rather than for oneself. Both in its choice as in accordance with God's will, and in the fervor with which we devote ourselves to its performance, the love of God should be the fundamental motive. The difficulty and the duration of the action generally mean an increase of merit and value, for they call for more effort and greater love. Still a facility acquired by the habit of doing good, does not lessen the merit of actions; on the contrary, insofar as such a facility is the result of a will more deeply in love with God, it means a greater merit and value.

One must be careful not to be misled by the external splendor of achievement or even by the spiritual fruit-fulness of one's works. Both these things can be quite deceptive. The former's is obviously mere vanity, the latter may be due to some other cause. The law of spirit-ual fruitfulness is a supernatural one. It is not always the priest who preaches the sermon that is responsible for the conversions produced by it. Insofar as he is the cause of its good effects, that is rather the result of his interior union with God than the excellence of his preaching.

[1] *Summa* i-ii æ; 114, 4.

Very often the real source of his success is to be found in the prayers and sufferings of some hidden soul. The words of Pope Pius XI to the Carthusians illustrate the point:

> *It is easy to understand how they who assiduously fulfill the duty of prayer and penance contribute much more to the increase of the Church and the welfare of mankind than those who labor in the tilling of the Master's field. For unless the former drew down from heaven a shower of divine graces to water the field that is being tilled, the evangelical laborers would indeed reap from their toil a more scanty crop.*[2]

These words are addressed to contemplative religions, but they apply to all Christians, and if by way of adaptation we alter the pope's phrase to "prayer and *patience*," it is clear that there is an unlimited scope for fruitful labor even in the life of the laity.

In regard to the supernatural fruitfulness of good works, it must be remembered that every single step that any soul takes towards God is the result of grace. The grace comes as the result of a whole chain of causes. It must first be merited by our Lord Himself; it must like all graces pass through our Lady's hands in some way or other; some of the saints may be involved in its impetration; some one or even many souls on earth may have had to pray and to suffer before that grace was applied to its object. It does not follow that the agent who is the instrument in applying that grace to a particular soul receives the greatest, or even any, credit for it. Should a priest who is not in the state of grace convert a soul by his preaching, none of the merit is his. Frequently, indeed, grace is brought to a soul by some apparently chance remark for which no one seems responsible. It should not, then, matter to us at what particular part of that long chain of supernatural activity God places us, nor should we be disappointed when we see no fruit for our works. Every act that unites us to God

[2] Apostolic constitution, *Umbratilem*: A.A.S., Oct. 15, 1924; cf. *Rerum Ecclesiæ*.

is fruitful: *He that abideth in me,* said our Lord, *the same beareth much fruit.*[3] If we remember that the most fruitful life of any human being was that lived by our Lady, and that her life was essentially ordinary, obscure, and laborious, we shall, perhaps, find a new value in the ordinary things in the day's round when done for God. Let us repeat the words of St. Thomas: "Just as in a living body the operation of one member promotes the welfare of the whole body, so it is in the spiritual (or mystical) body, which is the Church. Since all the faithful are one body the good of each is communicated to the others . . . whence it follows that whoever possesses charity, shares in all the good that is done in the whole world."[4] To share in every thing that is being done in the Church—all we have to do is to have charity—to love God; and that in practice means to do His will, no matter how ordinary it is. *And we cannot* obtain any greater share by doing anything else, no matter how magnificent. If we do achieve something, the chief merit of it belongs to somebody else. Not only can we not improve on God's plan as a plan; we cannot improve on it even as a plan for our own welfare.

There is, of course, a hierarchy of virtues and of good works; it is better to hear Mass than to fast. But that rather applies to the virtues and good works considered in themselves. Considered as part of the program of this individual person, the determining factor in their choice is a prudent submission to the will of God. Where this will is not indicated from external sources, it may be found in the inspiration of the Holy Ghost. It is not always an easy matter to recognize His voice. There are times when we feel impelled to do something, apparently by God, but the action proposed is against justice or authority, or in some way clearly wrong. Such impulses must be rejected. There are other times when, as a result of continued suggestion, we feel morally certain that God requires some particular service from us. In such

[3] John xv, 5.
[4] *Expositio super Symbolo Apostolorum,* art. 10.

cases advice is a safeguard, and in matters of importance—especially when other people are concerned in
the result of our proposed action—it should always be
sought. But when it is clear that we are not deceived
and that it is really God who is our mentor, we should
be careful to yield to His wishes.

There are, however, a number of occasions when we
cannot be certain. In such cases ordinary prudence should
be used, and care taken not to lose our peace of mind.
God will never be angry with us for failing to follow an
uncertain lead, and where His will is not clear, we
should never let our doubt be a source of uneasiness to
us or of estrangement from Him. He only expects a
reasonable service. The same principle applies to the
example of others. Sanctity is different in different persons, and the practices by which one saint has reached
holiness are not necessarily the right means for someone
else. We are not expected to imitate the saints in all the
details of their lives, nor are all the counsels for all. As
we have said above, the solution of these problems varies
from one case to another and we prefer to leave the
question open and even vague, rather than risk misleading one person by trying to give a definite lead to another.
Prayer, meditation, and a readiness to do what God wills,
always bring sufficient light for the next step.

It should be noted that what are called the inspirations of the Holy Ghost, those gentle urgings towards
certain practices, certain good works or certain renounce-
ments, are quite an ordinary method of God's action on
souls, and to our mind, one that plays a very large part
in His provision for the sanctification of the laity. St.
Thomas, commenting on the text: *Whosoever are led
by the Spirit of God, they are the sons of God*,[5] writes:
"The spiritual man is not only instructed by the Holy
Ghost what he should do, but his heart also is moved by
the Holy Spirit." Comparing this to the action of a
higher instinct, he proceeds: "The spiritual man is
inclined to do something not, as it were, by the prin-

[5] Rom. viii, 14.

ciple of his own will, but by the instinct of the Holy Ghost." St. Frances de Sales tells us that just as God has given animals those instincts which they need for their conversation and their natural action, so also, if we do not resist the grace of God, He will give each of us the inspirations necessary to live, to operate and to conserve us in the spiritual life.[6]

Of course, if we have made up our mind not to do certain things, if there are certain sacrifices we have definitely decided not to make, it is no wonder if God remains silent. And if we habitually reject His advances, there is a danger that He may refrain from appealing to us. Besides, such a habit of saying "No" to God must eventually harden our heart, and there is no greater catastrophe in the spiritual life than the hardening of the heart against God. It is, however, quite a different thing to feel the difficulty of co-operating with His suggestions. He is quite prepared to listen to us telling Him that we cannot do the particular thing He seems to want us to do unless He gives us the grace and the strength, and since He is a very understanding Father, He will even understand our hesitation to ask for that grace. But He has been generous with us, and we must be generous with Him; if we feel we cannot make the sacrifice He asks, at least let us force ourselves to ask Him for the grace and strength to do so. His answer may surprise us. Once every day at least, we should "catch God's eye." If we do that, we will sooner or later have to be honest with ourselves as well as with God, and the eye-shades of self-deception will be taken off, and then we will receive both the light and strength to do God's will. In passing, let us note there is hardly any better way of testing our own sincerity, and making sure of our spiritual health, than this daily practice of looking God in the face, so to speak, and listening to what He may have to say to us.

The other way in which God leads us and shows us His will for us, is in the course of events, in everything, in fact, which happens to us. Insofar as the par-

[6] *The Love of God*, vii, 10.

ticular individual is concerned, one may say that everything that happens to him is God's will for him, except,
of course, any act by which he personally sins. But even
the consequences of that sinful act are willed by God,
and as soon as one repents, God wills to ordain the end
of sin to good. Now God's permissive will and providence
extend to all our circumstances—past, present and future.
He has willed the circumstances of our origin, of our
up-bringing, of our education; He has willed all the
personal qualities we have—good and bad; He has willed
even our mistakes and our failures; in fact, there is absolutely nothing in our present situation—as long as we
are in the state of grace—which has not been accepted by
God's will. Of course, we are speaking here of what is
called God's "will of good pleasure"—His "permissions."
We do not say He directly willed our sins for example,
but He permitted them to occur, and He sees how they
can be turned to good.

Now one of the first acts of spiritual life—and an
act which, if generously performed, will advance us far
at one bound, and open a door for us to an undreamed
of peace—is to accept all God's "wills" for us, *to accept
our present situation in its entirety*. In this matter there
one can obey because God is supreme ruler; one can
decide just "to put up with it;" one can submit as to
superior force—"Well, if it must be so, it must be so";
one can obey because God is Supreme Ruler; one can
be resigned; one can take up an attitude of acquiescence,
or of conformity. All these are good in different ways.
But the highest of all ways of accepting God's will is a
joyous and cheerful abandonment into His hands. "To
abandon oneself is to renounce, to quit, to alienate oneself, to disappear, it is to yield oneself altogether without
measure, without reserve, and almost without noticing
what we do, to Him who has the right over us. To
abandon oneself is to pass away. . . . Abandonment is
the soul's Passover; on one side it is its immolation, on
the other it is its divine consummation."[7]

For the moment, we do not distinguish between mere

[7] Cf. Msgr. Gay, loc. cit., On Abandonment.

submission to God's will, and the joyous embracing of it that is the essence of abandonment. In one case we serve a kind master, in the other we throw ourselves lovingly into the arms of our tremendous lover. In either event, we are doing God's will in accepting the course of events. But we have to accept them in a common sense way. (Common sense, as we said, is an essential part of every act of the spiritual life. Theologians call it prudence.) For example, if illness comes to us—that is God's will; but it does not follow that it is God's will that we should remain ill. On the contrary, it is God's will that we adopt the ordinary measures to deal with the situation. In fact, a great part of the life of a layman is spent in reacting in this common-sense fashion to the events sent or permitted by Providence. *In doing so he is doing the will of God.* The important thing is that he should do so with faith, hope and charity, and humble submission. For it is exactly in this way, by evoking acts of these virtues, that God sanctifies us.

Obviously, an active faith is necessary to see in all things God's hand—but *the just man liveth by faith.*[8] And it may be admitted, that there are times when one's faith may have to be exercised by a vigorous and deliberate effort. The malice of men is so obvious in what befalls us, the course of events is so opposed to what we were quite certain were God's designs for us, the pain and the sorrow inflicted upon us or upon those we love by special trials are so keen, that we find it hard to convince ourselves that God "knows what He is doing." That is just the point. God *does* know what He is doing, and knows it full well. As Juliana of Norwich puts it, "God's plan is of a piece." It is perfectly designed to accomplish His purpose. But His purpose is unknown to us. Our Lord Himself warned us:

> *I am the vine, you are the branches. . . . I am the true vine: and my Father is the husbandman. Every branch in me, that beareth not fruit, he will take away; and everyone*

[8] Gal. iii, 11.

that beareth fruit, he will purge it, that it may bring forth much fruit.[9]

This purging or pruning action of the Father is what disconcerts us. We see an orchard in full bloom, and what has a more delicate charm? And yet those flowers must disappear if the branches are to bring forth fruit. There are many flowers in our life that seem of great value to us. In God's sight they are only flowers, and in His mercy He removes them that we may yield Him fruit. He alone knows the deep desires of our hearts, and He alone can satisfy them. We must trust Him absolutely if we wish to achieve our heart's desire. We are not only the children of God, but we are members of the Mystical Body of His well beloved Son in whom He is well pleased. Every single thing that happens is part of a plan for the development of that Mystical Body. The Three Divine Persons are continually directing events towards that end. The Father in His ruling of the universe is continually being a Father to the Body of His Son. The Holy Spirit is continually moving each of us interiorly that we may live the life of the Son. The Son Himself is continually pouring His grace into our soul that we may share His own life. Is it any wonder that all things work together for the good of them that love God?

The whole trouble is that—literally—we do not know what is good for us; and what makes the trouble still worse is that we think we do. We have our own plans for our happiness and too often we merely regard God as somebody who will help us to accomplish them. The true state of affairs is just the opposite. God has *His* plans for our happiness, and He is waiting for us to help *Him* to accomplish them. And let us be quite clear about it, *we cannot improve on God's plans.*

This whole subject of co-operation with God's plan as revealed in the course of events, and of the almost sacramental value of what He allows to happen to us, is one that could be discussed at great length. An incom-

[9] John xv, 1–5.

plete discussion might be misleading, because once one realizes the loving design behind God's providence there is a danger of adopting too passive an attitude, a danger of falling into that error called "quietism." We must take God's will as a whole. By "abandonment" we mean not only a cheerful submission to all that God permits to happen to us, but also a prompt, decisive and generous performance of all He requires us to do. There are certain things He wishes us to do; there are certain ends, He wishes us to aim at, although it does not follow that He wishes us to succeed in our aim; there are certain things He wishes us to put up with. For example, He wishes the father of a family to provide for the education of his children. That involves a certain expense, certain foresight, a calculation of means and ways, continual supervision, and perhaps certain alterations in one's original plans as a result of experience. God does not want the father to wait for His providence to take the lead; the iniative rests with the head of the family. But He does not command *success*. A father's attempt to educate his children may be partly frustrated by nonco-operation of the children, by mistakes on the part of the teachers, by illness, or by many other misfortunes. All God asks is that one should make a reasonable attempt. *The rest is God's business.* And the outcome of it all, whatever it may be, is God's will.

And because the rest is God's business, worry is usually a result of lack of confidence in God. We say usually; because some minds seem so constituted that they must worry over something. Yet, even in their case, something seems to be amiss. They are not responsible for the ruling of the world; why then worry over what they cannot influence? The type of worry which is more reasonable is where one is charged with responsibility and cannot decide what is the best course to adopt. The principle that applies here is that where God does not indicate His will, He expects us to use our own judgment and then to leave the consequences to *Him*. In such cases, we should make up our minds after asking God for help, and then leave the ultimate outcome to God. Really, our worry generally arises from the fact that we attribute far too great importance to our own share of the work in the partnership with God. We can always rely on Him to stand by us and supply for our own shortcomings. *Our sufficiency is from God.*[10]

Once a man has realized that God wills his happiness and that all that happens to him is ruled and regulated by God with infinite wisdom and power towards that end, and that all God asks of him is to co-operate with that loving will of His—then, that man has found the beginning of peace. And if he would be filled with that peace which is as a river, full, overflowing, rising up from the depth of his own heart, the peace which surpasseth all understanding, the peace which the world cannot give—let him devote himself to the practice of abandonment to God's will, always remembering that where God's will is to be done or to be accepted, Jesus Christ is waiting to share our doing of it. He always does the things that please the Father.

And if God's will for a man should mean death to himself—and for Jesus Christ it did—let him, nevertheless, abandon himself all the more joyously—for in shedding himself, he is putting on Christ. The Mass is the perfect picture of the Christian life. We offer ourselves to God and He gives us Christ. The more sincerely we offer ourselves and the more faithfully we carry out the promise contained in that offering by doing the will of God—the more closely shall we be united to Christ and, losing our old selves, the more wonderfully shall we find our new selves in Him.

[10] II Cor. iii, 5.

CHAPTER 16

Union with Christ in Our Neighbor

THE will of God contains all that is necessary for each of us to please Him and to reach those heights of holiness which He desires us to achieve. Nothing more, then, is necessary than to abandon ourselves completely to this will of God. But the use of the word abandonment must not be taken to imply merely a generous and open hearted acceptance of all God allows to happen to us; it is here used to cover that active fulfilment of God's will, by performing those things that He wills us to do, with cheerful and energetic promptitude. The first thing He asks of us is that we love Him with our whole heart and soul, and that we conform our wills to His. And He indicates His will in a special way to us when He says:

A new commandment I give unto you; that you love one another, as I have loved you, that you also love one another.[1] *. . . As the Father hath loved me, I also have loved you. Abide in my love. If you keep my commandments, you shall abide in my love; as I also have kept my Father's commandments, and do abide in his love. . . . This is my commandment, that you love one another, as I have loved you. Greater love than this no man hath, that a man lay down his life for his friends.*[2]

Here we have a manifestation of God's will which is so important that our Lord Himself made it the distinctive mark of His disciples: *By this shall all men know that you are my disciples, if you have love one*

[1] John xiii, 34. [2] John xv, 9–13.

for another.[3] No one seeking to live a Christian life can afford to neglect this command. Coming as it does in our Lord's farewell discourse, immediately after His explanation of Christian unity: *I am the vine, you are the branches,*[4] its relation with our membership of the mystic vine—with our incorporation in the Mystical Body —is obvious. Since Christ and His members form one vine, one body, we cannot be united to Him as to our Head unless we are also united to our fellow members as to an "extension" of Him. *Amen I say to you, as long as you did it to one of these my least brethren you did it to me.*[5] If St. Paul is entranced with the wonders of the unity of the Mystical Body, St. John the Evangelist is equally entranced with the wonders of fraternal charity; and fundamentally, the two ideas arise from the same mystery of our unity in Christ. St. John cannot get away from the thought. There is a well known account of his last days given by St. Jerome, when the aged apostle, whose inspired eye had once seen the vision of the Apocalypse, could no longer walk to his Church or even preach at any length. For all and sundry he had but one counsel and precept:—"Little children, love one another." Some of his hearers were moved by the constant repetition to inquire why he always repeated this advice. St. John's answer was simply this: "Because it is the commandment of the Lord; and if this alone is done—it is sufficient."[6] We cannot refrain from quoting his epistle on the subject:

Dearly beloved, let us love one another, for charity is of God. And everyone that loveth, is born of God and knoweth God. He that loveth not, knoweth not God, for God is charity. . . . If we love one another, God abideth in us, and his charity is perfected in us. . . . God is charity; and he that abideth in charity, abideth in God, and God in him. . . . If any man say, I love God, and hateth his brother, he is a liar. For he that loveth not his brother whom he seeth, how can he love God, whom he seeth not? And this com-

[3] John xiii, 35.   [4] John xv, 5.   [5] Matt. xxv, 40.
[6] Cf. Breviary, Feast of St. John.

mandment we have from God, that he, who loveth God, love also his brother.[7]

There can, therefore, be no true union with God unless we love also our neighbor. First of all, our neighbor is a member of the body of Christ, and we do not truly love Christ if we do not also love the members of Christ. Secondly, Christ delivered Himself for each of His members, and we, ourselves, cannot be united to Christ unless we share in *His* love for them. That is why He lays upon us the tremendous obligation to love one another "as He has loved us." We call it tremendous, for He loved us to the extent of laying down His life for us.

At first sight this seems to be an intolerable burden and an impossible obligation. But the service of God is a reasonable service, and He Himself has assured us that His yoke is easy and His burden light. If we examine this precept of love we shall find that the obligation, while extensive, is by no means insupportable. For though we are to love the members of Christ as He did, we must note that we ourselves are also members of Christ, and, therefore, we are bound to love *ourselves* in a truly supernatural fashion; and our first responsibility is for our own supernatural welfare. Further, we should note that though we are bound to *love* all, we are not bound to *like* anyone. It is true that our likes and dislikes can be offences against charity, insofar as they are wilful and inordinate; but there are many natural causes which produce a sympathy or an antipathy for which we are not responsible. What we are responsible for, is to see that these natural likes and dislikes do not interfere with the discharge of the obligations that justice and charity impose upon us in regard to our neighbor.

We are bound to love our neighbor insofar as he belongs to God. Therefore, our love for our own selves comes under the same principle. God died for our salvation, and hence our first duty of charity is to save our own souls. In desiring our own good, we should be

[7] I John iv, 7, 8, 12, 16, 20, 21.

guided by this principle; and we may, and often should seek health, pleasure, safety, learning, honor, fame and the goods of this world insofar as they assist us to reach our supernatural end. Insofar as these things come between us and God, or lead us away from Him to seek them their pursuit is not true Christian love of ourselves. Because we are personally responsible for our own salvation, we must put that first. The duty and the freedom to seek for other goods for ourselves may be modified by circumstances. Thus we are bound to take ordinary measures to preserve our own life; but we may sacrifice our life for the good of our neighbor. In a state of public emergency such as war, we may, in fact, be bound to endanger our life for the common good, and there are occasions when the saving of our neighbor's soul may oblige us to risk our own life. A priest, for example, would be bound even at the risk of his own life to administer the necessary sacraments to a dying man for whose salvation they were necessary. A mother may sometimes be bound to endanger her own life if there is no other way of ensuring the baptism of her child. What we are bound to do is one thing; what we are permitted to do, and would be praised for doing, is another. We may all follow our Lord's example of laying down His life for His friends.

We are bound to love all men. "To love," in this context, means to wish well to all men. Therefore, our charity must be sincere and interior, and we must will all men good equally insofar we must will them all salvation. In practice this means that we must not deliberately exclude anybody, friend or enemy, from our prayers, and that in a case of extreme necessity we should be ready to give them any help that is essential for them and which may be in our power. But, not all men have an equal claim upon our further charity. "Charity," says St. Thomas, "does not change the natural order, it perfects it." [8] Other things being equal, our own family has first claim, then our relatives, our friends and our bene-

[8] 3 *Sent.*, xxix, 7.

factors; and of a man's own family, his wife must come first, though her claim is not exclusive and may have to yield to special necessity.

This love of charity must be supernatural. We do not satisfy our Lord's new commandment by a natural love. It must be supernatural in its principle and in its nature. We must love our neighbor for God, and according to God. As the *Imitation of Christ* says: "That seems often to be charity which is rather natural affection; because our own natural inclination, self-will, hope of reward, desire of our own interest, will seldom be wanting."[9] That does not mean that a natural love or friendship cannot be supernaturalized, but it means that until the natural is subjected to the supernatural, we have not true Christian charity.

Having noted these two points, that our charity must be supernatural and that it may have to be limited in one order or direction by the higher claims of charity in another order or direction (for the natural must yield to the supernatural, and the stranger may have to yield to the relative), let us see how it affects our relations with the rest of human society. In the first place we have a duty to everyone even in our thoughts. Rash judgments and suspicion, envy and ill-will against one's neighbor, have no place in the deliberate thoughts of the true Christian. And in passing let it be noted that nearly all avoidance of evil and all practice of virtue must begin in our thoughts. If we deliberately allow ourselves to think evil, we shall soon find ourselves speaking evil and doing evil. Even in our thoughts and imagination we must apply the principles and ideals which we wish to be dominant in our daily life.

The faults of the tongue are innumerable, and it is noteworthy that even in people who are otherwise quite virtuous one often finds an uncharitable tongue. There is a wide field here for the practice of virtue and the quest of holiness. So much so that the Holy Ghost tells us by pen of St. James: *If any man offend not in word,*

[9] *Imitation of Christ,* i, 15.

the same is a perfect man.[10] Let us remember that every word we utter or every insinuation we make to the detriment of our neighbor is an injury done to Christ. There are occasions when one must speak unpleasant truths about one's neighbor—for example, in a law court, or to avoid greater evil—but, normally, we are not allowed to speak evil of him, even when what we say is true. The Christian man does his best to hide the faults of others, and will not listen to detraction. If detraction is wrong, calumny is still worse. And even quite good people do not seem to realize the responsibility they have for every single word they say about anyone else. Our neighbor's honor and good name, his professional reputation and his personal character, should be as safe in our mouth as in our Lord's. And it must be remembered that this is true even though we know that his private behavior does not justify his public reputation. There are, however, circumstances in which we may have to give someone a charitable warning. But all tale-bearing and mischief-making, all imprudent revelations of another's secret, all sowing of discord or exciting of suspicion are quite wrong, and are altogether incompatible with a true life in Christ. Not only do we separate ourselves from Him in the doing of these injuries, but we widen the breach inasmuch as these injuries are done to Him. We make public the very sins of which He has taken the shame upon Himself.

The really spiritual man is known by the kindness of his speech and still more by the kindness of his silence. He is always ready to find pity and sympathy for everyone. "To understand all is to forgive all," and no man who knows his own weakness and his complete dependence upon God's grace in the avoiding of sin, can ever be harsh with the faults of his neighbor. Even as human beings we should have a "fellow-feeling" for one another; but as Christians and members of Christ, our mutual sympathy should be much deeper.

Solicitude for the corporal necessities of our neighbor

[10] James iii, 2.

has always been characteristic of the fervent Christian. Whenever Christianity has taken root, it soon bears fruit in the form of countless organizations for the relief of the poor and the sick. The number of religious congregations which have such work as the external purpose of their organization (the primary purpose must always be the sanctification of the individual members) is quite striking. There is no need to draw the attention of the laity to this type of work. The Society of St. Vincent de Paul, and the Legion of Mary are world famous. What we would like to emphasize here, is the need for supernaturalizing such work, and the fact that the primary purpose of such organizations is the *individual sanctification of their members*. This latter fact is too often overlooked; and a lot of charitable work is done without real Christian charity as its motive. One can seek oneself in such work just as easily as in any other form of activity. A taste for publicity, for domination, for patronage, and for many other forms of self-exaltation, can seek its gratification even in Catholic Action. The true Christian seeks Christ; he tries to let himself be used as an instrument by Christ, to continue the charitable work of His days in Palestine when He went about doing good; and he tries also to serve the same Christ in the person of His members.

Christianity is really a sort of continuation of the Incarnation. Each of us is asked to give our Lord a further chance of satisfying His love for God and His love for men by living in us, and by performing in partnership with us, acts of charity—both to God directly in heaven and for His creatures here on earth. And our Lord wishes also to use us as a means of letting others show their love for Him through the things they do for us. We should note this double aspect of Christian charity. It should be done by Christ and by us in partnership with Him, to Christ and to His members united in Him. It will not be till we see Him face to face in heaven that we will perceive the full depth of meaning in His prayer to the Father at the Last Supper: *That the love where-*

with thou has loved me may be in them, and I in them.[11]

If we consider fraternal charity as a means of advancing in union with our Lord, we shall find in Him the model to which we must conform. If we truly desire to be one with Him we must obviously try to love our fellow men as He did. Now, that includes even our enemies. He forgave them all. He died for the very men who crucified Him. He prayed for them on the cross in the agony they caused Him. *Father, forgive them for they know not what they do.*[12] This forgiveness is not always easy in practice. Yet its importance and its urgency can be gauged from the fact that our Lord puts this amazing request on our lips in the *Our Father: Forgive us our trespasses, as we forgive them who trespass against us.* He makes us set as a limit to God's forgiveness of our sins against Himself, the same limit that we put to our forgiveness of our neighbors' faults against us. And He adds: *For if you will forgive men their offences, your heavenly Father will forgive you your offences. But if you will not forgive men, neither will your Father forgive you your offences.*[13]

This is an essential point in the spiritual life; and one that calls for frequent effort and watchfulness. We must keep a careful control over our thoughts to prevent any tendency to brood over the wrongs—real or imaginary—that have been done to us, and to avoid wishing evil to the person responsible or even taking deliberate pleasure in his misfortunes. When we are wronged, our external behavior has to be regulated by prudence, but we must be prompt to pray for the wrongdoer, as was Christ Himself. Few things make us so dear to God as this. And those whose love for our Lord is seeking expression, can find no better expression than praying for, and serving their enemies.

Of our duty in charity to assist our neighbor in temporal matters, there is no need to write here at any

[11] John xvii, 26.   [12] Luke xxiii, 34.   [13] Matt. vi, 14, 15.

length. All that we do for him is done for Christ, and, insofar as almsgiving is concerned, we must remember that once our own reasonable needs and those of our dependents are satisfied, we are only stewards for the remainder of our property and are under an obligation to assist our neighbor out of what is superfluous. This form of Christian charity is so well known that sometimes people think that it is, if not the only, at least its principal form. And modern society tends to judge the value of a man's life by the amount of good he does for his fellow men. The true Christian measure depends rather on what He has done for God.

But the result of popular misconception is that one often forgets that our principal duty to our neighbor is a supernatural one, and that the principal way of satisfying that duty is also a supernatural one. The most destitute man in the world is the man in the state of mortal sin. He cannot rise out of his sin without the help of a grace, which he cannot merit strictly for himself. The greatest work then of fraternal charity is that by which grace is obtained from God for those in mortal sin. And grace is only obtained by a spiritual life. The greatest service we can render our neighbor is to sanctify *ourselves*. In doing so, we become, if not a power house, at least a transformer station in the network of the distribution of grace. Elsewhere in this book, the words of Pius XI are quoted, showing the value of the contemplative life for the mission fields. The principle can be applied quite widely, and there is no limit to the supernatural service we can render our neighbor by a life of faith, hope, charity, humility, and abandonment to the will of God.

This principle of Christian charity, according to which Christ is replaced by His members, will be of extensive service in sanctifying the daily routine for those who wish to live a better and higher life. Our Lord can always be found in our neighbor, and loved and served in him. At first sight it might seem that the obligation arising from this identification of Christ with our fellow men is endless, but in practice it is by no means so unreasonable. Insofar as all mankind are concerned, the best service we can render them is to sanctify ourselves and to pray for them. It will be noted that the Church always prays in the plural: "pray for *us*"; we should include all men in such prayers. As is elsewhere pointed out in this book, every single step that any soul takes on the road to sanctification needs supernatural grace; all other instruments of sanctification—preaching, example, organization, reading—are of no avail, unless the soul obtains the grace to co-operate with them. This grace has to be obtained by prayer and sacrifice. It is true that the work of prayer and sacrifice has already been done by our Saviour Jesus Christ, and His Mother Mary. But God wishes to associate men with Him in His work of salvation, and so He makes us agents in the application of the fruits of our Lord's redeeming work.

Every single thing we do during the day, which is according to the will of God, can be used to bring down grace on men. The more anything runs contrary to our own will, the more closely does it resemble the cross by which Christ redeemed men. By willingly accepting such a share of the cross when He sends it to us, we lighten His load, and bring down His grace on men.[14] There are few works of fraternal charity so valuable as this. It has the further advantage, that we do not see the good we do, and hence the temptation to vainglory is not so obvious.

Here we would like to draw attention to a principle which is involved in all works connected with the

---

[14] It is reported that during the fourth apparition of Our Lady of Fatima, at Valinhos, on August 19th, 1917, she exhorted the children in the following words: *Pray, pray very much, sacrifice yourselves for sinners. Remember that many souls are lost because there is nobody to pray and to make sacrifices for them.*

Previously, on July 13th, she had told them: "Sacrifice yourselves for sinners. Say often, especially when you make sacrifices, 'Oh, Jesus. it is for love of You, for the conversion of sinners and in reparation for the sins committed against the Immaculate Heart of Mary.'"

apostolate or with the service of God. Apart from the direct praise of God, most works serve Him more or less indirectly; they have some purpose, some result to be achieved—which is intended as a means to glorify Him. Let us suppose that it is the conversion of some particular soul: and to simplify the issue, let us suppose that we have a clear duty to work for such a soul's conversion. The principle to be noted is this: God does not put a premium on success. In fact, in His service failure is often the greatest triumph. In the particular case under consideration, our efforts to serve Him lose nothing of their value in His eyes, when they do not meet with success. Their value as acts of love and service for Him is quite independent of their outcome. It is true, especially where we have a clear duty to strive for a particular purpose, that we have to use prudence in choosing means which are likely to achieve that purpose. But that is the end of our obligation. It is God who giveth the increase, and if He does not give it, that is His business.

It very often happens that the real fruit of our labors is gathered elsewhere. Some priest, perhaps, wearing himself out in a non-Catholic district and failing to produce any conversions, may be drawing souls into the Church in great numbers out in the mission field as the result of his apparently fruitless labors. Such a form of apostolate is quite common, and is obviously the only way which at present is available for the conversion of Russia. If, therefore, the efforts of ardent apostolic zeal are frustrated in one particular place, that is no reason to be despondent; if they are done according to God's will, they will surely bear fruit somewhere. It must never be forgotten that the principle of all fruitfulness is that given by Christ to His apostles: *Abide in me, and I in you. As the branch cannot bear fruit of itself unless it abide in the vine, so neither can you, unless you abide in me. I am the vine and you are the branches; he that abideth in me, and I in him, the same beareth fruit.* And it is important to remember how this fruitfulness is increased: *I am the true vine, and my Father is the*

*husbandman: every branch . . . that beareth fruit, he
will purge it, that it may bring forth more fruit.*[15] Very
often apparent failure in our work for souls is nothing
else than this purging action of the Father, to make us
bring forth more fruit elsewhere. We are always doing
enough for souls if we abide in Christ.

To some souls, our Lord makes is clear that He has
a special work for them to do. Occasionally, He asks a
soul to become a victim for the salvation of others. When
such a vocation is certain, one has a quite new field for
God's service. Our own view is that in this matter one
should wait for God to make His will clear; and such a
form of apostolic work should never be undertaken without the consent and authorization of some prudent director. Anyone who takes such a work upon himself without
an indication of God's will, may be guilty of pride and
presumption, and may find that he is left to carry a heavy
burden without the extra grace that lightens such a burden. We repeat, that as long as one abides in Christ by
doing the will of God, that is ample.[16]

It is not by the extraordinary, but rather by ordinary
things that we shall sanctify ourselves and help others.
The saints become saints by using the opportunities we
neglect and even despise. Without going to seek out
our neighbor, we can still find many opportunities of
exercising fraternal charity in the course of our day's
work. In everyone with whom we come in contact during
the day, Christ can be found, Christ can be loved, Christ
can be served. Faith, of course, is required, and so is
courage. But so also is prudence. Christ is to be served
in each of our neighbors according to the particular circumstances of our relations with each one. For example,
a teacher can see Christ in all his pupils. What he does
for each boy is done not only *for* Christ, but is done *to*

[15] Cf. John xv, 1–5.

[16] In a book entitled *Consummata,* Fr. Raoul Plus, S.J. has
given an account of the life of a young Frenchwoman, whose
story will show what can be done in the lay state. It is not everyone who has the same vocation, but most readers will find light
and encouragement in her words.

Christ. What then, about punishment? In the case of a boy who really deserves and needs punishment, the teacher is dealing with a sick member of Christ, and his position is something the same as that of a doctor or a dentist. He has to cause pain in doing good, and where it is his clear duty to punish, it would be a neglect of his duty to Christ, not to do so. Note what we say "where it is his clear duty." For if justice be a virtue, so also is mercy. And there is a very important general principle that should influence all our relations with our neighbors —especially with those who are young. The measure and the manner in which religion influences a man's life— the interest and zeal with which he pursues a spiritual life—depend very much on the habitual notion that he has of God. Now most of us form our notion of God from our experiences with those whom we meet frequently, especially from the treatment we receive from our parents and teachers. If they are harsh and "just" and strict, we find it difficult to be convinced that God is a loving Father and a merciful Saviour.

We all know the cringing, fearful way in which a dog shrinks away from our caresses if he has been previously ill-treated by others. One meets children whose arm goes up to ward off a blow as soon as anyone in authority approaches them. The same sort of attitude is often found with regard to God. He is thought of as a hard master, overexacting and meticulous, setting traps for His creatures, and almost only anxious to catch them in wrongdoing. No true love of God is possible with such a concept in one's mind. Yet such ideas can exist, and we must take care that we are not responsible for their formation. That is one reason why, if we must err in dealing with our neighbor, we ought to err on the side of mercy and kindness rather than of justice and rigor.

Kindness and mercy should characterize all our dealings with our neighbor. In the course of our daily labor, we may have to work with people, to work for them, to work under them, or to work in charge of them. In all cases we have a duty to do, certain responsibilities to remember. These we must observe conscientiously. But all should be done with kindness. If we have to refuse a request for help because of the prior claims of duty, we should do so kindly and gently. And, if we truly seek God, we shall not refuse to help when we are free to do so. It is said that the willing horse gets all the work. Even if that be so, the willing Christian will also get all the reward. But Christian charity, while demanding that we help our neighbor, also puts a limit to his claims. We have, for example, to look after the needs of our own soul first of all; and though on occasions we should never allow private devotions to come before the assistance of our neighbor, yet in the long run we must insist upon sufficient time and energy being left for our spiritual life.

This can be difficult in family life. The series of calls upon one's time from members of the family, from visitors, and from the hundred and one other sources of interference with one's plans, is almost endless. We may have to draw a line somewhere if we wish to keep up regular practices such as prayer and reading. Still, we should be on our guard against feeling that time devoted to family functions and to family fun is wasted. There is a proper measure in everything; and each has a right to his own private life for some part of the day. But those who live with their family need have no scruple in spending much of their time in sharing the life of the family.

If they maintain a healthy interior life, they can find Christ in their family, and be united to Him, even in family fun. To make a fourth at family bridge, to help to entertain some guests, to take a walk with one's parents and one's children— all such things can be more meritorious and more pleasing to God than private prayer or even, say, a visit to the Blessed Sacrament. A saint should be a very easy person to live with. Unfortunately, those who try to be saints are often quite the opposite. Might we refer them to the example of St. Jane Frances de Chantal? While she was still living in the world, St. Francis de Sales became her director. The result of his influence may be gathered from the comment of one of her servants: "The first director that Madame had made her pray three times a day, and we were all put out; but the Monsignor of Geneva (St. Francis de Sales) makes her pray all day long and no one is troubled.

Everyone who wishes to lead a spiritual life in the world, should read *The Introduction to the Devout Life* by St. Francis de Sales. The style may seem somewhat old-fashioned, and minor details of his practical direction may have to be tempered to fit in with changed social conditions, but there is no better book for the laity, and it has the particular merit of imparting that spiritual outlook which best accommodates itself to the needs of family life. It is urgent, at the moment, that Catholics should sanctify the family and the life of the family, for the influence of Christianity upon society depends upon its influence upon the family. Insofar as the family ceases to be Christian, Christian civilization will approach its end.

Two particular aspects of familiar relationships call for brief notice. The mutual relations of husband and wife will be dealt with in a separate chapter; here we would draw attention to the extensive possibilities of exercising Christian virtue and Christian perfection in the relations between parents and children. After their mutual obligations to one another, the next obligation on parents is towards their children. It is probably safe to say that the greater part of the life of the ordinary man and woman is occupied with these duties. What a woman has done for her children can be seen in her face. She has given of herself, of her very substance; she has renounced her young beauty and natural comfort; the very skin of her hands shows her devotion. It is true the woman who is a mother has a mellow beauty and a royal dignity that no other woman can achieve. But her sacrifice of herself is none the less courageous for all that. What we have always seems far more precious than what we may achieve. And the extent of the sacrifice involved can be measured by the dread and the repugnance that the modern woman feels for making it. In truth, both in the spiritual and in the temporal order, it is only by dying to oneself, that one can give life to others.

There can be no question that parenthood may call for heroic devotion. This is evident even if one only thinks of the continual tie that young children are to their parents, who can hardly leave their home without the anxious feeling that they must be back again quickly. Their pleasures are curtailed drastically. Time and money are at a premium, and modern life has little sympathy with those who recognize all their obligations to their children. The modern often view the mother whose main interest lies in her family, with amusement, if not with contempt. One can only thank Providence that women have an inexhaustible reserve of courage to meet these difficulties and overcome them. To their courage there is to be added the grace of the sacrament of matrimony by which parents can receive a share of our Lord's own strength and courage and love, for dealing with all the problems which arise from devotion to their family.

To illustrate the general by the particular, consider for a moment the sacrifices that parents have to face to make Christmas all that tradition says it should be for their children. The expense, the worry, the trouble, the patience, the fatigue, the bitterness of financial limitations to one's power of gratifying a child's dream—the list is endless. Think alone of what is involved in Christmas shopping, where a large family and a small income are involved. And the thought can easily arise, especially for the "detached" Christian: "Is it worth it all?" Of course, it is worth it all. It is done in memory of Christ; it is done to build up an idea of Christ; it is done *for* Christ; it is done *to* Christ! *Amen, I say to you whatsoever you did to these my least brethren, you did it to me.* When the New Year brings an end to those halcyon days for the children, this service done to Christ is the consolation that the parents should have in facing the expense.

In view of a life of things of this sort—who can

say that holiness is not possible in family life? Ought not the question rather to be, how is family life possible without heroic sanctity? There is no need to labor the possibilities of living a life of service of Christ by devoting oneself to one's family. St. Joseph, the greatest saint in heaven after Jesus and Mary, sanctified himself in no other way. He should be the model of all. If one omits the visits of the angels to warn him of special circumstances, there is nothing extraordinary in his life except his love of Jesus and Mary. His life is full of lessons for the discerning. He governed the Holy Family, although he was the least gifted of the three both by nature and by grace. He was an ordinary workman, and never achieved any noteworthy success. He did no miracles, he performed no extraordinary penances. He spoke no word that came down to us; he lived only a generation before the wonder-working apostles who took up our Lord's work of preaching and building up the Church. He stands silently beside that master of heroic penance, St. John the Baptist. Compared with these great figures he seems almost a nonentity, and yet his fame is still growing today in the Church, of which he is the universal patron, and its greatest saint after the Queen of Saints.

The other point to which we would refer is the place of friendship in the spiritual life. In quite a number of spiritual books, written for religious, one will find a condemnation, on various grounds, of particular friendships. From the point of view of the perfection of charity in the life of a religious community, such particular friendships are very objectionable. The preference for one, means to some extent an aversion for another; it makes impossible the ideal of regulating all our relations by the spirit of faith so that Christ should be found as easily in one person as in another. It interferes with the custody of the heart and with that perfection of detachment which should be the aim of every religious. And the origin of such friendship is by no means always to be found in Christian charity. But a lay person reading such books may easily form a false standard for his own life.

Even among religious orders friendship has had its defenders, and the Cistercian tradition that shone forth in St. Bernard, can be found in St. Aelred's famous work on *Spiritual Friendship*, which has appeared in English with an introduction by Fr. Hugh Talbot, O.C.R. To quote one line as an example: "Here we are, just we two; and Christ I hope, is between us." To this book we refer those who would know how instrumental friendship can be in reaching perfection.

People living in the world are in quite a different position from religious. What might be an unnecessary luxury for religious, could be for them a necessary aid. There are, of course, friendships of the wrong sort that lead one away from God; but there are friendships which can be of great spiritual profit, if they are properly referred to the love of Christ. *The Imitation of Christ*[17] gives us the true ideal, putting these words in the mouth of our Lord: "In *Me* the love of thy friend must stand; and for *Me* he is to be loved, whoever he be that appears to thee good, and is very dear to thee. Without *Me* no friendship is of any strength nor will be durable nor is that love true and pure, of which I am not the author." Thomas à Kempis, it is true, does demand a high degree of mortification in this matter, but one cannot apply the maxims of the religious life in their entirety to the life in the world. For some, friendship is a necessity, for others it might be a hindrance. Our love for our friend must be subordinate to our love for our Lord; and He may, perhaps, test our loyalty. All that we wish to do here is to reject the idea that the love of a creature is incompatible with the love of God. The Scripture tells us: *A faithful friend is a strong defence and he that hath found him hath found a treasure. Nothing can be compared to a faithful friend, and no weight of gold and silver is able to countervail the goodness of his fidelity. A faithful friend is the medicine of life and immor-*

[17] iii, 42.

tality, and they that fear the Lord, shall find him.[18] The idea that our Lady loved St. Joseph will come as a shock to many people, and yet she must have done so; otherwise she would not have been the perfect wife. One wonders whether popular misconceptions in this matter are the cause or the effect of the fact that most painters represent St. Joseph as an old man. That he was so much older than our Lady is a conventional assumption rather than a proved fact. Modern writers consider him to have been much younger than he is generally represented.

Our Lord Himself felt a need for His special friends. St. John is immortal as "The disciple whom our Lord loved"; Martha and Mary were loved by our Lord, and He sought the comfort and consolation of their house. The death of Lazarus, their brother, wrung tears from His eyes, and His love for him led to one of His most striking miracles. Even the saints have found profit in friendship; the association of St. Francis de Sales and St. Jane Frances de Chantal is a classical example.

But, as we said, the subordination of such love to one's love of God may have to be proved and tested. Even our Lady and St. Joseph had their trials when the mystery of the Incarnation became obvious to St. Joseph and had not yet been explained to him. Our Lord Himself set us an example when as a boy, because He must be about His Father's business, He left Mary and Joseph, who sought Him sorrowing. The lesson is clear: no human friendship must interfere with our Father's business.

The details of fraternal charity cannot all be discussed here, but we must return to the fundamental principle that true Christian charity is supernatural in its motive and in its purpose. To sanctify ourselves and to pray for our neighbor is our first duty to him. We can, if we feel called to do so, go further. We can offer our sufferings in atonement for his sins, we can offer our Lord love in reparation for the coldness of our neighbor. No one has such a claim upon our pity as the sinner; for without the grace of God, he cannot even repent of his sin, yet

[18] Ecclesiasticus vi, 14–16.

he has condemned himself to an eternal fate that is too appalling to consider. This need of sinners for our help should be ever present to us; there are few dispositions which put us so completely in harmony with Christ, who lived and suffered and died for sinners.

Closely allied with the needs of sinners are the needs of those outside the faith at home and in the mission fields. Both classes should have a permanent place in our prayers, and it is significant to note that even to the apostles, our Lord suggested prayer as the first means of converting souls. *Pray ye the Lord of the harvest; that he send laborers into his vineyard.*[19]

This is the purpose of true Christian charity, to save men from sin and to unite them to God. As Fr. Petitot says in his book *St. Teresa of Lisieux* (which will be of tremendous help in giving the reader a true notion of the value of spiritual works): "One of the most widespread and pernicious errors is to imagine that the merit of our life is proportionate to our labors and activity. In reality, the merit of our life and the efficacy of our apostolate is proportionate not to the amount of trouble we take, but to our holiness."

And the foundation of true charity is our union in Christ. To quote St. Augustine: "Extend thy charity over the entire earth if thou wilt love Christ, for the members of Christ are to be found everywhere in the world. If thou lovest only a part thou art divided; if thou art divided, thou art not in the Body; if thou art not in the Body, thou art not under the Head. . . . What is the use of believing if thou dost blaspheme? Thou adorest Him as Head, and thou dost blaspheme Him in His Body. He loves His Body. Thou canst cut thyself off from the Body, but the Head does not detach itself from its Body. 'Thou dost honor Me in vain,' He cries from Heaven, 'thou dost honor Me in vain!' If someone wished to kiss thy cheek, but insisted at the same time on trampling thy feet; if with his nailed boots he were to crush thy feet as he tries to hold thy head and kiss thee, wouldst

[19] Cf. Matt. ix, 38.

thou not interrupt his expressions of respect and cry out: what art thou doing, man? Thou art trampling upon me. . . . It is for this reason that before He ascended into heaven our Lord Jesus Christ recommended to us His Body, by which He was to remain on earth. For He foresaw that many would pay Him homage because of His glory in heaven, but that their homage would be vain, so long as they despise His members on earth."[20]

For when we reject the claim of our neighbor on our charity, we reject Christ; we even reject ourselves, for we, too, are members of Christ. Lack of Christian charity wounds ourselves as well as wounding Christ. The whole question is well summed up by a medieval English Cistercian, Isaac of Stella: "Therefore, my brethren, let this be your manner of life. . . . to converse in thought and desire with Christ in our heavenly country, and in our earthly pilgrimage to refuse no service of charity for the sake of Christ. Let us follow the Lord Christ in heaven in our dealings with the Father, uniting ourselves with Him in the quiet of contemplation. And let us follow Christ here below in our dealings with our neighbor, by extending our activity, multiplying ourselves, by making ourselves all things to all men.

"Let us despise nothing that is done for Christ, let our thirst be for one alone and be occupied with one alone, where Christ is one; and let us be ready to serve all, where Christ is many."[21]

[20] *Epist. ad Parthos.* 10; P.L. 35, 2060.
[21] *Sermon,* 51; P.L. 194, 1863.

CHAPTER 17

Union with Christ through Humility

A BANDONMENT to Divine Providence is but the outward expression of that virtue of humility which is the foundation of the whole spiritual life. We have already referred to humility as that by which the obstacles to the outpourings of God's goodness are removed, for *God resisteth the proud and giveth grace to the humble.*[1]

If one asks: "How am I to become humble?" the immediate answer is "by the grace of God," and that is indeed the truth. Only the grace of God can give us that insight into our own condition and realization of His exaltation that make for humility. But even though it be a grace, it is a grace with which we must co-operate. The first thing to do is to ask in prayer for the grace of humility, and to ask sincerely. The second thing is to accept humiliations when they come our way; but, let us never forget that there is an enormous difference between being humble and being humiliated. The next thing is to accept as lovingly as we can, our own limitations, our own defects, our own lowliness; and even to be resigned —if we cannot be glad—when these shortcomings become known to others. Human nature being what it is, all this is not easy; in fact, without confidence in God, it is morally impossible.

Confidence and humility always go together. One of the reasons why men are so anxious to exalt themselves —to overestimate their own value and their own powers

[1] James iv, 6.

—to resent anything that would tend to lower themselves in their own esteem or in that of others—is because they see no other hope for their happiness save in themselves. That is often why they are so "touchy," so resentful of criticism, so impatient of opposition, so insistent on getting their own way, so eager to be known, so anxious for praise, so determined on ruling their surroundings. They clutch at themselves like drowning men clutch at a straw. And as life goes on, and they are still far from being satisfied, their attitude borders on the feverish and the hysterical; whatever they may have got, they are certainly far from having found peace.

The attitude of the man who has true Christian humility is just the opposite. His hope is placed in God; he sees no hope in himself. He has not to worry about getting his own way; all that matters is that God should get His way. He knows that the less he has to do with the arranging of things, the more likely is it that things will turn out for the best. He is by no means spineless or inert. On the contrary, let him but once be certain that God wills him to undertake a particular work, and he will tackle it, no matter what it may be, because he knows his sufficiency is from God. He knows his life is a partnership: and whether he acts, or whether he lets God— or even other men—act, he trusts with unshaken confidence in God. And God never refuses to aid him, because such a man is not an enemy of His glory, as is the proud man.

Humility, in fact, is not so much self-depreciation as self-forgetfulness. It is a return to the simplicity of childhood based upon a realization of the fatherhood of God. It is to realize that our sanctification is the work of God, and that we are rather an obstacle to His work than otherwise. It is a realization, and a glad acceptance, of the fact that we have nothing which we have not received. The truly humble never desire to appear before God as workers who have accomplished all their tasks perfectly, and who therefore expect to receive their full wages as their due. Such workers, of course, will receive their just reward; if we appeal to God's justice, He will be just with us. But which of us dare stand in such confidence before the judgment seat of God and put all our hope in His just retribution? Such an attitude is the height of folly. The wise man closes his eyes to any good he may have done, and goes to God as to his Saviour, relying on His mercy and upon his own poverty. For that is the claim or title which our Lord recognizes to the kingdom of heaven. *Blessed are the poor in spirit for theirs is the kingdom of heaven.*[2]

The truth is that we do not understand the value of our own weakness. We want to be conscious of our strength, and we want others to be conscious of it also; we want to do great things—for God, we say—and we want others to know that we have done them: we want to acquire a store of merit and an armory of virtues so that we can feel secure in our own spiritual riches; we want good to be done—but we want to have the doing of it ourselves so that we may be rich in what we think are good works. We forget what the Holy Spirit writes:

There is an inactive man that wanteth help, is very weak in ability, and full of poverty: Yet the eye of God hath looked upon him for good, and hath lifteth him up from his low estate, and hath exalted his head. . . . Trust in God, and stay in thy place. For it is easy in the eyes of God on a sudden to make the poor man rich. The blessing of God maketh haste to reward the just, and in a swift hour his blessing beareth fruit.[3]

As Fr. Clerissac said to a friend, "it is our emptiness and thirst that God needs, not our plenitude."[4] The right attitude is that of St. Paul: *Gladly will I glory in my infirmities, that the power of God may dwell in me.*[5] The wise man prefers to be conscious of his own weakness, and even tries, at least, to be glad when others perceive it, for then the glory of his works belongs to God

[2] Matt. v, 3.   [3] Ecclesiasticus xi, 12, 13, 22–24.
[4] Clerissac, *The Mystery of the Church;* cf. Introduction.
[5] Cf. II Cor. xii, 9.

and not to himself; he has no wish to do great things, but rather to love God greatly in doing little things; and since he only seeks to please God, he is indifferent to what others may think of his achievements. He has no regard for any store of merit and virtues he himself may possess, because his whole security is placed in his own poverty and in the riches of God's mercy; and while his zeal for God's glory keenly desires that good works be done, for it is a matter of indifference to him by whom they are done as long as they are done for God.

There is perhaps no point in which the attitude of the Catholic is—or at least, should be—so opposed to the spirit of the time as in this matter of humility. The whole trend of modern standards is to put all value in personal achievement and self-exaltation. Men live and work for the end that they may think well of themselves and that others may be forced to acknowledge their value and their achievements. The superficially minded are content with applause; whether it be merited or not, whether it come from the discerning or from the easily impressed, does not make much difference to them. Those who have more vision, judge themselves by higher standards: they seek the approbation of the competent few, and are even indifferent to the applause of the mob. Yet, it does not follow that their pride is any the less on that account. The real value of a man is what he is in the sight of God; no human judgment can affect that.

But in trying to react against this pagan pride that the world preaches, the lay Catholic has to be prudent. There is a difference between the practice of humility in a religious and in a layman. The religious has a poise and a background given to him by the habit he wears and the status of the order to which he belongs. He can be forgetful of himself even in his contact with men, and unconsciously rely upon his membership of a religious organization. He does not have to stand upon his feet, so to speak. The layman is in quite a different position. If he is to defy the trend of the times, and stand against the tide of public opinion as he must nowadays, he has need of quite a considerable measure of poise and self-respect, of consciousness of his own worth and of his own importance. This consideration may mean that the practices of humility suggested for a religious are not always suitable for the laity. This is especially true in those countries where Catholicity is despised or where it is only beginning to raise its head after years of persecution. It is true that the proper foundation of such a poise and self-respect is supernatural, but the supernatural does not dispense with the natural, and there is need for considerable prudence in these matters.

There are, however, many ways in which pride can manifest itself which can be avoided even by the layman without any compromise to his status. In speech, pride leads a man to talk of himself and of his own affairs and to seek esteem in various ways. Sometimes it is by open boasting, at other times by a mock modesty that only succeeds in drawing more attention to oneself. Some men are quite adroit in turning the conversation to topics in which they can display their knowledge or ability. The patronizing person is generally a proud person, as also are those given to airs of superiority, to studied phrases or to a magisterial tone. There are those who insist upon maintaining their own opinion, those who cannot let any slip pass without correcting it, those who are only too glad to correct others; all such are generally proud. Contemptuous sarcasm and mordant wit often come from pride, though it is quite surprising to what limits shyness or nervousness can sometimes drive men who are really not proud. The meanest form of self-exaltation is that which seeks itself by decrying others. The proud do not like to hear others praised; they are only too ready to point out the feet of clay in those who are renowned; and, what is perhaps their most characteristic note, they cannot bear contradiction or correction.

However, just as the exterior display of humility does not always mean that one is really humble, so it does not always follow that all such defects are really due to pride. Sometimes it happens, especially in the inexperienced, that there is an inner uncertainty—a feeling of one's own shortcomings which leads to external extravagances that pass for pride. There is, for example, a boyish boasting that is really due to consciousness of one's own lack of years. There is a youthful quest of admiration that is often the result of a painful feeling of inferiority. For that reason, as well as for the love of God, we should be reserved in our judgments about one another. The external crust of apparent pride often covers a surprising depth of humility.

In the practice of humility, it is a very sound principle never to display a humility that is not sincere. It is far better and far more humble to let one's pride appear where there is no danger of scandal, than to assume a humility that is not ours. For that reason, the cultivation of humility should commence in the interior. It will be learned by keeping good company, and the best company is that of Jesus and Mary. If we but read the life of our Lord as that of a friend, we cannot help being influenced by His constant example. Frequent meditation on the Passion will bring us more quickly to humility than anything else, and while humility is dependent upon true self-knowledge, such knowledge is better obtained by studying what God is, than what we ourselves are. The continual remembrance of God is one of the best ways of ensuring humility, for humility is really reverence for God, and advance in humility means advance in reverence for God. Here again we find that the Christian life is but a continuation of the Mass. In the Mass, we offer sacrifice to assure God that we are nothing and that He is all, to offer Him our adoration and our reverence. If we are sincere in our protestation we shall maintain that attitude of humility of heart during the rest of the day.

The practice of this humility of heart is capable of many degrees, and the practice of each degree could be realized in many ways. It is not within our scope to draw up a complete program here. In this, as in all such matters, we prefer to suggest an attitude of mind, and to leave the manifestation of it to the individual judgment. Where there is real humility of heart, conduct and speech cannot be affected by it. Still, perhaps some examples of the practice of this virtue will help to make the notion of true humility clear.

The avoidance of all those manifestations of pride which we mentioned above would be sound forms of practical humility. To speak as little of one's own self or affairs as possible; to mind one's own business; to avoid curiosity; not to want to manage other people's affairs; to accept contradiction or correction; not to insist upon one's own opinion unless truth or justice require it, and then to do so moderately, but with courage; to pass over the mistakes of others, to cover them up, even, where prudent, to accept them (for example, in pronunciation); to yield to the will of others, where neither duty nor charity nor genuine Christian principle is involved; to hide one's own ability or talents; to avoid ostentation; all such are works of humility that are within the powers of all. One can, however, go further. To accept blame when innocent, to accept insults or injuries, to accept being slighted or forgotten or disliked, not to seek to be specially loved or admired, not to be put out at one's own clumsiness or mistakes, to be kind and gentle even under provocation, never to stand on one's dignity save where Christian prudence demands it, to accept correction gladly, to yield in discussion even though one is right, not to be self-opinionated or self-assertive; all these are praiseworthy. But if we remember first that humility is reverence for God, and secondly that it is not only an imitation of Jesus, but a perfect way of giving oneself to Him, one may be ready to go still further.

To be glad, for example, at being despised, to thank God when one is humiliated, to rejoice in one's lowliness, to be patient with one's own failings, to meet failure with a ready smile, to glory in one's infirmities; here love is becoming ardent, and union with Jesus is growing more intimate. Insofar as any of the practices mentioned above are only in the exterior, their value is not great; their true value comes from the humility of heart which leads to them. To develop this genuine humility, it is important always to practise humility and its associated virtues *in one's thoughts*. Reveries, day-dreaming and castles in the air, for example, designed to exalt oneself will hardly lead to true humility. Brooding over humiliations, over failure, over one's shortcomings; trying to retrieve one's mistakes in one's imaginings, trying to excuse oneself, refusing to admit one's error, even being dishonest with oneself, putting the blame on somebody else; all these things are contrary to humility. In fact they could be dangerous; and could lead first of all to an entirely false notion of oneself, and even to a "near-neurosis" of some form or other. In passing, it might be no harm to point out that the practice of Christian humility and of its inseparable associate, Christian confidence, based as they are upon the true relations between man and God, is one of the best ways of curing such ills. And it would be well to make it clear that what moderns call an "inferiority complex" is not humility. The former exaggerates one's defects, and morbidly refuses to accept them; humility is truth and a glad acceptance of the truth.

There are other ways in which pride can manifest itself, of which those who seek humility should be at least suspicious. Ambition—especially ambition for showy success—is often the fruit of pride. The desire to control affairs, to be in a position to manage others, to make one's own will prevail, often comes from that form of pride which has, perhaps, the deepest of roots: the love of one's own judgment. Even when we yield externally, we are still convinced in our heart that "we knew best." The man who sees things in a supernatural light is very slow to take responsibility for arranging affairs, even where he has reason to believe that from the merely natural point of view, he is best equipped to form an opinion or to decide. Still, it can be that a humble man may feel it his duty to assert himself, especially when he sees that those who are arranging things have no supernatural outlook, and then he should act with courage, but gently though firmly.

There is another case where humility insists on holding the reins, and that is where God's will has made a particular man responsible. The father, for example, is head of the family, because he is the person responsible.

Quite often he has not got the best judgment, and in any event, prudence and love demand that he take counsel with his wife; but the final decision should be his. And he can insist upon it in all humility, for there he has the "grace of state." This means that where God has made a certain man responsible for deciding, He will see to it that those concerned do not lose by submitting to his decisions, if their motives in submitting are correct. Humility, too, need not prevent Catholics from taking their due share in public life, or from cultivating their professional reputation. What it does demand is that they faithfully ascribe their ability and their success to God, and never cease to lean upon His aid. Even in the most extreme case of insistence upon one's rights, humility of heart must never be absent.

It is, however, in loving our Lord, that our humility will fully flower, and it is in being humble that our love will fully flame. For Jesus is not only a tremendous lover, He is also in the best sense of the word a jealous one. He is especially jealous of our independence, even if our independence is only sought for in our thoughts. This divine jealousy is not the same as that prompted by vanity and self-love which one sometimes finds in human love (though not all human jealousy is as petty as that ; it is the jealousy of a lover that knows that He—and He alone—can give happiness to His beloved, and who knows that full happiness is impossible except in complete dependence upon Him. After infidelity, there is nothing hurts so much in human love as aggressive self-sufficiency, even when it is found more in external assertion than in interior reality. The mere desire for independence is at least a limitation to one's love—and where love for Jesus is concerned, there can be no limitations. *Thou shalt love the Lord thy God with thy whole heart and thy whole soul, with all thy mind and all thy strength.* Thomas à Kempis puts these words on our Lord's lips:

What more do I ask of thee than to try to give thyself up entirely to Me? Whatever thou givest besides thyself is nothing to Me: I seek not thy gift but thyself! Just as thou couldst not be content without Me, though thou possessest everything else; so nothing thou offerest can please Me unless thou offerest Me thyself! . . . Behold, I offered My whole self to the Father for thee, and have given my whole Body and Blood for thy food: that I might be all thine, and thou mightest be all and always Mine. But if thou wilt stand upon thy own strength, and wilt not offer thyself freely to My will, thy offering is not perfect, nor will there be an entire union between us.[6]

Our humility and obedience are but the exercise of our love and desire for Jesus; they are but means of giving ourself completely to Him, as He does to us in the Mass, and that is what, by our Communion and assistance at Mass, we signify our readiness to do.

For that is the whole spiritual life—a love union with Jesus, in which each of the lovers, the divine and the human, give themselves completely to one another. It is not so much a question of acquisition of virtue, of performing heroic deeds, of amassing merit, of bearing fruit in the Church; these things are excellent, especially insofar as they come from love. But nothing less than our very self in its entirety will satisfy the Heart of Jesus, and all He asks is that we give Him our whole self in all poverty and nothingness. The great way to do that is the way shown by Jesus and by Mary—by love through humility and abandonment.

This way has again been brought to men's notice in our own times by the life of St. Thérèse of Lisieux. There can be no doubt that she was raised up by God to show us the true way to holiness. One would hesitate about citing the life of an enclosed contemplative as a model for the laity, were it not for the insistence with which more than one pope has stressed the universality of her message of what is called "spiritual childhood." Her life really marks a true renaissance in the history of spirituality. Its importance cannot be exaggerated. Let us quote Pope Benedict XV in his discourse regarding

[6] *Imitation of Christ,* iv, 8.

the heroicity of her virtues.[7] *There,* he exclaims, referring to spiritual childhood, *lies the secret of holiness . . . for the faithful throughout the entire world. . . .* And he proceeds to give a complete description of this spirituality from which we quote brief passages. Taking as an example the confidence of a child in its mother's protection and its certainty that she will treat it in the way best suited to its needs, the Holy Father proceeds:

So likewise, is spiritual childhood fostered by confidence in God and trustful abandonment into His hands. . . . Spiritual childhood excludes first the sentiment of pride in oneself, the presumption of expecting to attain by human means a supernatural end, and the deceptive fancy of being self-sufficient in the hour of danger and temptation. On the other hand, it supposes a lively faith in the existence of God, a practical acknowledgment of His power and mercy, confident recourse to Him who grants the grace to avoid all evil and obtain all good. Thus, the qualities of this spiritual childhood are admirable . . . and we understand why our Saviour Jesus Christ has laid it down as a necessary condition for gaining eternal life. One day the Saviour took a little child from the crowd, and showing him to His disciples, He said: "Amen I say to you; unless you be converted and become as little children you shall not enter into the kingdom of heaven."[8] . . . "Who, thinkest thou, is the greater in the kingdom of heaven? . . . Whosoever shall humble himself as this little child, he is the greater in the kingdom of heaven." And again on another day, Jesus said: "Suffer little children to come to me, and forbid them not; the kingdom of heaven is for such. Amen I say to you, whosoever shall not receive the kingdom of God as a child shall not enter into it."[9]

The Holy Father continues:

It is important to notice the force of these divine words, for the Son of God did not deem it sufficient to affirm positively that the kingdom of heaven is for children—Talium

---

[7] Cf. Discourse of Pope Benedict XV, Aug. 14, 1921.
[8] Matt. xviii, 3.   [9] Cf. Mark x, 14–15.

est enim regnum coelorum—or that he who will become as a
little child shall be greater in heaven, but He explicitly
threatens exclusion from heaven for those who will not become like unto children. . . . We must conclude then that
the Divine Master was particularly anxious that His disciples
should see in spiritual childhood the necessary condition for
obtaining life eternal.

*Considering the insistence and the force of this teaching,
it would seem impossible to find a soul who would still
neglect to follow the way of confidence and abandonment,
all the more so, we repeat, since the divine words, not only
in a general manner, but in express terms, declare the mode
of life obligatory, even for those who have lost their first
innocence. Some prefer to believe that the way of confidence
and abandonment is reserved solely for ingenuous souls
whom evil has not deprived of the grace of childhood. They
do not conceive the possibility of spiritual childhood for those
who have lost their first innocence.*

And the Holy Father proceeds to show that our Lord's
use of the words "be converted" and "become" indicate,
that a change is to be made, and that therefore the words
apply particularly to those who are no longer innocent.
He continues:

*Any such thought as that of reassuming the appearance
and helplessness of early years would be ridiculous; but it is
not contrary to reason to find in the words of the Gospel the
precept addressed alike to men of advanced years to return to
the practice of spiritual childhood. During the course of centuries, this teaching was to find increased support in the example
of those who arrived at heroic Christian perfection precisely
by the exercise of these virtues. Holy Church has ever
extolled these examples in order to make the Master's command better understood and more universally followed. Today, again, she has no other end in view when she proclaims
as heroic the virtues of Sœur Thérèse de L'Enfant Jesus.*[10]

May we add the words of Pius XI at her canonization:

We today conceive the hope of seeing spring up in the

[10] Cf. Laveille, *St. Teresa of Lisieux,* Cap. XII.

souls of Christ's faithful a holy eagerness to acquire this evangelical childhood, which consists in feeling and acting under the empire of virtue as a child feels and acts in the natural order. . . . If this way of spiritual childhood became general, who does not see how easily that reform of human society would take place which We set before Us in the early days of Our pontificate?

Many books have been written to broadcast St. Thérèse's message. No adequate summary of it can be given here. The reader is referred to her own autobiography, to Msgr. Laveille's biography of the saint, and to Fr. Petitot's book, *St. Teresa of Lisieux.* Since however we believe that this is the way of sanctification for most of the laity, we shall quote some passages from Mgr. Laveille's work,[11] in the hope of inducing the reader to seek further information from the mass of literature already available on the subject.

"God," he writes, "is a Father, and the burning ardor of His love surpasses all human tenderness. [He Himself assures that His love is far beyond that of any mother.[12]] . . . It follows that the surest means of gaining His Heart is to remain or become again a little child in His eyes, that is to say, to recognize our nothingness in His sight, to lay our poverty before Him, to make ourselves truly little in the presence of His Majesty, confiding without fear in His sovereign goodness so that we may move Him to generosity towards us. . . .

"This secret appears simple; it contains nothing which can inspire fear in the feeblest Christian heart. It is essential, however, to discern clearly the true signification of the actions enjoined by this method. First, there is the recognition of our incapacity and poverty. But this can be recognized, and at the same time hated, reviled. What is necessary is that we willingly proclaim our nothingness in regard to the greatness of the Almighty. In other words, the surest disposition to draw from the Father in heaven a kindly smile is *humility of*

[11] Laveille, *St. Teresa of Lisieux,* chap. XII, pp. 305, *et seq.*
[12] Cf. Isaias xliii, 25.

heart by which we really and truly love to see ourselves as we are and look with joy into the depths of our lowliness." [St. Thérèse explains: "To be little means not attributing to self the virtues that one practices, believing oneself capable of anything; it means recognizing that the good God places this treasure of virtue in the hand of His little child to be used by him when he has need of it; but always it is God's treasure. In fine, it means not being discouraged about our faults, for children fall often, but are too small to do themselves much harm."]

"This disposition is, alas, comparatively rare, even among Christians. The greater number are, indeed, willing to admit their weakness, but only to a certain point. They credit themselves with real personal strength, on which they are content to rely while all goes well, only to fall into discouragement at the first serious obstacle they meet with. They have not understood that the child's strength lies in its very weakness, since God is inclined to help His creatures in proportion to their recognition and humble avowal of their natural helplessness. . . ."

"A second characteristic trait of spiritual childhood is *poverty*. The child possesses nothing of its own; everything belongs to its parents. But is it not precisely this absolute want of all things which moves the father to provide for every necessity, especially if the child is insistent in drawing attention to its excess of misery? When this state of penury has ceased through the child's growing up and commencing to earn his own livelihood the father, be he ever so affectionate, discontinues his bounty." [For this reason St. Thérèse never wished to grow up spiritually, "feeling incapable of gaining for myself life eternal, for I have never been able to do anything for myself alone." . . .]

"In the same way, the soul will gain everything by possessing nothing and looking to God for all. She must, however, accustom herself to await the coming of each day for the gifts thereof, asking nothing except what is needed at the present instant, because the grace required is, in God's designs, an actual grace, to be given at the opportune moment. . . . The poor in spirit, when once in possession of God's gifts, be they spiritual or corporal, will guard against any proprietorship over them, for they belong always to God, who has simply lent them and is free to take them back as He wills. . . ."

"Finally, one who chooses the 'little way,' must be resigned to remaining poor all his life. By this he will imitate the dear saint, who, while multiplying her acts of virtue, did not concern herself with storing up merits for eternity, but labored for Jesus alone, giving over to Him all her good works to purchase souls." St. Thérèse's own words are full of consolation: "to love Jesus, to be the victim of His love, the more weak and miserable we are, the better disposed are we for the operations of His consuming and transforming love. . . . The sole desire of being a victim suffices; we must, however, be always willing to remain poor and weak. Herein lies the difficulty! . . . Let us love our littleness, let us love to feel nothing. Then shall we be poor in spirit, and Jesus will come to seek us, be we ever so far away. He will transform us into flames of love." [13]

"Besides humility of heart and the spirit of poverty, something more is required. *Confidence,* unbounded, unwavering confidence in the merciful goodness of the heavenly Father is the infallible means of inclining His Divine Heart to compassion and bounty. With St. John of the Cross, St. Thérèse repeated from her heart: "From the good God we obtain all that we hope for."

"The chief practical conclusions from this doctrine is that a soul initiated into this 'little way' must confide in the divine mercy regarding past faults, however grave and multiplied they may have been, and that he must look to the same mercy for the pardon of his daily faults. . . . This confidence is necessary in failure; the futility of human actions draws pity from the Divine Heart. It is equally required in darkness and aridity. . . ."

In fine, St. Thérèse wished that no bounds should be set to our hopes and desires of attaining to holiness,

[13] Sixth letter to S. M. du Sacré Coeur.

supporting her words by reference to the merciful omnipotence of "Him who being power and holiness itself would have but to take a soul in His arms and raise it up to Him in order to clothe it with His infinite merits and make it holy."[14] And asserting more definitely the efficacy of confidence even in arriving at the highest perfection, she does not hesitate to add: "If weak and imperfect souls like mine felt what I feel, not one of them would despair of reaching the summit of the mountain of love."

This way of humility, of self-forgetfulness, of reliance on God's own holiness, is the royal road to sanctity—for everybody. The spiritual life is not so much a work of acquiring virtue and merits, as of getting rid of oneself; in fact, it is not so much a getting rid of oneself as a putting on of Christ. No more excellent commentary on St. Paul's doctrine of the Mystical Body of Christ which we outlined in the earlier chapters can be found than the life and teaching of St. Thérèse of Lisieux. Every one should study her doctrine, but let us add a word of warning; one must not let the childlike language and manner of the saint hide the fact that she was a woman in whom grace had forged and tempered a will of steel, a woman whose very childlike charm hid sufferings that are beyond all telling. And, if one may judge by the extraordinary honors the Church has showered on her in a few short years, she became one of the greatest saints the Church has known, by a life in which there was nothing extraordinary, in the usual sense of the word. Yet her way is recommended to all by the highest spiritual authority upon earth.

Humility, we repeat, is the royal road to sanctity; but it must be joined to unbounded confidence. We only forget ourselves to remember Christ, of whom we are members, and who loved us and delivered Himself to death for us. Humility is the great way of repairing the fall and failures of the past. There is no shortcoming for which it cannot more than compensate. To

14 *Story of a Soul*, chap. XI.

which effect, we quote the words of a Cistercian Abbot, Blessed Guerric, a disciple of St. Bernard, with a modern Cistercian's introduction to them:[15]

"Humility has a very special property of its own; it not only ensures that the other virtues are really virtues, but, if any one of them is wanting, or is imperfect, humility, using that very deficiency, of itself repairs the deficiency. Therefore, if something seems to be lacking in any soul, it is lacking for no other reason than that the soul should be all the more perfect by its absence, for virtue is made perfect in infirmity. *Paul,* saith the Lord, *my grace is sufficient for thee.*[16] He for whom the grace of God is sufficient, can be lacking in some particular grace, not only without serious loss, but even with no small gain, for that very defect and infirmity perfects virtue; and the very diminution of a certain grace only makes the greatest of all God's graces—namely, humility—present in a fuller measure and more stable way. Far, then, O Lord, from thy servants let that grace be—whatever it may be—which can take away or lessen our grace in thy eyes *(gratiam tui),* by which, namely, although more pleasing in our own eyes, we become more hateful in Thine. That is not grace, but wrath, for it is only fully fit to be given to those with whom Thou art angry; in whose regard Thou hast disposed such things, and that because of their simulation, thrusting them down at the very moment of their elevation and rightly crushing them even while they are raised on high. In order, therefore, that that grace alone, without which no one is loved by Thee, should remain safe in our possession, let Thy grace and favor either take away all other grace from us, or else give us the grace of using all properly; so that having the grace by which we serve Thee pleasingly with fear and reverence, we may earn the favor of the giver through the grace of the gift, and that growing in grace, we may be truly more pleasing to Thee."

To sum up a long chapter let us repeat again with

15 Cf. *De Beato Guerrico,* by P. Deodatus de Wilde, O.C.R.
16 Cf. II Cor. xii, 9.

St. Paul, *Gladly will I glory in my infirmities, that the power of Christ may dwell in me,*[17] and let us be convinced that no matter what we have lost, what we have ruined, or how far we have wandered into the wilderness from the right path, God can give us back all we have lost or damaged. God can show us a road—or, if necessary, build a new road for us—that leads from our present position, whatever it may be, to the heights of sanctity; humility is the Philosopher's Stone which changes all our losses into the gold of God's favor. He can do *all* for us, and He will do all if we co-operate with this grace. What then does He ask of us? Nothing but blind faith, confident hope, ardent love, cheerful humility, and loving abandonment into the arms of our tremendous lover!

[17] II Cor. xii, 9.

CHAPTER 18

Christ's Life-Giving Cross

T HEY *that are Christ's,* writes St. Paul, *have crucified their flesh, with the vices and concupiscences thereof.*[1] "Know you not," he exclaims, "that all we who are baptized in Christ Jesus, are baptized in his death."[2] Prat's commentary on this text is a useful summing-up of our theme and a good introduction to our next point. "We live," he writes, "in proportion as we are associated with the life of Christ: Now it is in His death that Jesus Christ makes us participate in His life: we live in Him only so far as we die in Him. This takes place *de jure* on Calvary [and also may we add, in a manner at Mass], *de facto* at baptism. Baptism [and we again add, the Mass] applies to us the fruit of Calvary. In it [and in the Mass] Jesus Christ associates us, in a mystical, yet very real way, with His death and His life. By associating us with His death, He neutralizes the active principle which sin had implanted in us, and which constituted the old man; by associating us with His life, He destroys all the germs of death and confers upon us the privilege of endless life: life of the soul and life of the body, life of grace and life of glory. No doubt we possess in hope only a portion of these favors, but *hope confoundeth not.* God wishes to perfect His work in us, and He binds Himself to do so by granting us a certain pledge of His fidelity, we have only to let ourselves live."[3] Rather, we should say, we have only to let Christ rise to life in us.

[1] Cf. Gal. v, 24.   [2] Rom. vi, 3.   [3] Prat. loc. cit., i, 222.

Let us quote Prat still further: his sober words carry
an amazing truth. "To be baptized into Christ is not
simply to be made subject to Him, like a slave to his
master, or like a liegeman to his lord, nor is it merely to
be bound to Him by an oath like a soldier to his general,
nor even to be consecrated to Him as a temple to a
divinity, it is still more and above all to be incorporated
with Him, to be immersed in Him, as if in a new
element, to become part of Him as another self." And
noting the phrase *in the death of Christ,* he adds: "In
fact, we are associated with Christ and become members
of Him just when He Himself becomes the Saviour. Now
this moment, in the case of Jesus, coincides with that
of His death, symbolized and mystically realized for us at
baptism [and in another way, in the Mass]. From that
time on, *we have everything in common with Jesus
Christ,* we are crucified, buried, and raised from the dead
with Him, we share His death and His new life, His
glory, His reign, and His heritage."

Prat summarizes St. Paul's thought thus: "The sacraments are efficacious signs which produce *ex opere operato*
what they signify. Now baptism represents sacramentally
the death and life of Christ. It must therefore produce
in us a death, mystical in its essence but real in its effects,
death to sin, to the flesh, to the old man, as well as life in
conformity with the life of Jesus Christ risen from the
dead." [4]

We are here in contact with a great mystery, and we
note that independence of the time sequence to which we
have previously referred. In some way we died to ourselves with Christ on the cross and rose to new life in
His Resurrection. This death to our old selves and resurrection to life in Christ are sacramentally repeated and
renewed at baptism. The same mystery is more or less
re-echoed every time that we offer ourselves up to Christ
at Mass and receive His life in Communion. And the
same mystery thus expressed in baptism and in the Mass
must characterize our whole life. We signify it—we

[4] Loc. cit.

promise it—at Mass; we must mean what we say—we must keep our promises. If we remember that before Chirst with His life was given to us in baptism, a renunciation of our own life—insofar as it was connected with the world, the flesh, and the devil—was made on our behalf, we shall have some idea what our obligations are. The sacrifice of the cross, which is made ours in the Mass, was a complete summing-up and expression of what the whole of our Lord's life had been on earth. Baptism is for us a complete summing-up and expression for us of what our whole life on earth must be: the death of our old self, which was crucified on the cross with Christ, and the development of the life of Christ in all our actions. *He must increase but I must decrease;* [5] there is hardly any better formula. The "old man"—as St. Paul calls our fallen self—is crucified with Christ on the cross, is condemned to death, so to speak, in baptism and even given a death-wound there, and is offered up in the Mass for destruction; it still remains for us to carry out that sentence of death and destruction, and to fulfil the offering made at Mass.

This has to be done by mortification. Let us be quite clear. Mortification is no mere negative thing, it is the getting rid of self in order to allow Jesus to live His life in us, and to enable us to share His life fully. The evil effects of the sin of Adam still remain in as much as our passions and our lower appetites are not properly subject to our will. They clamor for satisfaction, rebelling against control, and if they are not checked they grow from strength to strength and carry us away into sin. In order to submit ourselves completely to Christ, we have to be masters of ourselves. To put things in a homely fashion, we are like a man driving a donkey; either he drives the donkey or the donkey drives him. We either rule our passions or they rule us. To rule our lower appetites, we must not only be determined not to allow them any unlawful satisfaction, but even to refuse them some lawful gratification, for it is well known that one who only

[5] John iii, 30.

says "no" to himself when the law says "no" to him, will soon lose his authority over himself and become unable to say "no" even when necessary.

There is no living a Christian life without that degree of mortification which is sufficient to prevent our lower appetites from leading us into sin. We are speaking now in general terms. We include under these appetites, the desire of bodily pleasure, of ease, of comfort, of gratification, of admiration, of knowledge, of pleasing others, of revenge, of achievement, and all those attempts which self-love makes to control and dictate our actions. Where the satisfaction of the desire is forbidden, there is obviously no question of living the life of Jesus in the action which gratifies it. As a result of original sin, it is only by a constant struggle that we can keep control of ourselves. And if these desires are habitually gratified they will soon become masters of our lives. Obviously then, we must establish at least sufficient authority in our self-government to remain masters of ourselves. In this way we are co-operating in the work of undoing the effects of Adam's sin, which lost for our first parents the gift of integrity, and leaves us under the necessity of maintaining a continual struggle to keep our lower appetites and passions in subjection.

Good habits have an important part to play in this matter; they facilitate greatly the performance of good actions, while bad habits interfere considerably with proper self-government. We cannot here enter into details of this aspect of mortification, but the question is fully discussed in the general literature of the subject; what we would stress, is the importance of motivation in dealing with habits, and the need of having a positive aim and ideal which will move our will in the matter. What is often called a weak will is really the will of one who has not developed sufficient motives or ideals to move it. There is practically no normal weakness that cannot be overcome by proper motives and ideals. For an emergency, so to speak, one may seize upon any motive that will deter the will from a particular sin, as a means to a higher end; but, because of the importance which the love of God has in the merit of our actions, it is essential to develop motives which flow from it, and which will act as a permanent driving force for the will. There is no stable virtue without such motives.

The personal love of Jesus, leading us to be ready to remove all obstacles to His full life in us and to His sharing in our every action, is probably one of the best motives. From a different point of view, we might be led by the same love to regard mortification as the removal of the obstacles to our perfect sharing in the life of His Mystical Body, which arise from the efforts of our own nature to assert itself. Each one, with the help of the Holy Spirit, should form his own personal ideal. It is important that it should be an effective and gripping one. Everyday experience affords many examples of the complete change in character and habits produced even in weaker men, by a strong personal motive such as arises, say, from war, from love, or from a new responsibility. That is but another reason why we are so insistent on the need for daily reading and reflection, and for the early development of a tender, personal love for our Lord.

It need not be thought that all pleasure must be shunned by one who would live with Christ. We are men, not angels, and some pleasure is necessary for us. In fact when one realizes the nerve-racking rush and rattle of modern life, its provincial superficiality and shallow insincerity, its unutterable boredom and its deadly monotony, and when one considers those worries that the difficulties of each day bring to the mind of anyone who has responsibilities, it may seem that there is even more need for the relaxation of pleasure today than formerly. That is a question that need not be settled here. But, in any case, there is a lawful measure and manner of pleasure that is both necessary and praiseworthy, and which can be shared with our beloved. He Himself told us: *As long as you did it to one of these my least brethren, you did it to me,*[6] and surely each of us is one of these

[6] Matt. xxv, 40.

brethren; in fact, we are members of Christ Himself, so that what we do to ourselves is done to Him! Therefore, all good recreation can be holy and can be offered to God. We can take Jesus with us even on the path of pleasure; we can have Him beside us in all our amusements, sharing in them all, as long as they are within the limits set by the will of God.

The ideal aim in all mortification is to avoid any action, thought, word, or deed, which Jesus cannot share and make His own. We must never forget that from our baptism, we have all things that He did in common with Him, and only He could tell us how He in turn longs to share fully every single moment of our life. Mortification, then, is not performed in any morbid sense of self-hatred, or contempt of the body; it is not a mere negative thing, a foolish frustration and self-suppression. It is something quite positive; an "assertion" of Jesus rather than a denial of self; for we only deny ourselves to find Him, that He may live in us and that we may be united to Him. And we should remember that He wishes even to share our thoughts, so that interior mortification must not be forgotten.

The principal way of denying oneself in order to be united to Jesus is by humility. We insist upon this, despite the fact that corporal and external mortification is often presented as the first stage of the spiritual life. A man can be highly mortified in his body, master of all his passions, ready to defy all human respect, undaunted by suffering or hardship, indefatigable in good works—of the external sort—and even given to long "prayers," and withal be as proud as the Pharisee in the Gospel and, therefore, hateful in the sight of God. Far, far, better to evade a mortification saying to God: "How unmortified I am," than to perform it, saying to oneself "How wonderful I am!" An experienced observer found the famous nuns of Port-Royal "as pure as angels, but as proud as devils."

Still the danger of pride does not dispense us from carrying out the "crucifixion of the flesh" promised in baptism. Nor does the need and lawfulness of some pleasure exempt us from resisting the tide of the times in which people are living for pleasure. We must have at least sufficient self-control to avoid sin. But our vocation as Christians, our baptism, our participation in the Mass, our union and identification with Jesus, lead us further than that. It is impossible to be intimate with Jesus, to know Him, to know His story and to know His views, without feeling some desire to share His sufferings. *Despised, and the most abject of men, a man of sorrows, and acquainted with infirmity.*[7] *O all ye that pass by the way, attend, and see if there be any sorrow like unto my sorrow.*[8] *I looked for one that would grieve together with me, but there was none; and for one that would comfort me, and I found none.*[9] *I was wounded in the house of them that loved me.*[10] A mere sense of fellowship, a desire to be like our friend, a wish to lighten His burden, would lead us at least to accept sufferings when they come, and would probably have the further effect of producing in us a certain uneasiness at living a life of pleasure.

But there is a deeper motive to be found. St. Paul writes to the Colossians: *I now rejoice in my sufferings for you and fill up those things that are wanting of the sufferings of Christ, in my flesh, for his body, which is the Church.*[11] He had written to the Corinthians: *I chastise my body, and bring it into subjection, lest perhaps, when I have preached to others, I myself should become a castaway*[12]; in this latter case he merely wishes to avoid sinning personally. But the filling up of what is wanting of the sufferings of Christ is quite a different matter. The text does not mean that there is any insufficiency in the Redemption as wrought by the Passion and Death of Christ; it refers rather to the role of suffering in applying that Redemption to individual souls. Every grace that comes to men from God has to be merited by Jesus Christ, and comes from Him to us. He

---

[7] Isaías liii, 3. [8] Lam. i, 12. [9] Ps. lxviii, 21.
[10] Zach. xiii, 6. [11] Cf. Col. i. 24. [12] I Cor. ix, 27.

has associated His Mother, the Mother of Sorrows, with Him in the work of Redemption, so that at least in the application of its fruits she always has a part. But He seems to have made the application of these fruits of His Passion partly dependent also on the prayers and sufferings of the other members of His Church. This is evidenced by St. Paul's readiness to suffer for his flock. The reports of the requests made by Our Lady of Fatima are in full harmony with this view.

And our Lord Himself includes this readiness to suffer in the conditions He lays down for His followers: *If any man will come after me, let him deny himself, take up his cross and follow me.*[13] He adds immediately: *For he that will save his life shall lose it, and he that shall lose his life for my sake, shall find it.*[14] There is an obvious reference here to the need of forgetting oneself and forsaking one's own life in order to be united to Him and to live His life. Does He not liken the kingdom of heaven to *a merchant seeking good pearls: who when he had found one pearl of great price, went his way, and sold all that he had, and bought it.*[15] But He also expects His followers to share in His work of expiation and satisfaction. His reply to the request for the first places in His "kingdom" is: *Can you drink the chalice that I drink of?*[16] Indeed, even now He often asks chosen souls to become victims of reparation for the sins of the world and for the direct insults offered to God and to His Son. And if He sends such souls sorrow and associates them with Him so closely in His work of Redemption, it is only because He wishes that they should earn greater glory and closer union with Him in Heaven. Indeed, even without being so chosen, no one can truly say he loves his Saviour, if he does not feel ready to embrace the sufferings God sends him, in order to lighten the load that the Saviour had to bear in the Agony in the

---

[13] Matt. xv, 24.   [14] Ibid.

[15] Matt. xiii, 45–46. The Latin text is full of significance: *dedit omnia sua.*

[16] Mark x, 38.

Garden. We should not let the time sequence disturb us. God's foreknowledge is above all time and just as He suffered by the sins we commit today, so was He comforted by our share in His work.[17]

This is a most fruitful field of apostolate for the laity. Even in the ordinary day's round, they can exercise the apostolate, and, like the heart in the human body, they can associate themselves in the work of "circulating" the life of Christ in the souls of His members, by prayer and suffering. They must keep in mind, that in doing so, they are dealing with *primary* causes; those who actually preach or minister grace are often only *secondary* causes—mere instruments in applying the grace someone else's prayers and sufferings have obtained. Here is the work for any layman, which does not call for anything out of the ordinary beyond the patient acceptance of God's will.

Suffering has other effects that are of great value. It satisfies for our own sins, it purifies our soul, and it deepens and strengthens our character and our personality. It gives us an insight and a power of sympathy for our neighbor that can be acquired in no other way. In fact, it opens to us the interior life of Christ Himself, and in doing so unites us still more closely to Him. Often, too, sharp suffering is a turning point in our lives, and leads to the commencement of new fervor and new hope. Even in the natural order its deepening effects are well marked; it brings out all that is good in us, and, in an extraordinary way, it can lead to happiness and peace. False standards are shattered and our eyes are opened; we are raised to a new height of dignity, of magnanimity, of serenity, of noble moral perfection.

To quote Fr. Faber: "Nothing condenses life so much as suffering. Nothing precipitates so much the great labor of experience. Nothing so endows the faculties of our nature with the most magnificent increase. A life of joy, is for the most part, spent superficially and without any solid gain. There are few acts of heroism in a state

[17] Cf. *Miserentissimus Redemptor.*

of joy, although joy has also its profound lights which are full of God. But it is affliction which makes saints." [18]

These are the reasons why a man who comes to the service of God must prepare his soul for tribulation. God is a tremendous lover, and love knows no half measures. Love will not be satisfied with anything short of all; no degree of union short of the closest possible, will satisfy it. In fact, if it seeks less, or if it is satisfied with less, it is not love. God will not be satisfied with anything less than everything: *Thy whole heart, thy whole soul, all thy mind and all thy strength.* Jesus will not be satisfied until we are transformed completely into Him. And to that end He sends us suffering, so that we may be united to Him and be transformed completely into Him.

On our part, if we but really loved Him and really understood Him whom we love, we would rejoice in suffering. To love, in fact, is to suffer; for love demands union, and is tortured and torn to its very depths by even the slightest defect in union. What then must be the suffering of those who truly love God while in exile here on earth! And after death, no exterior fire in purgatory is anything like the interior fire of suffering that burns in the hearts of those souls who have glimpsed their beloved God and are not yet united to Him.

This very suffering in purgatory is God's merciful provision for the purification of those who have not completed their transformation here in this life. No one can enter into that blissful union of love with God which is heaven, until he is perfectly transformed into Christ. That should be the normal term of our life here below; death should be merely the removal of the very last vestige of self remaining after a lifetime of gradual transformation into Christ. Unfortunately, such is not usually the case. We have, we persuade ourselves, other things to do in this life; we have our work, our career, our friends, our loves, and our talents; we have our own life to live—so we fondly imagine. And so when it all comes to the end, we are not ready; we have no wedding gar-

[18] Faber, *At the Foot of the Cross*, The Sixth Sorrow.

ment, we have no oil in our lamps. Like the famous five—we have been foolish!

The wise man hopes that God will accomplish this transformation for him here on earth. And, if he be willing to rely upon God's grace and accept the sorrows and sufferings sent to him by God's loving and fatherly providence, he will find that God sets about that work of transformation here and now. And what is more, he will probably find like St. Teresa of Avila, that it is the first of our crosses that is really the hardest. Once he has learned to suffer in union with Jesus, he has discovered a new happiness, hitherto undreamed-of, and he begins to see what our Lord meant when, promising eternal life to those who renounced all for His sake, He added the assurance that they would *receive a hundred times as much, now in this time.*[19] But really we should not be surprised at this discovery; our Lord Himself assured us that His yoke was easy and His burden light. *Why will we not take God at His word?* The pity of it all is that people are so often frightened by the thought of the suffering that they may have to endure in the service and search of God, while in fact such sufferings are usually no greater than those which men often endure to ensure worldly success or the attainment of some cherished end—to say nothing of the fact that half-hearted service is the hardest service of all. Courage has its own reward in these matters. There is in the spiritual life a relief that comes in time, something very similar to the athlete's "second wind." After a certain amount of effort it seems to the runner that he cannot possibly go one step further; he has then to force himself to endure the strain and to continue his efforts. Very soon, however, his system readjusts itself to the new demands that are being made upon it, and he experiences that sense of relief and consciousness of new strength known as "second wind." A similar renewal of one's strength come under like circumstances in the spiritual lif Our motto should be: *Do manfully!* And let it

[19] Mark x, 30.

forgotten that pleasure is not happiness, nor is suffering sadness. All the saints' lives are full of joy—a joy that the world does not know, a joy that surges up in a man's heart and wells up like a river, overflowing and overwhelming his whole being till his very soul sings a canticle of joy. Only the lovers of God can understand the Ninth Symphony.

And in passing let it be added that these lovers of God share Beethoven's difficulty in finding adequate expression of their feelings. To express his joy Beethoven had to make use of words and the human voice in that famous orchestral work. To express their love for God, His lovers can find no more adequate way than of suffering. For suffering intensifies love and manifests it. Our Lord Himself went far beyond the measure of suffering necessary to make strict atonement for our sins. The Cross is the expression of His love. One cannot see into the heart of the lover, but suffering gladly and joyfully borne for the sake of the beloved is the lover's age old resource to manifest his own heart and to touch the heart for which he longs. Let it be added that there is a special poignancy and immeasurable depth in our Lord's sufferings which has no counterpart in the sufferings of the human lover. Where love is unrequited, or where it fails to find full or even adequate response, there is always the cold comfort of the possibility that the very failure to respond is merely an indication of the inherent impossibility of finding full satisfaction or return. There are hearts so centered on themselves, that they can only be a source of grief and misery to those who love them. Our Lord knew that there is no heart, no character, no soul so cold, so hard, so selfish, or so self-sufficient, that He could not set it on fire, if that heart would but give itself to Him. He knew that the very suffering which the hardness of each particular heart was causing Him could be the very means of His meriting for it, of softening it, and giving it a power to love far beyond reckoning. *With God all things are possible.* He knew that He can make success of every single soul whose love He seeks. But

. . . *thou wouldst not.* That is what breaks His Sacred Heart! For suffering that is inevitable is not so keen as that caused by the will of another. To realize that one's own happiness, or, as in this case, the happiness of one's beloved, could be realized by the mere consent of another who *can* give it but *will* not—that is what pierces the very depth of the heart and rends it in an agony of pain.

And it is exactly for this purpose—to make a success of us, to kindle this fire of love in our hearts—that He allows suffering to come to us. He can take away our hearts of stone, and give us hearts like His own. Sufferings—the sufferings *He* sends—will do that, if we take them in the proper manner. But we must accept them rightly; for suffering can destroy any greatness of soul we may have and make us narrow, bitter, hard, and incapable of love, if we do not accept it properly. What then should our attitude be in suffering?

To determine our proper dispositions in suffering we should first of all note that suffering in itself and for its own sake is not good, nor is it willed by God as such. Its value lies in the effects it has upon the soul, and the acts of which it is the occasion. Also it may be noted that suffering generally owes much of its painful aspect for us to some attachment we have to a created good, either in ourselves or in others. To accept suffering when it comes as an inevitable evil, may only be a mere sickly expression of spineless impotence, it could be the surrender of defeat, a fatalism that is far from Christian. But even Christian acceptance of suffering can vary. St. Bernard describes three different attitudes: "Those who are beginning in the school of fear, carry the cross of Christ with patient submission; those who are progressing in hope, bear it willingly and readily; but those who are consumed with love, embrace it with ardor." [20]

The patient submission of the first group is a resignation which excludes all murmuring; despite our repugnance, we will what God wills. Tears may flow, but even though our eyes are blurred we see the hand of God

[20] St. Bernard, *Serm. de S. Andrea.*

our sovereign Lord. We may pray for relief, we may seek help, but still: *Not my will, but thine, be done.* We imitate the divine model in Gethsemani, who in His love for us let us see His human repugnance to the sorrows of His Passion.

The second group go further. They not only see the hand of God their sovereign, but they recognize it as the hand of their loving Father. Their faith and hope convince them that God is acting for their good. If His pruning knife is painful, yet He is only ensuring the fruitfulness of their life. They endeavor to co-operate with God. They try to thank Him, they praise His providence, they conform themselves to His will and actively follow His lead. They remember that they are the bread and wine of Christ's priestly sacrifice in their souls, and that it is in suffering that He transforms them into His own Body. They love Him, and if, being human, they must seek sympathy, they prefer to seek it from Him. To their fellow men they are silent. This silence in suffering, *when prudent,* is a great virtue; though there may be times when the relief of speech is not only necessary but also praiseworthy.

The lover, however, embraces the Cross, and delights to share the life and even the death of his beloved. It is not the suffering as such that he loves; that would be the desire of a diseased mind. It is rather the one who suffered. For the lover seeks no reasons; if Jesus suffered, that is enough; His lover must suffer too. There are souls for whom it can happen that the greatest suffering is not to suffer. St. Teresa exclaims: "Either to suffer or to die." St. John of the Cross sings in limpid poetry: "I die because I do not die." This seems unnatural; but when every other attachment is gone, when every simple tendency of the heart and will is to the beloved, no created joy can satisfy the heart. In fact even the truest and the greatest joys of creatures can only hurt, for the lover sees in them all a faint image of the beloved— whom he has not yet found in full union, for whom he longs, and without whom he cannot find rest or happiness.

But as with all human desires, there are many different reasons for this glad embrace of the Cross. Love must be told; it must express itself. In fact the love that does not know that urge to expression is hardly love at all; it is perhaps some sort of secret pride in one's own tastes or one's own benevolence. Now suffering gives expression to love as nothing else can; hence the relief it can give to the bursting heart that can know no joy but that which it can share with its beloved, and would rather suffer with Him, than be full of all else without Him.

Listen to St. Andrew going to his crucifixion: "Hail, O Cross! Receive the disciple of Him who hung from thee— my Master, Christ! O good Cross, so long desired and now awaiting my thirsty heart. In tranquil joy and exultant security I come to thee! Do thou, also exulting, receive me the disciple of Him who hung from thee! Thou hast received the beauty and loveliness of the members of the Lord; do thou now receive me and take me from men and join me again to my Master, so that He who by thee redeemed me, may by thee also receive me."[21] It is not to be expected that all will be able to summon up such enthusiasm as St. Andrew, just as it is not to be expected that all will meet the same extreme fate. But there is one thing which can be expected: that if anyone greets even the smallest cross which God sends him as St. Andrew did, he will find his cross very much lightened and will perceive a joy that may open to him a new realm of happiness, for he will discover a wonderful sense of fellowship with Jesus in suffering.

Our Lord Himself warned us: *If any man come to me, and hate not his father, and mother, and wife and children, and brethren and sisters, yea and his own life also, he cannot be my disciple. And whatsoever doth not carry his cross and come after me, cannot be my disciple. . . . Every one of you that doth not renounce all he possesseth cannot be my disciple.*[22] When we remember that these are the words of Him who commanded us to

[21] Cf. Breviary, Nov. 30.   [22] Luke xiv 26, 27, 33

love even our enemies and to honor our father and our mother, it is obvious that there is a Hebrew figure of speech in the use of the word "hate." The meaning here, of course, is that we must love God above all these and let no love of the creature interfere with the love of the Creator and all that it asks of us. Suffering came into the world by the free act of man's will in turning away from God. And much suffering has its ultimate origin in the love of the creature. Now God is our lover. He will not be satisfied with part of our heart; He will not share our heart with any single one of His creatures. We may love them in due measure, but always in complete subordination to our love for Him, always ready to renounce any or all of them as soon as His love demands it. That is His desire. Unfortunately we are full of attachments, we have given our hearts to many things, and God in His merciful goodness provides in His government for our lives for the breaking down of these attachments. Advance in the spiritual life, advance in the quest for Jesus, advance in union with Jesus, consists principally in two things: more and more detachment, and more and more purity of intention.

To produce this development is the purpose of God's providence, and is the result of our abandonment to His will. To this progress we must now turn our attention. But let us insist that in all this question of mortification and suffering, there is no question of mere negation. We mortify ourselves to embrace Jesus; we welcome suffering for love of Jesus, because it transforms us into Him, and by detaching us from His creatures, gives Him our whole heart. As in the case of St. Andrew, the Cross joins us and unites us to Christ.

Suffering should be a matter of joy rather than of sadness; in fact, so much do we feel that to be true, that even where there is only question of those voluntary mortifications or acts of self-denial by which one brings one's self into subjection, and breaks the bonds that tie one to creatures—we would say that the rule for such mortification is to perform only those acts that one can do cheerfully and without losing one's peace of mind. *The Lord loveth a cheerful giver.*[23] To give cheerfully is a grace from God, which He will cheerfully give to those who sincerely ask. St. Francis of Assisi gave us his notion of perfect joy when he said: "More than all graces and gifts of the Holy Ghost, which God gives His friends, is to deny oneself and, for the sake of Christ's love, to suffer pain, injury, disgrace, and distress. For, in the other gifts of God we cannot glory, because they are not our own but God's, whereas in the cross of trial and suffering we can glory, for it is our own."

At the risk of apparent contradiction, we add an assertion that may seem strange after all we have said of suffering; yet truth and prudence compel it. To do the will of God, whether it be in joy or sorrow, in pleasure or in pain, is a greater thing than to suffer. To do the will of God, so readily, so eagerly, so lovingly, that we do not even notice whether it accords with our own will and desires, is the height of self-denial. To accept our own imperfection in the manner in which we accept the will of God can be a tremendous act of self-denial. In fact, "it is a pure grace from God and one of the greatest, to suffer in a petty way, to conquer in a feeble manner, that is to say, with a sort of spiritual feebleness; humbly and with self-contempt, and to be so discontented with ourselves that we do not believe that we ever do anything well. This discontent with ourselves is very pleasing to God, and His content should be the basis of our own. Nothing would give us any further anxiety if we found our sole satisfaction in pleasing and satisfying God."[24] To ensure a proper perspective we refer the reader back to Bl. Guerric's doctrine at the end of the last chapter, and we also quote Msgr. Gay: "Holy spiritual childhood is a more perfect state than the love of suffering, for nothing immolates a man to such a degree as to be *sincerely* and *peacefully* lowly. The childlike spirit kills pride far more surely than the spirit of

[23] Cf. II Cor. ix, 7.
[24] De Caussade, *Letters*, Bk iv, no. 12.

penance." The apparent contradiction disappears if we remember that the fundamental reason both for suffering and for humility, is to give ourselves to God and to be transformed into Him. Whatever achieves that best, is the more perfect. And one cannot improve on the will of God as a means of sanctification whether He sends us joy or sorrow. It is His will—and that is all that really matters.

CHAPTER 19

Union with Christ in Prayer

HUMAN affairs and human relationships seldom stand still—they develop one way or another; and human friendship especially can never be quite static—it either grows or fades. The same is true of our friendship with God, as far as the human side of that friendship is concerned, and it is especially true of that part of our friendship with God which manifests itself in private prayer. We have already noted the course of the development of prayer; we must now return to consider the subject in a little more detail.

The usual manner of praying which the beginner has to adopt is that which is best called discursive prayer. In this prayer, by "discourse" of the reason—that is, by consideration and reflection—we bring ourselves to produce acts of prayer: faith, hope, love, sorrow, resignation, admiration, or gratitude, to name but a few. Needless to say, not all these acts are necessary; any one would suffice if it occupied us for the whole time of prayer. The amount of consideration required depends upon a number of circumstances; but if one is faithful to daily spiritual reading and reflection, one should soon develop a facility to produce acts of prayer after a short consideration.

In the beginning our time of prayer is nearly all given to considerations; as we advance in intimacy with God and in understanding of His ways, the acts, or "affections," as they are called, take up an ever increasing part of the time of prayer and eventually predominate. This kind of prayer is generally called affective prayer, and sometimes develops to such an extent that hardly any consideration is necessary to produce acts; the acts come quite easily. These acts are the real prayer; the consideration is only an introduction, a means to an end. In some cases, there are occasions when this kind of prayer is possible even with those beginning their spiritual course. When, however, it becomes characteristic of one's manner of praying, it generally denotes some advance in the spiritual life. But this fact should not prevent beginners from talking to God in their own words as often as they are able to do so. The different stages of prayer are by no means mutually exclusive, nor are they sharply divided from one another.

All prayer, of course, presupposes grace, for it is a supernatural act. Yet its development may follow natural laws, and it seems natural that as one grows in understanding of spiritual things and becomes more intimate with God, long formulae and many words should cease to be necessary in our conversation with Him. Our expressions become less complicated; one act includes many others, sentences are replaced by words, words may even be replaced by looks, and our whole prayer becomes much simpler in its nature. One can remain in God's presence without the need to use many words; silence, in fact, seems the best expression of the fullness of our heart, and such silence can be a perfect prayer. Prudence and caution are of course necessary to avoid reveries and daydreaming, but prudence must not be overdone in this matter, and when one feels the need to pray in this way, there should be no anxiety in doing so, even when it means an absence of distinct acts. The whole question needs a much more detailed treatment than can be given it here, and we would refer the reader to what we have written on it elsewhere.[1]

Everyone who wishes to live a spiritual life should acquire a correct notion of the development of prayer. It is a capital error, and one that can be responsible for

[1] Fr. Eugene Boylan, O.C.R., *Difficulties in Mental Prayer.* cf. also de Caussade, *On Prayer.*

much harm, to imagine that there is no intermediate form of prayer between point by point meditation and infused contemplation. And we think it also seems to be a mistake to assume that these stages of prayer—discursive prayer, affective prayer, simplified prayer—are mutually quite exclusive. It would, we think, be a mistake to hold, for example, that before passing on to the use of affective prayer, one should have completely finished with discursive prayer. It would seem that any of these three ways of praying may present themselves —and may even be necessary—at almost any stage of spiritual development. It is the one which predominates that is usually in harmony with the extent of one's progress, and that determines one's "state" of prayer.

This development in prayer seems, as we have said, to be partly a "natural" process. However, it also depends upon grace and presupposes a certain development of the spiritual life. Simplified prayer, for example, is incompatible with habitual sin, or with frequent refusal to follow God's grace. Facility in making genuine acts is closely connected with one's sincerity and fervor, and with the purity of one's conscience. Prayer is not to be considered as something completely separated from, or independent of the rest of the spiritual life. It is but one branch of the tree; and while one tree may differ from another in the relative size and shape of its branches, yet the life of each branch in each tree depends upon the life of the tree itself.

The conditions necessary for advance in prayer are generally considered in relation to the fourfold purity upon which the health of our spiritual life depends: purity of conscience, purity of heart, purity of mind, purity of action. Purity of conscience results from our avoidance of sin, and from our general conformity with God's will. Purity of heart is achieved by keeping our heart for God, and avoiding or suppressing all *inordinate* attachments, that is, attachments that are not according to His will. Purity of mind arises from a continual control over one's thoughts and memories, and from a frequent but gentle effort at recollection. Purity of action requires that we watch carefully the motives and intentions that animate our actions, and endeavor to direct all our intentions in our work towards God, so that we may act only for His love and according to His will.

This fourfold purity is endangered by a weak purpose, slack rein on our thoughts, a loose control of our imagination, an only half-hearted resistance to the lead of inclination or impulse, or above all, by an unguarded heart. Custody of the heart is one of the most important rules in the spiritual life. The best way to develop this fourfold purity, this single-mindedness and single-heartedness, is to become enamored of Jesus Christ. One should build up an idea and a memory of Him which will hold one's attention; one should be resolutely and courageously determined to follow His lead; one should, above all, give Him one's whole heart. If this is done with generosity and with decision, one's whole life will soon be purified, and advance in prayer will be rapid.

So far we have described progress in prayer as if it were a natural psychological process, depending, of course, upon grace. Somewhere, however, during this process, God may intervene to lead the soul to ascend still higher in the paths of prayer. One is not directly conscious of His intervention, but one is painfully conscious of its effects. One can no longer "pray"! When the time for prayer comes, the mind seems to have lost all its power of action. There are no good thoughts, no good affections; complete sterility and aridity reign, and ordinary effort cannot dispel them. This powerlessness of the mind is only evident at the time of prayer. At other times the mind functions with normal vigor. At prayer, however, it seems dead; the imagination may run riot, and the senses may clamor for earthly things. But in some obscure way, the will wants God.

This latter point is important. The other phenomena could be the result of sin, of infidelity, of tepidity; and if the powerlessness of the mind were general, some natural cause would probably be its origin. But if the will still wants God, and does not want anything else, then we have a very safe sign of God's action in the soul. The soul must be careful, henceforth, to second God's action, and not to interfere with His work by trying to proceed on its own. God has changed His manner of presenting Himself to the soul. His grace no longer carries any appeal or effect for the senses and the imagination, or even for the intellect. He is working deeper in the soul, and only the will is affected by His operations.

The will must second this action by an attitude of loving faith. There is no use whatever in trying to form good thoughts, or to stir up pious feelings. In fact, it would be a mistake to make such attempts, as well as being useless. God wants our loving faith, unadorned by anything else. And He wants us to realize that we are completely helpless without Him. *Not that we are sufficient to think anything of ourselves as of ourselves, but our sufficiency is from God.*[2] We can only live by faith, and look at God by faith, and, one might say, love God by faith. We are like a mother sitting in the dark near her sleeping child. And like that mother we are *not* inactive. We love. And we love God, not our own piety or prayer. And that is what God wants.

We go to prayer to give ourselves to God. Here in this form of prayer is the way to do so. There is nothing here to pander to self-satisfaction; there is nothing here that would attach us to the gift, rather than to the giver. We have nothing to do but to believe in God, and to give ourselves up to His will in our complete helplessness. There is no lower form of prayer which is so sanctifying as this prayer of faith, and it is by no means uncommon.

There is some difficulty in following the literature of prayer at this particular stage. Terms differ, and opinions differ. A book by Fr. de Besse, O.F.M.Cap.: *The Science of Prayer*, is one of the few that really give help at this point. The works of Fr. Gabriel of M. Mary Magdalen, O.D.C., on St. John of the Cross,[3] and especially that on

[2] II Cor. iii, 5.

[3] Cf. *St. John of the Cross—Doctor of Divine Love and Contemplation*, which includes the work on *Acquired Contemplation*.

Acquired Contemplation, will be found of great help and encouragement. There are quite a number of books which might be read with profit; but considerable discretion is necessary. Firstly, all writers do not attach the same meaning to the terms used on this subject, and their discussion of prayer is affected by lack of agreement as to its nature. Secondly, even where two writers are in agreement as to terms and theory, their practical suggestions may differ, because they may be dealing with different stages of development of the same type of prayer. The reader will have to select what applies to his own case, and remembering that few men travel exactly the same road, he need have no scruple in rejecting what does not apply to him or even what seems to contradict his own decisions. Obviously, advice from a competent and understanding guide, who is ready to adapt his counsel to the particular needs of his client's case and not to impose upon him his own personal views, should be sought if it is to be had. Where it is not available, constant recourse to God for grace, will enable one to solve the problems of prayer sufficiently for the needs of the moment. There will always be a certain obscurity and dissatisfaction in this condition, and there is so little to be done at the time of prayer, that one's fears of wasting time or being deluded are always recurring.

What often happens in this condition of affairs is that one decides that more effort and initiative are needed and makes various attempts at meditation or at affective prayer. Sometimes, by a violent effort which cannot be sustained for long, the attempt succeeds momentarily, but the reaction when that effort fails—as it must fail —is all the worse. Then the really dangerous temptation comes:—to abandon all attempt at private prayer as waste of time and devote the time to reading or to good works. Such a decision, if it were adopted permanently, would be fatal, and, unless God interferes by His merciful providence, could easily mean the end of all advance in the spiritual life, if not the beginning of its decay.

At all costs, the decision to persevere in devoting a set time to private prayer daily must be made and carried out inflexibly. It does not matter if one can do no more than remain on one's knees for the period and only battle with complete lack of success against distractions; *one is not wasting time.* There is no use whatever in making violent efforts to engage the imagination and the mind with good thoughts and ideas; God no longer makes any appeal to these faculties. There is nothing left for the soul to do but to fall back on the three theological virtues of faith, hope and charity. And in practice it is faith that should be one's aim; it will lead to love.

What most of us overlook is that these three are the fundamental virtues of the spiritual life. The other virtues derive their full vital value from the influence of these three in various ways; these three are really the life of the soul and of its virtues. And God, as it were, strips off all else, and only leaves us the essentials. And whatever we might desire to achieve, there is nothing else we can do at the moment but to use these essential virtues, leading as they do to humility and abandonment to the will of God. One might describe this condition by representing God as peeling off the outer shell and rind—which is ourself—to expose and free the real divine interior of our soul; because these theological virtues are the fruit of the divine life of our soul. The process is really a "denial" and a crucifixion of ourself, and an "assertion"—one might almost call it a resurrection—of Christ in our stead.

This process is but typical of the plan of the whole spiritual life, and a comparison might help us to visualize it. When a prepared photographic film is properly exposed to the action of the light coming from a certain object, certain parts of that film are transformed so as to become capable of forming an invisible or latent image of the object. Under the action of a developer, this transformation is made actual and stabilized. After development, the untransformed material in the film is removed by another chemical solution. Something of this sort occurs in the spiritual life and, in a special way, in the life of prayer. There is, for example, in our prayer, an element that comes from God. Under the influence of the divine light and the divine action there is a living image of the divine prayer produced in us, inside our own prayer, so to speak, by a transformation of part of it. This is "developed" and actualized by the action of God's grace, and then He "dissolves" away the untransformed part of our prayer by a long purifying action, during which the divine "image" may as yet be invisible. Meanwhile we have to live and pray by faith until the shadows retire and the day of the divine image dawns. When the dark night is over we shall see the glory of God's mercy and love in the new life and prayer He has wrought in our souls. And in this, prayer is only typical of the rest of the spiritual life: a divine infusion, a transformation of part of ourself into Christ, and a removal, in this life or in the next, of what is left of our old self.

Our own notions of perfection are often full of error. We imagine holiness as the perfecting of our own life; whereas in fact it is the perfecting of the life of Christ within us. We imagine that the really important part of a life of holiness is the good works we perform and the fruit they produce; whereas the thing that primarily matters is the love, the *supernatural* love, with which they are performed. There can be very much self-seeking, even in a quasi-spiritual way, in good works. God wishes to change all that and to make our works originate in Him and tend towards Him. He is the Alpha and the Omega; He must be the beginning and the end of everything, as indeed we profess Him to be every time we assist at Mass. Let us never forget St. Augustine's marvelous summary: *There shall be one Christ loving Himself.*

Our prayer is really a continuation of what we try to say at Mass; it should be the expression of our whole life, which in turn should be in accordance with what we express by the Mass. There is very little solid worth in protestations of love and submission made in prayer if the rest of our actions during the day are done from self-love and by self-will. One might say that just as God gives us the Mass as an expression of our complete submission to Him and expects us to conform our life to what we profess in the Mass, so, to a certain extent, in this prayer of faith, He so moulds our prayer, that it tends to become a true expression of what *should* be the really important part of our life: faith, hope, charity, humility and abandonment to God's will.

Our very inability to pray, is a perfect prayer; our very inability to express ourselves is the best expression of ourselves; our very inability to see God, to hear Him, or to "feel" Him, is the very best vision of God, the very best hearing of God, the very best "feeling" of Him. For God is above all we think Him to be. As the mystics say, we know Him by not knowing Him. So that even this failure in prayer gives us truer knowledge of God and of ourselves, than did the prayer of former days when God was so vividly present to us, and when our love for Him was seemingly so full that it defied words.

What we have to do at the hour of prayer in these times of aridity and helplessness, is to be *gentle* with ourselves. We make a quiet act of faith; we believe in God, we believe in God's interest in us, and we believe that He sees and hears us. We accept His will in all its details, especially in the dereliction which we experience. We put our whole reliance on the prayer of Christ of whom we are members, and with whom we have all things in common, especially His prayer; we rely on the spirit of Christ, who is within us and prays in us in an ineffable way. In other words we quietly and gently, begin to abandon ourselves, and to unite ourselves to Christ, by relying on Him alone. *He is our all!*

As to our mind and imagination, we may find it possible to quiet them by use of a book, or some formula of prayer, or by fixing them upon some good object. Even if they are occupied with divine things, they have very little to do with our real prayer. It is, however, much more likely that we cannot anchor them; in which case all we can do is to try to see that our *will* does not follow their wanderings, but is brought back gently to God by a simple act of faith. Until God gives us more grace there is nothing much more that we can do at prayer except to be patient with God, and to be patient with ourselves. Patience has a perfect work, which in this case is to detach ourselves from ourselves, and unite us to Christ; *His* life, *His* merits, *His* prayer, are what we must rely on.

Our best hope of helping ourselves lies outside the time of prayer, by humility, detachment, great purity of intention in all our works, and a ready correspondence with God's grace and providence. He is working for our detachment from all creatures—even from ourselves. All His providence is directed to that end. We can be just as much attached to our spiritual goods and attainments, to our spiritual joys and powers, as we can be to the temporal. For complete union with God, and for the bearing of "more fruit," these attachments must be purged.

This process is described in two famous books by St. John of the Cross: *The Ascent of Mount Carmel* and *The Dark Night of the Soul.* They can be of great help to souls who are faced with such difficulties at prayer. But there are certain points about these two books that should be noted if one is to read them with profit. First of all, St. John is describing the plenitude in order to show the participation; as he tells us: "here we have described the highest that may happen, because in that is comprehended all else." [4] Secondly, he is dealing with a soul who is determined to reach the summit of divine love and who is prepared to stop at no sacrifice necessary for that end. Thirdly, he has a habit of saying things in quite an absolute fashion in one place, and qualifying them elsewhere; so that isolated texts may mislead if they are not taken in conjunction with the rest of his works. Fourthly, the relations between *The Ascent of Mount Carmel* and *The Dark Night of the Soul* must be properly understood.

These two books are not two separate and successive chapters of a continuous story, such that the first must be

4 *Spiritual Canticle*, S. xiv, 2.

ended before the next is commenced. They are rather two different aspects of the same process of advance towards God, and of detachment from all else. *The Ascent* describes the soul's own part in the work—the active part; *The Dark Night* describes God's work, which is the passive part of the process. These two parts dovetail in with one another and mutually interact in such a way that one cannot be completed without the other. In fact, there are certain stages of the active part that cannot be even commenced until the necessary stages of the passive part have occurred. To put it in another way: the soul is not expected to perform all different works of detachment (or attachment to God, as we prefer to regard it) outlined in the *Ascent*, without getting considerable help from God, which help only comes in course of the process of purification wrought by God which is described in the *Dark Night*. The two processes dovetail into one another. As one advances by the grace already given and one's own strength, God comes to one's assistance by His work in the soul and adds new strength to one's forces. He is the principal agent in the work and His part is an ever increasing one. Therefore, no difficulty whatever, real or imaginary, should ever deter us or shake our confidence. We must never forget our Lord's words; *With men this is impossible: but with God all things are possible.*[5] Is not the very name that the prophet gave to the Redeemer: *Emmanuel—God with us?*[6]

It is true that the whole process of advance may be summed up in one word—detachment. This word however only hides the real truth; for detachment is but a means to an end, or rather, it is the reverse side of the real end and process, namely attachment. If we have to detach ourselves from various creatures and from our own self, from our own will, from our own ways, from our own judgment, from our own strength, from our own pleasure, from our own achievement, from our own life, spiritual as well as temporal—it is only in order to become completely attached to Jesus. Attachment to Jesus is the royal road to detachment from self. A bride

[5] Matt. xix, 26.   [6] Cf. Matt. i, 23.

does not leave her mother—she rather goes to her husband. Still for practical purposes, especially when it is remembered that our own attachment to our tremendous lover is to be made in the darkness of faith, it is well to keep both aspects of the transformation in mind.

One of the best ways of understanding the process is to look at its purpose. The purpose of this detachment is to achieve complete union of love with God. St. John of the Cross tells us: "This state of divine union consists in the soul's transformation, according to the will, in such a manner that there may be naught in the soul that is contrary to the will of God, but that in all and through all, its movements may be those of the will of God alone." . . . "The union and transformation of the soul in God does not always exist, but only where there is equality of love. . . . This takes effect when two wills, the will of God and the will of the soul are conformed together, neither desiring aught repugnant to the other.[7] "In this state of union, all the operations of the memory and of the other faculties are divine. God then possesses the faculties, being completely master of them by their transformation into Himself, and it is He himself who moves and commands them according to His divine spirit and will, and this is done in such a manner that the operations are not distinct, but those that the soul operates are of God and are divine operations."[8]

What else is this, but the full development of the life of the Mystical Body of Christ in His member? And this full development *must* take place before one enters heaven. We say this, lest it should be thought that such a union is only for very special souls. In his prologue, St. John of the Cross says: "We propound a doctrine substantial and solid, which will serve for *everyone* who wishes to attain the spiritual spoliation here described."[9] The pity is that we do not wish; to us, as to Jerusalem, our Lord can address His heart-broken complaint: "and thou *wouldst* not!"

To what extent we may hope for advance towards

[7] *Ascent*, I, c. xi, 3; II, c. v, 3.
[8] Ibid., III, c. i, 6.   [9] Ibid., Prol. 8, 9.

this union, is a question we shall consider in the next chapter. Here we would stress the absolute necessity of resolutely persevering in devoting the set time to prayer daily, no matter how unsuccessful our attempts may be. And we must be careful not to waste our energy in fruitless attempts to pray. Let us be satisfied with our failure. That is our prayer. The whole spiritual life at this period may become completely arid and repugnant. Any attempt to produce "fervor" by violent efforts will only result in a reaction that will make things worse. We have to look to God for our salvation, and to live by faith; and to learn by faith something of the full meaning of the words: *My God and my All.*

There is a dialogue between an enquirer and a statue cited in *The Love of God* by St. Francis de Sales,[10] which will bring comfort to those souls who are powerless at prayer, for St. Francis makes the statue typify the soul in this condition. To the question why it stays there doing nothing, the statue replies: "Because my master did not place me here to do anything but simply remain motionless!" Asked what advantages it has from such a proceeding the statue replies: "I am not here for my own interest or service, but to obey and to accomplish the will of my master and maker, and that is enough for me." Asked how it can be satisfied to content a master whom it cannot see, it replies; "I do not see him . . . but my master sees me here and likes to see me here, and that is all I want to make me happy." To the protest that it should at least desire to have the power to do some better service for the master, the reply is that it desires nothing except to do the will of its master: "I desire nothing else as long as ever my master wishes to leave me here, because my sole happiness is in contenting Him to whom I belong, and by whom I am what I am."

This quaint comparison from the great Doctor of Devotion should encourage us. Such a state is one in which there is nothing left for self love. There *is* activity —faith, hope, charity, humility, and abandonment are

[10] Bk. VI, chap. xi.

in full action; but the activity is such that the soul is unable to take any complacency in its own achievements, and that is an enormous gain; for until we become detached from this self-complacent pleasure of achievement even in spiritual things, our union with God cannot be complete.

This way of praying perfectly expresses the Christian way of living, stripped of all unessentials. In it we find the five virtues that we regard as fundamental: faith, hope, love, humility, and confident abandonment to the will and good pleasure of Him who is our God and our all.

Those who seek help in the literature of prayer may be confused by the different meanings attached to the word "contemplation" and the different opinions expressed about the possibility of achieving certain forms of prayer for which the word can stand. As to its meaning, one should note that some Ignatian writers use the word to denote a certain concentration of one's attention on, say, an incident in our Lord's life, by forming a vivid mental picture of the incident, and applying one's different faculties to it. In this sense we say, in the Rosary, "let us contemplate in this mystery how our Lord suffered in the garden, etc." This is quite an ordinary form of meditation and is available even for beginners.

There is another use of the word contemplation to denote an infused form of prayer, given to us by God, which represents a great advance from the elementary ways of making mental prayer. In St. Teresa's works, the word is always confined to those forms of prayer in which God's action is perceived by the soul. St. John of the Cross uses the word in a much wider sense than St. Teresa, to include also a state of prayer in which there is indeed a special action of God upon the soul, but in which this action is generally unperceived by the soul. The only apparent effect of God's action is to produce aridity and difficulty in prayer. One of the best treatments of this subject will be found in the work of Fr. Gabriel, O.D.C., already mentioned.

The same author gives a very good and helpful discussion of the question: who are called to these higher forms of prayer? He sums up his own conclusion, which however should be taken in its context, thus: "Infused contemplation, even of a very high order, is not a grace to be excluded from the outlook of spiritual persons; it does not belong to the realm of the extraordinary; it is wholly desirable because it is a very great help to sanctity and, in this world, it is the "connatural" crown of a holy life. But, for all that, it would be wrong to teach souls that without this contemplation they will never be saints. Also, it would be rash to promise souls graces and spiritual consolations which, perhaps, in His all-wise counsels, for some reason unknown to us, God does not intend to grant them. Hence there is a contemplation which is never, or scarcely ever, wanting after due preparation; there is another which is simply connatural and ordinary. Both may be called 'normal,' but this same word must be understood in two senses." [11]

Our chief aim in quoting Fr. Gabriel is to draw attention to his works, which we consider of the utmost practical value and importance. Our own view is that there is a type of prayer of very great value, which may be properly called contemplation, to which no particular baptized person who is willing to co-operate with God's grace, can say that *he* is *not* called. Every one so disposed may laudably and properly hope and work to reach such a height of prayer, even in the world; and even though God may, perhaps, withhold, or seem to withhold, the grace of this prayer, one may rest assured that in faith, hope, charity, humility, and complete acceptance of God's will *even on this point of prayer,* one can achieve the highest form of union with God, for by these virtues we can live the life of Christ, who is our holiness, and in whom is God, reconciling and uniting us to Himself.[12]

[11] Fr. Gabriel of St. Mary Magdalen, O.D.C. *St. John of the Cross—Doctor of Divine Love and Contemplation.*
[12] Cf. II Cor. v, 18, 19.

CHAPTER 20

Confidence in Christ

IF God is *our* God, and if God is our *All*, there should be no limit to our confidence and hope in Him. Yet, as a matter of experience, one sees that it is often through want of confidence that men turn away from the pursuit of perfection. They feel that "that sort of thing" is for the chosen few; they themselves are not "the stuff that saints are made of!" This is a complete misapprehension. Granting the limitations of ordinary human nature, those limitations have no restrictive power on the "super-nature" that is God's grace.

Discussing the measure of charity, St. Thomas lays down the principle: "There is no measure to be set in the end to which we tend, but only in the means." [1] The Scripture sets a very high aim when it says: *Be ye perfect as also your heavenly Father is perfect.* [2] Our Lord put no limit to the love He asked from everyone: *Thou shalt love the Lord thy God, with thy whole heart and thy whole soul and with thy whole mind and with thy whole strength.* [3] Since it is commanded, such a love must be possible. And, in any case, love that puts limits to itself is no love at all. As St. John of the Cross says: "He who loves cannot be satisfied if he does not feel that he loves as much as he is loved." [4] And St. John is not afraid to suggest the possibility of the fulfilment of this desire even in loving God; for he says: "Though in heaven the will of the soul is not destroyed, [for we never lose our own personal identity,] it is so intimately united

---

[1] *Summa*, ii-ii, 148, 3. [2] Matt. v, 48 [3] Mark xii, 30.
[4] *Spiritual Canticle*, S. 38. (Lewis' translation).

with the power of the will of God, who loves it, that it loves Him as strongly and as perfectly as it is loved of Him; both wills being united in the one sole will and one sole love of God. Thus the soul loves God with the will and the strength of God himself, being made one with that very strength of love wherewith it itself is loved of God. This strength is of the Holy Ghost."[5] St. John even considers that some foretaste of this union is possible here on earth.

The point for us to notice is that in the culmination of our union with God, all our power and strength come from His Holy Spirit. And the same is true throughout the whole of the way towards that union. From the very first moment of our spiritual life, all our power and strength come to us from the Holy Spirit, who is the living flame of the love of God for God, and who abides in our souls for our sanctification and our assistance. Those who wish to study St. John of the Cross cannot do better than to commence with the small works of Fr. Gabriel of St. Mary Magdalene,[6] from which we quote:

Hence the way of perfect love, is not a way reserved only for the few; none are denied entrance; it stands open to all souls of full good will. All may aspire to the fullness of the love of God; it is enough that they be willing to scale the path which leads them there: the way of *giving*, of total abnegation. As St. Teresa holds: God gives Himself wholly to the soul which gives itself wholly to Him.[7]

Let us add the words of Pope Pius XI:

All men of every condition, in whatever honorable walk of life they may be, can and ought to imitate that most perfect example of holiness placed before men by God, namely Christ, our Lord, and by God's grace arrive at the summit of perfection, as is proved by the example of many saints.[8]

[5] *Ibid.*　　　　　　　[6] Referred to in the last chapter.
[7] Fr. Gabriel, O.D.C., *St. John of the Cross.*
[8] *Casti connubii.*

One reason why we have drawn attention to these heights of the spiritual life, is because it will help to bring home to the reader the real agent in the work of our perfection. Such a sublime end is clearly beyond the powers of any human being. Therefore it must be *God's* work, not our own! And in fact the whole spiritual life is a gradual replacement of one's self by God, always, of course, leaving our own personal identity intact. Obviously, according as this replacement of the human by the divine proceeds, the strength at our disposal increases, and the possibilities of further advance grow greater with each step.

Therefore, all we have to do is to concentrate on the first step and *never to consider the difficulty of the next one.* This is a principle of capital importance. Each need brings the necessary grace from God; He will never give us a store of strength in which we can take complacency; and we cannot carry tomorrow's cross with today's grace. But once we realize that all our crosses are to be carried by grace, then there is an end to all discouraging calculation of one's own strength. We go then with confidence to the throne of grace.

We must never forget that the spiritual life is a partnership—a partnership with Jesus, a partnership with God. We have at our disposal all the power and love of the Holy Ghost to sanctify us and to energize us, for He is the soul of that one body to which we belong. We have at our disposal all the power of God the Father—the omnipotent Father of the Son whose body we are. He rules the universe, He regulates every single thing that happens to us or in us, no matter how small, and co-ordinates everything to work together for one end, the good and benefit of the body of His Son. Our needs are the needs of Christ; whatever the Father does to us is done to His Son, and for that Son's sake there is nothing that He will not do. So that everything inside us and outside us is controlled and arranged for one purpose— that of our complete union with Jesus. The Three Divine Persons are at work, in our soul and on our soul and in all that happens to us, and all that work is regulated by one single will—the will of God. There is only one thing left to our responsibility, and that is our own will. God will always respect our wills' freedom of choice. We can choose to do His will or to do our own—to be with Christ or to be against Him.

The folly of choosing wrongly should be obvious. To quote Fr. Lallemant:

"There is a void in our heart which all creatures united would be unable to fill. God alone can fill it; for He is our beginning and our end. The possession of God fills up this void and makes us happy. The privation of God leaves in us this void and is the cause of our wretchedness. Before God fills up this void, He puts us in the way of faith; with this condition, that if we never cease to regard Him as our last end, if we use creatures with moderation, and refer to His service the use we make of them, at the same time contributing faithfully to the glory which it is His will to draw from all created beings, He will give himself to us to fill up the void within us and make us happy. But if we are wanting in fidelity, He will leave in us that void, which, left unfilled, will cause our supreme misery." [9]

But it takes us time to learn by experience what we should know by faith:—that our hearts were made for God, and will not rest until they rest in Him. Like Francis Thompson, we are afraid "lest having Him we should have nought beside." It is only after many mistakes and failures that we realize our folly and find the right road. Still even these mistakes—even our sins—can be used for our good. Whether we think of them as gaps and empty places in our past which God can fill up—for all evil is lack of due entity; or as marks which, by changing the pattern, God can fit into the design according to which He is weaving our whole life; or as splashes of misapplied color, which the divine artist can employ to form part of a new picture; or as a dye which can be mixed with God's specially chosen coloring for

[9] Fr. Lallemant, S.J., *Spiritual Doctrine*, chap. I, p. 27.

our soul in order to give it the exact hue which He seeks; whatever view we take of the past, we must never, never, let any of our past sins, no matter how great or how grievous, interfere in the slightest with our unlimited hope and complete confidence in God, or with our aims and plans for the future. The heights of divine love are always accessible.

For that reason we must be resolute and optimistic in taking the first step, and in looking to God's fatherly providence for the rest of the journey. The perfection of detachment is the work of a lifetime, and is only achieved gradually. We are not obliged to renounce all creatures, absolutely, but we are asked to make God our ultimate end in our use and our love of them. Our Lord never ceased to love His Mother; St. John was His chosen friend until the end; and yet for all their excellence, they were only creatures.

In fact it is a favorite device of the devil, whose machinations we must never leave out of our calculations, to drive the beginner to excess in the matter of detachment. The result is that human nature reasserts itself even more strongly than before and one's last state is worse than one's first. In all this work we must never advance beyond grace. As one bishop of our times puts it: "There is an offside rule in these things; get in front of God's grace, and—suddenly the whistle blows and you pay the penalty!" Our business is to second God's grace and to follow its lead by generous co-operation.

If we are generous in co-operating with God's prompting from within our soul as well as with His providential indications from without, we shall find that He uses creatures to lead us to Him. As a matter of fact, every creature owes its origin to God, and anything of good that is to be found in each one is but a faint image of God's own beauty. There is no charm that any creature has, that cannot be found in a higher and more perfect way in God. All creation shows forth His loveliness; and what we find lovable in the creature is really the creature's resemblance to God. Creatures thus can lead us to God; their danger is that their charm may prevent our love from going further, and even lead us to prefer them to God. That is why custody of the heart is so important in the spiritual life. The truly spiritual man can love all creation; but he loves God above all, and he loves all else because of God. This principle will help many sincere souls to solve the difficulties that arise from too narrow a concept of the detachment necessary for the pursuit of perfection.

God is continually using creatures and the course of events to lead us to himself; and He does this often without our knowing it. In fact, there are times He seems to disguise His action so that we often think He has forgotten or abandoned us, or that He is leading us astray. The just man must live and pray by faith, and it is especially in regard to God's providence that his faith will have to be exercised. The path God traces out for us is often quite unexpected; He leads us backwards and forwards—this way and that way; He often seems to have changed His plan completely. He appoints—quite clearly we think—this particular work for us or that particular aim; and then He seems to arrange His whole providence to prevent us achieving it. He even seems to waste our whole life, to destroy our works, to take away all our means of serving Him. Yet we must never lose our confidence in Him, and the more contradictory His ways seem, the more complete our trust in His fatherly guidance must be. He knows what He is doing, and He alone knows it. There is not a single thing in our life or our circumstances which is left to chance, not a single event that He does not supervise.

We really never exactly know where God is leading us; and we must eventually give up all attempts to know. Very often our own ideas are quite wrong; we are thinking of great works for God, but God is thinking of great love from us. We do not realize the truth of the words of St. John of the Cross:

An instant of pure love is more precious in the sight

of God, and of the soul, and more profitable to the Church than all other good works put together, though it may seem as if nothing were done.[10]

The most valuable part of our life is often that which we esteem least, and the good works in which we think to have done great things for God and His Church, may have little real value in His eyes.

There is a mysterious lesson to be learned from the Gospel story of our Lord's life on earth. He became man to save the human race, to instruct men, to preach His Gospel, to found a Church, to establish a doctrine and an organization that should last forever. His own life was planned in all its details by the divine wisdom for that very purpose. Yet, how that plan contradicts our notions! We find that, born in obscurity, He—as we might foolishly think—"wastes" thirty years of His life in Egypt and Nazareth, first as the son of a workman and then as a workman himself when He grew old enough. After reaching thirty years of age, He spends three short years—He knew the duration of His life in advance— in the work of preaching His Gospel and instructing a handful of simple folk to form a nucleus of His Church. Then He allows the whole work to end in the apparent failure and shame of the Crucifixion, dying in degradation on the cross, deserted by all His followers, save only His Mother, a few women, St. John, and apparently a few friends in the crowd!

In fact the most surprising thing about His life is not what He did, but all that He left undone. And His whole anxiety seems to have been to complete His public ministry quickly in order to press on to His death. His whole reliance for the result of His life work seems to have been placed on the power and fruit of His death, rather than on the power and fruit of His life. If anything stands out from the Gospel story, it is our Lord's zeal, rather to die for His Father's glory than to live for it!

Let us not forget that He is our model. Very few

[10] *Spiritual Canticle,* S. xxviii, Note.

of us, however, are called to imitate His public life. But all are called to reproduce His hidden life, according to our condition. All, too, have to learn the lesson of His preference for death rather than life, and all must be prepared to follow His example. For, if the truth can be told in a few words without exaggeration, it is not so much the extent to which we *live* for God that is important, as the extent and generosity with which we *die* for Him. Most of us are called, like the Holy Innocents, to confess to God's glory *moriendo non loquendo*—by dying rather than by living—by the interior life rather than by the active ministry. There are some souls—and their number seems to be increasing today—who are called to die the violent death of martyrdom for God. But there are a great number more who are called to die for God the slow death of humility and abandonment to His will. The trial of the first is short and sharp; that of the latter may last long years, for they shed their blood drop by drop.

Our Lord warns us that it is by abiding in Him that we shall bear much fruit, and He adds that the Good Husbandman will purge us so that we may bring forth *more* fruit. We must be prepared for this purgation by God; a lively faith will be needed to co-operate with it. Sometimes the hand of the Divine Husbandman is quite evident, and whatever instrument He uses, every time any branch of our life or of our powers is cut off or pruned, it is clear that it is He who is at work, and no great effort is needed to see and kiss the loving hand of our Father who is in heaven when some person or event interferes with our plans or our possibilities. Such submission, however, becomes much more difficult, when, one by one, apparently *all* the branches are removed, and we seem to be left with no means of bringing forth fruit for God or of living for Him. This is the hour for the just man to live by faith. The *branch* of ourself which God intends to bear fruit is invisible to us. We must live then by faith in God; He is our hope, our life, and our love; we must live by *Him,* and not by ourselves. In fact, *He* is our God and our all.

This is of essential importance in that case where the divine action takes a form that is by no means uncommon —one in which the hand of God is by no means evident at first sight. God often prunes us by letting us *wither.* Instead of cutting off the branches, He cuts off the sap that seems necessary for their life. Sometimes things go so far that the whole man seems to wither away, even spiritually, and one feels like Lazarus after four days in the tomb. This is a moment which calls for a very definite correspondence with God's grace; because it is a grace, a great grace. In these circumstances, we must by a deliberate effort exert our faith, to see His hand and His love in all that befalls us; we must exert our hope, to trust in Him for everything we need for His glory and our own sanctification; we must exert our love, to cleave to Him in that union of will and humble emptiness of self, which is the true abiding in Christ, and one union with God that matters here below. Note we say *exert,* because these circumstances call for a very definite and determined *decision.* We must *decide* to believe in God; we must *decide* to hope in Him; we must *decide* to love Him; we must *decide* to trust Him; we must *decide* that Christ is our life, and God is our all.

Human nature however will rather tend to imitate the two disciples on the road to Emmaus after the final "failure" of the Crucifixion. "We hoped . . . and look what is left to us!" The answer our Lord gave them is no less for our ears than for theirs. *O foolish, and slow of heart to believe. . . . Ought not Christ to have suffered these things and so* [mark the word]—*so to enter into his glory?* [11] And, are not we members of Christ? . . . Is the servant above His master? Did not our Lord say to Martha, when Lazarus was in the tomb: *I am the resurrection and the life. He that believeth in me, although he be dead, shall live! Believest thou this? . . . Did I not tell thee that if thou believest thou shalt see the glory of God?* [12]

In truth, the just man is obedient to death, but he lives by faith; for faith is the proximate principle of

[11] Luke xxiv, 25, 26. [12] Cf. John xi, 25, 40.

union with God here below. And our faith must be exercised despite everything—even despite our own insignificance.

When we study the lives of the saints, we seem to find that apparently they were all "great" souls. They either followed God from their youth and, like the Little Flower, never refused Him anything; or else, even in their sins, they showed a "greatness" and thoroughness which after their conversion, seems at first, to have been the cause of their heroic sanctity. Once converted, they never looked back. Such greatness of soul, we know is not ours; we have not even the grit to be great in sin. Their determination, their thoroughness, their whole-heartedness, have little in common with our faint-hearted futility. Even in our sins, we are merely mean and treacherous; we try to have it both ways; we have no generosity in doing good, or even in doing bad; we are inconstant and inconsequent; we are failures. The counsellors of despair are quick to remind us what our Lord said of those who were neither hot nor cold—that He would begin to vomit them out of His mouth because they were lukewarm, and we get the impression that there is no conversion, no hope of advance, for the tepid.

That is just where we must stir up our faith and glory in our infirmities. Even if our sanctification is difficult—and there is no reason to admit that it is, for such a soul has a proximate disposition for a very high degree of humility—we must not forget that our sanctification is to be more the work of God than our own work, that God's plan is to glorify himself by His mercy, and that mercy is most glorified when it is exercised towards great misery. The more difficult the work and the less claim we have on God's help for it—the more will His mercy be glorified in making us saints. Therefore, our very hopelessness is a reason for hoping without limit!

That is a principle that must be carried very far. The Canaanite woman who came to our Lord asking for the cure of her daughter received no answer at first, and the disciples wanted Him to send her away. When she persisted, our Lord insisted that He *was not sent but to the lost sheep of Israel;* and she was not of them. But she came and adored Him, and despite His apparent harshness, she humbled herself, making herself less than the dogs to which He seemed to compare her. Our Lord finally yielded, saying, *Woman, great is thy faith; be it done unto thee as thou wilt.*[13] Here we have an example of our Lord himself excluding someone from the scope of His official appointment and yet, eventually, yielding to her faith.

The words of our Lord after the death of Lazarus have already been cited, where our Lord asked Martha to believe in Him, despite the death of her brother. No matter how spiritually dead we are—if we believe in Him—we shall live. But when discouragement takes possession of us, any condition that requires fulfilment on our part seems to destroy our hope. We find it hard even to believe. There is, however, still a remedy, and room for hope.

Let us recall our Lord's first miracle at the wedding feast in Cana.[14] The wine failed; and our Lady turned to our Lord and drew His attention to the awkward situation, saying *They have no wine.* Our Lord gave her a mysterious answer, which, in its English form, may seem harsh: *Woman, what is that to me and to thee? My hour is not yet come.* The first part of the reply has to be understood according to the idiom of the Aramaic tongue; the second part is a clear affirmation that the appointed time for working miracles had not arrived. Yet, our lady, quite unperturbed, calmly tells the attendants: *Whatsoever he shall say to you, do ye.* They obeyed; and we know the result. The water they provided was changed into excellent wine.

The whole spiritual life is summed up and manifested in this incident. Our Lady's extraordinary power is obvious. The effect of doing God's will is clear, and it is noteworthy that this is the one precept our Lady ever gave any of her children. If we do "whatever He shall

[13] Matt. xv, 24, 28. [14] Cf. John, ii.

say to us" the water of our miserable self, will be changed in the wine of His new creation. But for the moment we would stress the fact that His explicit declaration of the limitations of the divine plan, did not prevent Him altering that plan at His Mother's request. *So there are no absolute limitations to the working of divine grace.* And even if there were, they are not absolute for our Lady. She is blessed because she believed.[15] And if our faith is weak, we have but to have recourse to our Mother, and tell her "we have no wine." She will provide.

So that if all authorities, all our friends, all our advisers, all books, and all examples, our very innermost self, seem to conspire to tell us that we are not such as are called to the marriage feast of the lamb, to the heights of holiness; even if our Lord himself seemed to say that we were neither of the time or the number to whom He was sent—we must still persevere in our faith, in our hope, in our love, in our humility, and in our abandonment to His will. *There is nothing that God will not do for a loving, confident faith.* And even if we feel that we have no faith, our Lady has more than enough for both of us. And, we have our Lord's own word for it, that she is *ours.*[16] She will manage the matter of our lack of wine like a good housekeeper. But our Lady's housekeeping needs a chapter to itself.

Let us consider this fear that we are not the stuff out of which saints are made in the light of the teaching of St. Thomas. Discussing the question whether charity is infused according to the capacity of our natural virtues, he states: "The measure of each thing depends upon the cause of that thing: for the more universal cause produces a greater effect. Charity, since it exceeds the proportion or capacity of human nature, does not depend upon any natural power but only upon the grace of the Holy Ghost who infuses it. And therefore, the measure of charity does not depend upon the condition of nature, or upon any capacity of natural virtue, but only upon the will of the Holy Ghost distributing His gifts according

<hr>

[15] Cf. Luke i, 45.   [16] Cf. John xix, 27.

to His will. Thus St. Paul writes to the Ephesians.[17] *To everyone of us is given grace, according to the measure of the giving of Christ.*[18] And by way of removing any limitation that could be based upon the dispositions which usually precede the infusion of charity, he answers that such dispositions are also under the influence of the Holy Spirit *Who hath made us worthy to be partakers of the lot of the saints in light.*[19]

And we can draw encouragement from his discussion of the question whether there is any limit to the increase of charity (which is the bond of perfection). There are only three reasons for which it could be limited, either on account of charity itself, or of the agent producing charity, or of the soul receiving charity. He continues: "None of these three puts any limit to the increase of charity. Charity itself has no limit, for it is a certain participation of uncreated charity which is the Holy Ghost. The agent producing charity is of infinite power, being God himself. Likewise, there is no limit fixed for this growth by nature of the subject (receiving it); because always when charity grows, the ability for further advance is yet more increased. Whence it follows that no limit can be fixed to the growth of charity in this life."[20] So there is no limit set to our progress by our nature. The only two limiting factors are God's will and our own; and if we abandon ourself to God's will, the only limit comes from God's loving decision. To Him we can certainly leave that decision in full confidence.

We have dealt with this question at some length, because it is of essential importance that no soul ever let any circumstance whatever interfere with his unlimited confidence and hope in God. There is a close connection and interaction between humility and confidence. A man who realizes God's mercy can put his whole hope in God and be honest with himself about his own weakness. A man who only knows God as a strict judge and who feels that his only hope is to be placed in

[17] Eph. iv, 7.
[19] Col. i, 12.
[18] *Summa* ii-ii, 24, 3.
[20] Cf. *Summa* ii,ii, 24, 7.

his own righteousness and strength of purpose, dare not be honest with himself; and since humility is truth, he will not achieve true humility. Only the man who knows God can afford to know himself. And, in another sense, only a man who knows himself, will know the full depth of God's liberality and extraordinary love. Knowing this, he will then advance to the higher degree of humility which consists in not only knowing one's own nothingness, but in being glad of it.

Confidence, therefore, must always animate our spiritual life. It is especially necessary during that stage of progress in which God begins to purify the depths of our soul and prepare it for greater things. God's providence always works towards the same end of detachment from self and from creatures, and of attachment to Him; but He does not always work in the same way. Sometimes, He detaches the soul step by step, so to speak, taking one "tentacle" from a creature and attaching it to Himself before going on to deal with the next attachment. He will even use a creature as an intermediary, and raise up our standard by attaching us for the moment to some superior creature, but only as a means to ultimate attachment to Himself. For example, He will use the desire for knowledge to detach us from the desire of sense pleasure: He will use the desire of physical skill and achievement to detach us from lower satisfactions.

At other times, God works on a wider front and first loosens, so to speak, all the stones of the building, which later comes down with a crash on the occasion of some special trial. All our attachments are gone at once. Here again He may use an intermediary, and replace a multiplicity of attachments by one outstanding one, which at a later stage He removes, and seizes our whole heart for himself. There is no limit to His ingenuity, and there are no obstacles He cannot overcome. No matter how low we have fallen, how mediocre we are, or how far we have wandered from the high road into the swamps of sin; He can always build a bridge that will give us a way of reaching the goal He sets for us, and He can always supply us with the strength to do so.

In leading us on to union with Him in prayer, His action can be quite disconcerting. Prayer, as we saw, is capable of development. Given good will, purity of life, and daily reading and reflection, prayer first of all becomes more affective; we talk to God with a certain facility, and then we begin to talk to God quite simply, with but few words, which, however, can mean quite a lot. Quite a large part of the time of prayer can be spent in silent adoration and love. Somewhere in this process of development—it is not necessary to specify where—God is wont to intervene; and the result of His intervention is that prayer as we knew it, first becomes more difficult, then dries up, and ultimately becomes impossible. All sense of God's presence is gone, all facility in making acts and persevering in silent prayer disappears. A general distaste for spiritual things may come over us. Spiritual reading seems, at best, useless and may even be very distasteful. Spiritual exercises become nothing but weary tasks, almost drudgery; the mind is incapable of good thoughts, and all fervor seems to have gone.

Now, as we have already said, such a development could be due to sin, to infidelity, or to tepidity. If so, an honest examination of one's conscience will reveal either a definite fault, or, in the case of tepidity, a very definite laxity all around which, however, presents fairly definite points for improvement. But it frequently happens that nothing definite can be found. There is a general, vague, indefinite sense of things being wrong, but one cannot put one's finger on any particular fault. This vague feeling of uneasiness need not worry us.

We have already discussed this state of affairs at prayer in the last chapter. We return to it here, to urge the capital importance of an unwavering confidence in God's loving guidance and action to lead us to himself, and in His infinite mercy which will forgive all our infidelities; for in this condition one can see oneself so clearly that one may be quite overwhelmed at the sight, and, losing confidence in God, may give up the spiritual life and seek consolation in creatures. If one falls at this stage, one will probably fall very badly. One must go to extremes if one is to intoxicate oneself sufficiently with pleasure to drive out even temporarily the remembrance of one's need for God and one's horror of oneself. But even if one fall, one must return with confidence to God. *Where sin abounded, grace did more abound.*[21] God understands one's position far better than any human being, and always is ready to forgive.

The soul must persevere in this arid prayer and in the service of God despite distaste, with absolute confidence and reliance upon Him. Nothing gives Him so much glory and pleasure as these dry acts of devotion to His will. This is a time of great merit for the soul and great profit for the Church. There is nothing of self-seeking in such service.

If one persevere in prayer despite the gloom of winter, the spring will come eventually. And one will hear the voice of one's lover: *Arise, make haste, my love, my dove, my beautiful one and come. For the winter is now past, the rain is over, the flowers have appeared in the land.*[22] For one can then say in very truth with the Spouse in the Canticle: *Behold, my beloved speaketh to me. . . . My beloved to me, and I to him who feedeth among the lilies, till the day break and the shadows retire.*[23]

The grace of prayer, which formerly had caused such aridity in the soul, now extends its reign, and its effects become noticeable; it extends to the other powers of the soul, and distractions cease, it touches the very heart, and fills it with peace and joy and love. A new life opens before the astonished eyes of the soul, and one counts the past years of winter as nothing. Then one truly loves, one is truly loved, and one not only knows one's love, but one knows one's tremendous lover.

[21] Rom. v, 20.
[22] Cant. ii, 10–12.
[23] Cant. ii, 10, 16–17.

CHAPTER 21

Marriage and Holiness

S o far, in our discussion of the fulfilling of the life of Christ that is in our soul from baptism, we have made little mention of the usual type of external good works that are generally considered a major part of the spiritual life, such as social work and philanthropy. One of the reasons for our silence is because these works are only really valuable for sanctification when they arise from an interior life of union with God. *If I have not charity it profiteth me nothing.*[1] There is further the fact that too many Catholics consider such works to be the essential part of their Catholic life— whereas these works are merely one of the possible external expressions of the true spiritual life which, like the kingdom of God, is within us.

There is also a certain lack of due perspective in our estimation of the relative importance of such works. Sunday, we all admit, is a day for certain religious exercises. On week days the more fervent will adopt certain voluntary practices, daily Mass, or a visit to the Blessed Sacrament, for example. If something further is desired, it generally takes the form of some social work. Once that is done, there is generally a vague feeling that religion has purely a negative concern with the rest of the day; that the most one can do with the rest of one's time, as far as religion is concerned, is to avoid sin, and possibly fit in a few extra prayers.

Now, since we are members of Christ, this view is

[1] Cf. I Cor. xiii, 3.

obviously wrong; for we are His members—and He is our life—in everything we do. So that every single action of our lives should come under the influence of our religion. And so should our relations with every single person we meet during the day, for they must all be regulated by Christian charity. And if we seek for a further exercise of that Christian charity, we should begin with the person who has the greatest claim upon that charity. And that person is not society in general. For the most important person in the world to a married man should be, and must be—his wife. Therefore, after their personal practices, the spiritual life of married people— in its external expression—begins in their relation with each other; and this relation is always one of its most important expressions and certainly that which is primary.

No romantic novelist, no poetic idealist, no impractical dreamer, has ever dared set so romantic an ideal for married love as God does by the pen of St. Paul:

Let women be subject to their husbands, as to the Lord: because the husband is the head of his wife, as Christ is the head of the Church. He is the Saviour of his body. There-fore, as the Church is subject to Christ, so also let wives be subject to their husbands. Husbands, love your wives as Christ also loved the Church and delivered himself up for it; that he might sanctify it, cleansing it by the laver of water in the word of life that he might present it to himself a glorious church, not having spot or wrinkle, or any such thing, but that it should be holy, and without blemish. So also ought men to love their wives as their own bodies. He that loveth his wife, loveth himself. For no man ever hated his own flesh; but nourisheth and cherisheth it, as also doth Christ the Church; because we are members of his body, of his flesh and of his bones. For this cause shall a man leave his father and mother, and shall cleave to his wife and they shall be two in one flesh. This is the great sacrament, but I speak in Christ and in the Church.[2]

In other words, not only is the love and mutual sur-

[2] Eph. v, 22–32.

render of Christ and His Church the model proposed by God for the love and mutual surrender of husband and wife, but their union is also a "sacrament" of that union of Christ and His Church. Writing on this very point Pius XI reminds husband and wife that the love of Christ for His church should be their model. He continues:

> This precept the apostle laid down when he said: "Husbands, love your wives as Christ loved His Church"; which of a truth He loved with a boundless love, not for the sake of His own advantage, but seeking only the good of His spouse.

The Holy Father continues:

> Their love then, is not that based on the passing lust of the moment nor does it consist in pleasing words only, but in deep attachment of the heart which is expressed in action, since love is proved by deeds. This outward expression of love in the home not only demands mutual help, but must go further; it must have as its primary purpose that man and wife help each other day by day in forming and perfecting themselves in the interior life; so that by their partnership in life they may advance ever more and more in virtue, and above all that they may grow in that true love towards God and their neighbor, on which dependeth the whole Law and the Prophets.
>
> For all men of every condition, in whatever honorable walk of life they may be, can and ought to imitate that most perfect example of holiness placed before man by God, namely, Christ, our Lord, and by God's grace arrive at the summit of perfection, as is proved by the example of many saints.[3]

We would draw the reader's attention to the last passage of the above quotation. It contains a sufficient refutation of a widely current error, which suggests that marriage is not a state in which sanctity can be sought or achieved. For we see that not only *can* married people "arrive at the summit of perfection," but they *ought* to

[3] *Casti connubii.*

do so; so far from being an obstacle, their married life is a means to this end.

It is clear that Christian marriage is a union of love, both natural and supernatural. It would be highly imprudent to assume that the sacramental power may be properly invoked in advance, to make a success of a union that is doomed to failure from its very conception by a lack of any degree of that mutual love which moves a man and a woman to give themselves completely to one another. Let it not be thought that marriage is a mere physical union. To quote Pius XI:

> By matrimony the souls of the contracting parties are joined and knit together more directly and more intimately than their bodies, and that not by any passing affection of sense or spirit, but by a deliberate and firm act of the will, and from this union of souls by God's decree, a sacred and inviolable bond arises.

What really happens then in true Christian marriage, is that a man and a woman abandoning their own individual life, give themselves completely to one another, as Christ does to His Church (only think of Christ giving Himself in Holy Communion!) and together form one new unit, living one new life. They are not only two in one flesh, they are two in one life.

The standard then set for married love by St. Paul is very high. The man is to love his wife, *as Christ loved the Church and delivered himself up for it.* And Christ delivered himself up to death, even to the death of the cross, for His spouse the Church. And St. Paul connects that very headship of the family which he gives to the man with his willingness to deliver himself up for his wife, where he writes: *He is the saviour of his body.*

This, you may say, is an ideal beyond human attainment. Perhaps. But marriage is not a mere human union. It is a supernatural union, a sacrament that gives grace—that sharing of Christ's strength—to enable the two partners to achieve this ideal. In point of fact it takes three to make a happy marriage: a man, a woman, and

God. And there is a sense in which it could be said that these three are one. For they are certainly one in Christ.

Marriage, being a sacrament, not only gives that increase in supernatural grace which is the effect of all the sacraments, but it gives a special grace and assistance for all the difficulties and decisions that belong to married life. That is the reason why we can set such a high ideal before husband and wife. It is indeed a superhuman ideal. But the strength at their disposal is superhuman also. They must, therefore, rely on that strength that comes from God, and not upon themselves. And they must develop that "superhuman" life—their spiritual life—by suitable exercises. Perhaps it may seem old-fashioned to suggest that these exercises should be done in common. But there are many old-fashioned things that are of a value quite misunderstood by the moderns. This is one of them. If then we here point out some of the human difficulties that arise in married life, it is to indicate the need for the continual use of and reliance upon the supernatural means which the sacrament of marriage places at one's disposal. And if in a limited space, we confine ourselves to the relations of man and wife, rather than to those of parent and child, it is because the former is one that is most often forgotten.

The man and the woman are both members of Christ; to receive the grace of the sacrament they must be living members in the state of grace. Otherwise no supernatural love between them is possible. Just as two cells in the human body unite to form one, which is the beginning of a new human life, so two people in marriage become one in Christ, and one with Christ, to the end that the life of Christ may be fruitful—that a new member may be given to Christ.

For there are certain special features in Christian marriage. It is a contract; and that contract is a sacrament of which the man and the woman are ministers. But unlike many other contracts, its terms and its purposes are not determined by the contracting parties; they are already fixed by the law of nature and the law of God. Marriage may be approached under the influence of various motives, some better than others; but once accepted, it must be taken as it stands. And as it stands, its primary end is the begetting of new members of Christ and their formation in Christ for heaven; and that end must never be frustrated by unlawful means. Its secondary end, the mutual completion and perfection of the man and the woman in Christ, has its own importance which is often overlooked, but it can only be pursued as long as its primary and natural result is not positively and unlawfully prevented. Otherwise the union is not union in Christ.

That being always remembered, we would like to stress here the spiritual aspect of the secondary end, that which concerns the man and the wife. First of all, let us get rid of the heretical notion that there is anything sinful or shameful about that physical expression of married love, which forms the matter of the marriage contract. There is a peculiar feeling, vague perhaps, but none the less prevalent, that marriage merely gives a license to do something that is really unlawful and indecent, a toleration of a necessary evil, a mere concession to fallen nature and human weakness. Such a feeling is completely false.

Not only are the intimacies of married life free from sin or shame, they are actually holy. Read again the text of St. Paul quoted above, and remember that the Holy Spirit is the real author of these words, and note that He chooses the intimate union of married life as a symbol and a "sacrament" of the union of Christ and His Church. How can there be anything that is not altogether holy about such a union, unless human malice deform it from its true nature? Let us once and for all get rid too of the notion, so harmful to the spiritual life, so heretical in its origin, and so widespread today, that there is anything intrinsically wrong in pleasure as such. God forbid! God made pleasure, man made pain. God shares the pleasures of His creatures. All pleasure, that is not inordinate, no matter how intense it is, can be offered to God. What is lawfully done to one's neighbor or to one's self is done to Christ. Our Lord insisted that St. Gertrude should take grapes when she was ill, and assured her that the pleasure she thus gave to herself was given also to Him. It is only when pleasure becomes inordinate—that is contrary to the will of God—that it is wrong. And no one can live without some pleasure, just as no one can live without some food and some rest.

Love demands expression and love is nourished by expression, and that is true even of the most spiritual love. And the love of a man for his wife is a unique love and demands a unique expression, and God has provided an unique expression for it and has attached intense pleasure to it. And God has gone further still. For He has arranged that by that very act of expressing their love for one another, husband and wife become partners with Him in the work of producing a new creature. They produce the body, and God infuses the soul. And that is only the beginning of their work of partnership. For they have the privilege and the duty of bringing that new creature to the maturity of the life of Christ, when as an independent Christian, formed by their care and love, and molded by their example and teaching, it shall work out its own way to complete union with God in heaven.

Marriage then implies a complete donation of one partner to the other, and a love that symbolizes the love of Christ and His Church. The very obstacles put by human nature to the fulfilment of this ideal can make marriage the foundation of an intense spiritual life. For it will soon become apparent that neither party is an angel; both are human. And the love and sacrifice demanded on both sides are so great and so costly that the questions soon arise: "Is any human being worth all that?"; "Can any human being give all that?" The answer lies in the fact that it is not a mere human being who gives, nor is it a mere human being who receives. Each one loves, and sacrifices self, in partnership with Christ; each one is loved and is served, in union with Christ. Beyond her husband, and in his heart, the wife sees and loves and serves Christ. Beyond his wife, and in her heart, the husband sees and loves and serves Christ. The strength to go on, to give all the substance of one's house for love and count it nothing, comes from Christ and is used for Christ. Christ is the lover and Christ is the beloved. For, even in marriage, "there shall be one Christ loving Himself."

In fact the very difficulty of the situation throws one back on Christ, we seek strength in union with Him. Only the perfect Christian can be the perfect lover. And the disappointment which is inevitable in all human affairs—the seeming inability of the other to return the love given—leads one to look further for the perfect lover—the tremendous lover—who is Christ. For by falling in love one realizes that all one's happiness is bound up with "somebody." And it is often only after the comparative failure of that "somebody" that one learns to know the real "Somebody," who is Christ. When the inevitable separation from one's partner comes—as come it must, for part of the day at least— and one realizes that things have lost their meaning because there is no one with whom to share them, one is forced either to fall back on the distraction of work or pleasure, or else to advance further, and to develop that union with Christ which is latent in all Christian souls, and by which one can always share everything with Him who made all things.

Even in a perfect partnership, human limitation will become evident. Even there, effort is always necessary to build up new links and associations, to forge new bonds, which will defy the corrosion of custom and time. Love can never merely be taken for granted; it does not stand still; it lives and develops—or else it dies. But even at its best, love must be supernaturalized. Properly understood, there is a sense in which one might say that husband and wife should be to one another a "sacrament" of Christ. All that is lovable, all this is pleasing, all that is beautiful in each other, is merely a pale reflection of the charm, the beauty, the lovableness of Him in whose image all things are made. There is a time in the life of some who are fortunate, when the beauty of all creation is summed up for them in one person. The song of the bird in the summer evening, the crystal beauty of the young night sky, the merry dance of running water, all and each of those heart-touching charms of nature that made the poet sad, have but one message for the fortunate lover who has learned that all things in the world are but things and infinitely below the worth of persons, and that there is only one person who for him sums up the glory of all creation. These things will pass, and the foreshadow of their passing will sadden his heart if he does not learn that all these, and even the one in whom they are all contained, are in turn the expression of the beauty of Him who made them, and whose love they affirm and reflect. For husband and wife are not merely symbols of Christ and His Church, they are the "sacrament" thereof, and in some mysterious way they share in the reality which their union symbolizes.

Unfortunately, not all marriages are so perfect. It may be mere cynicism that is responsible for the saying: "There is always one who loves, and one who lets oneself be loved," yet too often it contains a measure of truth. Literature gives ample expression to the pain of unrequited love; and the half-requited love that is only too common in marriage, is one of the keenest forms of participation in the Passion of Christ.

Few things can hurt so much as the heart that demands love, and which is still so much in love with itself that it cannot and will not give itself in return. For love demands that one make one's own the joys and sorrows of the other. The lover finds happiness in giving himself, in making some one else happy. But that happiness is shattered if he is forced to realize that his devotion is merely accepted, and not returned; that it is used against himself; that it is accepted merely out of self-love, and used to nourish self-love. That, it seems, is what broke our Lord's heart in Gethsemani. And we, His members, have often to share in that suffering, in our work for souls, in our friendships, in family life, and in many human relationships.

It is in such cases that an interior life becomes so

essential for marriage. To love is to become capable of considerable suffering, and human limitations make it fairly certain that he who loves much will suffer much. *The disciple is not above the master.*[4] Where painful disappointment with another is felt, it is always well to turn the searchlight of criticism on one's own self, to see what is the attitude of one's own heart towards God. The love of man and wife should be the image of Christ's love for the Church. Sometimes God allows the love, or lack of love of one partner for the other, to be the image of that other's love, or lack of love, for God. If one thinks one is badly treated, the question should immediately arise: "Is that, perhaps, how I treat God?"

This is but a typical example of the way that God will use creatures to show us His love for us, to elicit our love for Him, and to show us our lack of due love for Him. In this way our relations with creatures—and especially the relations of man and wife, whether happy or unhappy—can be a continual support and incitement for progress in the spiritual life and in union with God.

For those who have discovered that the only thing that matters in this life or in the next—the only thing that can give true happiness—is to love and to be loved, married life can be a source of continual and untold suffering, even when on the surface it appears to be a success. What women may have to suffer in this way, is beyond the power of any man to describe. There are husbands who consider their wives as glorified housekeepers or secretaries, as an ornament in their home and a hostess at their table, a social acquisition, a mere means of pleasure and self-gratification, in fact as anything, but as what a wife really is: another and better self, a partner in living, one who is a continual influence for the development of all that is good. So few men realize that a man's wife is his best friend. So few men realize to what an extent their family life, and in particular that part of their family life which they share with their wife, should be the principal part of their life in this world.

4 Matt. x, 24.

They work for their own "advancement"—whatever that may mean. They have a "career," and they feel everything else must be subordinated to that.

One wonders to what extent educators are responsible for this folly. How many boys leave school with the idea that if they are not going into religion or the priesthood, they can do no better than carve out for themselves a career of worldly "success!" What a return to offer God for all He suffered for us! It is true, of course, that it is desirable that Catholics should stand in society as an asset to it, and that they should have the poise and assurance that success brings. This is especially true in a society where Catholicity is despised or where it has just emerged from a state of seige or of persecution. To that extent, the policy of our educators is, perhaps, justified. But God forbid that we should make an end of what can only be a means to an end!

It is also true, that, although a man's wife has first claim upon his devotion, she has not got the only claim. He has a duty to his parents and to the society to whom he owes his origin and development. In the particular case of a man whose work is of Catholic importance such a work has an added claim upon his time. But if he is married, he is married. And he must devote himself in the first place, adequately and generously to his wife and family. It is utterly wrong, for example, on the excuse of important social work, to rush out on all or many evenings of the week after the evening meal to some philanthropic work or meeting, or even to some exercise of devotion. Yet one often finds good Catholics doing that. The point is they are giving away something that is not their own; they are stealing from their wives to serve—as they imagine—God. God does not want such service. Far, far better for a man, and more meritorious, to spend the evening at home with his wife, or to take her to some entertainment which they can both share, and so to develop and manifest his love for his wife and their community of life. He will find Christ in his wife on such occasions more certainly, more fruitfully and more intimately, than he will in all his needy neighbors, or even—we would venture to say—in a visit to the Blessed Sacrament. For Christ is present and is to be received, wherever His will is to be done. And His will is that they whom He has joined together should not be put asunder by any man.

There are other sufferings that women have to undergo in secret. There is the shy husband who will not tell his love, the timorous man who is afraid to let his wife know his love for her, the man with that peculiar, but by no means unusual, habit which makes him set his face and assume a mask of solid indifference when his wife shows her affection for him in any way, despite the fact that there is a song in his heart that seems unending. There is the husband who has no tact, there is the husband whose sense of humor manifests itself by teasing. There is the man who always patronizes his wife, and who will never show her any deference in public. But there is no need to extend the catalog. It could not be completed even in a book. It is, however, clear, that nothing but a deep spiritual life will enable a woman to sustain such continual disappointment and suffering, and still remain happy. God, however, can always fill the void in her heart.

However, it is not always the man who fails to reach ideal standards. Not every single wife brings to marriage a sufficiently high ideal of self-surrender and self-sacrifice. And failure on the woman's side has more far reaching consequences than on her husband's. For a man needs two women to perfect him, his mother and his wife. If his wife fails him because of her self-centeredness and unwillingness to sacrifice herself, he has an especial need of the spiritual life. The Mother of God must come to his aid to repair what her daughters have spoiled.

Both man and wife have need of a spiritual life to succeed in their own individual part, and to sustain the effects on them of failure by their partner. Both men and women tend to live their life before a "gallery"—a small group of acquaintances—before whom they play their part, whose applause and whose approval they seek, by whom they are swayed and influenced. Only frequent contact with our Lord in prayer, in reading, and in the sacraments, can prevent the ruin of married life where such a circle of critics and admirers lacks a true Catholic outlook. This is especially true with regard to the wife. There is no greater enemy of married happiness than the wife's women friends. Unless she is a woman of character and of spirituality, she dresses for them, she lives for their applause, she learns from them, and takes her thoughts and her ideals from them. It would be hard to exaggerate the possibility of harm that can come from such a source.

This is especially true today. Women are not prepared for marriage at school. They are dependent on their acquaintances for their whole philosophy of married life, and that philosophy always tends to take its tone from the current fashion of so-called thought. This is not the place to discuss careers for women, or women's place in public life. They undoubtedly, have a very important role to play. But, apart from special circumstances arising out of need or misfortune, few Catholic married women can take up a career after marriage without thereby advertising their failure as women and their failure as Catholics. That may seem too strong, but one feels the necessity of reacting against the errors of the times. It is one thing for a married woman whom God has not blessed with children to find occupation for her leisure; it is quite another thing for her to make a career the first interest of her life. The parable of the talents is often quoted in this connection. The first answer to that is that if her talents are clamoring for development, let her not marry; marriage, in the modern phrase, is a "full-time job." The second, and more fundamental, answer is, that the fundamental talent in every Catholic's soul is the life of Christ, and for a married woman, that is to be developed inside marriage and not outside it. Beside that talent, all others pale into insignificance.

The woman who marries, intending at all costs to retain her own career, or who absolutely refuses to be dependent on her husband, does not know the meaning either of Christian marriage or even of true human love. If she is in love with anybody, it is with herself. Marriage means abandoning one's self to enter into one new life, shared with her husband. There cannot be two "careers" where this is only one life. Nor can there be independence. For man and wife are dependent upon one another for everything. Where there is love, all joy or pleasure that cannot be shared, loses its value. There is no need here to give the true name of such unions where independence of life is insisted upon, but that should not prevent clear thinking as to their nature. Further, it must be remembered that as regards their work and their place in civil society, husband and wife are in different positions. The husband has a direct connection with the civil economy, the wife is integrated into it only through her husband. To put it another way: husband and wife form one unit; and the wife's role in that unity is to assist her husband, not to rival him; she must be an accompanist as regards his public life.

St. Paul's exhortation to wives to be subject to their husbands as the Church is to Christ, raises much comment. Let it be noted that the husband to whom St. Paul wants a wife to be subject is one who, he insists, must love her so much, that he is ready to lay down his life for her, and who actually does give his whole life to her. One must understand what this "subjection" really means. A woman does not lose her personal liberty or freedom or dignity in marriage. She is not bound to obey her husband's every request if it is not in harmony with right reason or with the dignity due to a wife. She is not a minor, nor immature, nor incapable of judgment. As Pius XI says, this subjection merely *forbids that in this body which is the family, the heart be separated from the head to the great detriment of the whole body and the proximate danger of ruin. For if the man is the head, the woman is the heart, and as he occupies the chief place in ruling, so she may and ought to claim for herself the chief place in love.*[5]

[5] *Casti connubii.*

The wife is not her husband's servant. They are partners. They complement and supplement one another. She has a right to her opinion and her husband ought to take cognizance of it. It is not because he is the more expert or more intellingent, or has the better judgment or the greater courage, that the ultimate decision is his; for in fact, the contrary is often the case. The real reason is because where there are two minds in partnership, someone must take responsibility for their work; God has made the husband the responsible partner; therefore he must have the ultimate authority.

He has the grace of state. This is a notion that has been lost sight of in the world today, but which is of essential importance in the spiritual life. It comes to this in practice. Where God has appointed someone to decide things for others, those others may securely follow his decisions where they are in accordance with reason and inside the limits of allotted authority; and they may be sure that God's providence will adjust itself (or has adjusted itself, if one prefers to look at it that way) so that in the long run, things work out best as so decided. This is not inspiration, although it often does mean a special help to decide correctly. But it is one way of finding out the will of God, and putting one's part in life in perfect harmony with the rest of His providential symphony.

There is a passion, if one may call it such, prevalent nowadays for managing other people's affairs. It tends to show itself very much in family life. With a reckless assurance and a smug self-sufficiency, men and women "arrange" other people's plans, and order other's lives, without any thought of their own unwarranted interference with the guidance of Providence, or with the individual's personal rights and development. One finds many examples in marriage, where women "manage" their husbands by any or all of the inexhaustible variety of weapons and tactics at their disposal. Commands, browbeating, *faits accomplis*, silence until it is too late to alter plans, public arrangements where protest is impossible, private coldness when consent is refused;—the list is endless.

These are all symptoms of pride and show an ignorance of true spirituality and even of the true functions of a wife.

The true woman rules by submitting; she humbles her husband by the generosity of her love. She strengthens him by her dependence, she builds up his character by throwing responsibility upon him; she is queen of his heart by her love. Now the woman who leaves her throne to do by masculine crudeness and guile what she cannot do by feminine love and tact, admits her own incompetence, and in the modern phrase, "lets herself down," very, very badly. Not only herself, in fact, but also her husband. Not only her husband, but also Christ. For in refusing to be subject to her husband or to be loyal to him, she is also refusing to be subject to Christ or to be loyal to Him. And her plans and achievements of this sort always go wrong in the long run; for she is working against God. The harm done by such a policy is incalculable.

One great difficulty in married life arises from the tendency to measure one another's sacrifices and to try to lessen one's own because of the apparent insufficiency of those of one's partner. Now it is impossible to strike such a balance, because one is trying to equalize different things—one is measuring the reality against the appearance. On one's own side, one has a vivid realization of the interior cost entailed in making the exterior sacrifice. For the other side, however one can only guess the cost, which is often much higher than it seems to be. The result is that the estimate is too low, and one's own actual investment is correspondingly reduced below what is really necessary, which causes corresponding reaction on the other side. One, in fact, is trying to balance the apparent large size of the metal of one's own five-cent piece against the hidden value of the partner's apparently tiny dime.

How different is the ideal of Christian love. *If a man should give all the substance of his house for love, he shall despise it as nothing.*[6] As soon as one starts to count

[6] Cant. viii, 7.

the cost, that is the beginning of the end of love. True love is reckless. Those who are afraid to tell their love lest they be called upon to live it, or lest it be used against them, should take a lesson from the Crucifix. No love has ever been abused as the love of our Lord for us has been. We assume it, we trade upon it, we even allow ourselves to sin because of His mercy. Yet our Lord went to endless suffering in order to try to convince us of His love for us. He even carried the manifestation of His love for us "to death . . . even to the death of the cross."

The ideal is a high one, and the difficulties of married life are far from negligible. To realize this, it is only necessary to remember that every single word or gesture in married life calls up a whole chain of associations, some pleasant, some quite unpleasant; each word may be the last straw in a series of unspoken sufferings, that leads to an outburst altogether out of proportion with the immediate occasion—which is often too ridiculous to be spoken of—and yet which has its real reason in quite considerable anguish of heart. Only the continual grace of God can make such a life successful. Only the grace of God can make it possible for a man or a woman to live, as it were, in front of a mirror, with somebody who knows one in ways better than one knows oneself, who can see through all one's self-deception, and realize all the motives behind one's every action.

Another example is that of the incalculable sacrifice which is necessary to maintain that candor and mutual trust without which marriage is a mockery. It is so easy to use reservations, to evade questions, to use half-truths, and so difficult to have the courage to lose "face" for the moment by candor, for the sake of building up that mutual trust which in the long run is so valuable and so essential to married life. Many marriages fail merely because the husband or the wife begins to suspect the veracity of the other's replies and excuses. Yet no one can deny the difficulty of constant candor. Still the very difficulty of such a life, is a foundation for confidence in its sanctifying power. And sanctified it must be. Marriage is a secret society. Public society is formed by secret societies. And unless such secret societies are formed in Christ, Christ will not be formed in public life.

We have said little about the responsibility of parents to their children. The subject would need a book. Let it suffice to say that all that is done for the child is done for Christ. And it should be evident that one cannot give life, without giving oneself. The seed must die if it is to bear fruit. The truth of that is written in the face of every mother; her self-sacrifice is written large in her eyes.

One final word. There is one thing that must be done in marriage for the child and for each other that is often overlooked. The whole of any man's spiritual life is influenced principally by the idea which he has of God. Now that idea is formed chiefly by the example and model of one's parents' love and kindness, and in later years by the love and kindness of one's partner. No lower standard can be safely set for husband and wife—for father or mother—than to be "another Christ." That is the burden of this whole book, and that is why we insist upon applying all the principles of the spiritual life and allotting the highest of its aims to Christian marriage, for in loving as in being loved, Christ is our perfect supplement and partner. And in marriage, as in all else, we may sum up the essentials of the spiritual life and of union with Christ in five points: faith, hope, charity, humility and generous acceptance of God's will. Thus do we put on Christ, and He is "all in all." So much so, that the ideal of Christian marriage can be stated in St. Augustine's words: *And there shall be one Christ loving Himself.*

CHAPTER 22

Mary, the Mother of the Whole Christ

As Adam and Eve stood by the tree in the Garden of Paradise, having ruined the whole human race by their pride and disobedience, God promised a new Eve and a new Adam, saying to the devil: *I will put enmities between thee and the woman, and thy seed and her seed: she shall crush thy head, and thou shalt lie in wait for her heel.*[1] So too, as the new Adam and the new Eve were together on Calvary, God spoke again and revealed the part of the new Eve in the promised regeneration. But this time, the new Adam was nailed to the tree of the cross; and it was He Himself, both God and Man, who gave utterance to His dying bequest, saying to the new Eve: *Mother, behold thy son,* and to the disciple, St. John, in whose person He addressed the whole human race: *Behold thy Mother.*

This was but the climax on earth of that association of Jesus and Mary in the painful work of Redemption, which first becomes evident in the humble and obedient virgin's consent when the angel Gabriel announced to her that she was to be the Mother of Christ. At the invitation of the fallen angel in Paradise to disobey, Eve, by associating Adam with her in her pride and disobedience, had ruined the life of her children; in Nazareth, at the angel's word, Mary, by her humility and submission accepted her share in her Son's work of restoration and thus commenced to fulfill her vocation as the new Eve and the mother of men. In that scene, as

[1] Gen. iii, 15.

throughout all her life, she sets us an example of faith, hope, charity, humility and abandonment to the will of God.

It is true that in a sense this association with Jesus began even at the very first moment of her own existence, for she was preserved from the stain of original sin, through the forseen merits of her Son. Her sanctity, her merits, her life and her work, were completely dependent upon Christ. She is his perfect work. She is the only one human person who was entirely and ardently subject to God's will. She is the only one human person whose humility never failed for one instant to be perfect. She is the only one human person who never failed to love God with her whole heart and her whole soul, with her whole mind and with her whole strength. She is the only one human person who completely fulfilled God's plan on earth, and whose being and life perfectly corresponded to the idea that God wished to realize in her, so that she could truly say of herself to St. Bernadette: "I am the Immaculate Conception!" For in her was God's conception realized—immaculately!

The angels themselves cannot adequately sing her praises. We can do no more than to say that in Mary, God the Father found a worthy daughter, in her, God the Son found a worthy mother, and in her, God the Holy Ghost found a worthy spouse. If there is any human being who can truly be called "another Christ"—it is Mary, the Mother of Christ. We would even feel justified in saying that of her, more than of all others, it could be said, "that in her there was one Christ loving Himself."

She alone was exempted from the stain of original sin. From the very first moment of her conception she was "full of grace." So much so, that many theologians believe that even then, her initial grace was greater than the final grace of the angels and saints put together. Certain it is that her life on earth gave God more glory than the rest of all creation—her son's human nature alone excepted. So that if all else were lost, it would be no more than a drop of water beside the ocean of grace and glory that Mary represents. She is the Immaculate Conception in every sense of the word, and she alone would mean the success of God's creation. But if we commenced to sing the glories of Mary, we should never finish, save through the despair that comes from complete failure. We must confine ourselves to considering her place in our own lives. There is no better way of summing that up, than by saying that Mary is the Mother of the Whole Christ.

"The Whole Christ" is St. Augustine's phrase for the Mystical Body. "All men are one man in Christ, and the unity of Christians constitutes but one man. . . .[2] And this man is all men and all men are this man; for all are one since Christ is one[3] . . . There is but one man who reaches out unto the end of time.[4] . . . This is the *whole Christ,* Christ united with the Church."[5]

Jesus Christ, as we saw, came on earth in the role of the new Adam to repair the ruin wrought by the old Adam. His method of including us in the fruit of His redemptive work is to make us members of Himself. For us was He born, for us did He die, for us did He sanctify Himself—that we might die in Him, that we might be born in Him, that we might live in holiness in Him. In that work of Redemption God followed a plan which ran in what we might call "parallel opposition" to the plan of the fall. With the new Adam there is associated a new Eve; and as Eve brought death to the whole race in as much as she was their Mother, so Mary, the new Eve, should become our mother in order to give us life. Pope Leo XIII cites in support of this principle, "the unanimous consent of all Christians in every age," even referring it back to the fathers and the apostles.[6] Let us take the official statement of Pope Pius X:

Is not Mary the Mother of Christ? She is therefore our Mother also. All must accept this principle—that Jesus, the Word made flesh, is also the Saviour of the human race. Now, as the God-man, He possesses a human body like other men; but as the restorer of the human race, He has a spiritual or Mystical Body, as it

[2] *In Ps. xxxix,* 2.   [3] *In Ps. cxxix.*
[4] *In Ps. lxxxv.*   [5] *In Ps. xc,* 2.
[6] Rom. xii, 5.

is called, which is the society formed by those who believe in Christ. 'We many are one body in Christ.'[7] But the virgin did not conceive the Son of God solely in order that, by receiving human nature from her, He should become man; but also that, through the nature which He received from her, He should become the Saviour of men. It was for this reason that the angel told the shepherds: 'This day is born to you a Saviour, who is Christ the Lord'.[8] Consequently in this same womb of this most pure mother, Christ both took to Himself flesh and also united to Himself a spiritual body, formed of those who were to believe in Him. Hence Mary bearing the Saviour in her womb, can be said also to have borne all those whose life was contained in the life of the Saviour.

All we, therefore, who are united to Christ, and, as the Apostle says, are members of his body, of his flesh, of his bones,[9] have issued from the womb of Mary as a body united into its head. Hence, albeit in a spiritual and mystical fashion, we are all said to be children of Mary, and she is the Mother of us all. She is our Mother, spiritually indeed, but truly Mother of the members of Christ, which we are.[10]

We are dealing with a mystery, of which we have yet but seen only the beginning; and whose fulness will hardly be revealed till we are one with Christ and His Mother in heaven. Three aspects of this mystery are noted in recent papal documents. First, Mary is our Mother, because she is the Mother of the Head of the Mystical Body, the Mother of Him in whose life our life is contained. But the fact that she gave us Him who is the source of our spiritual life by no means exhausts the mystery.

Secondly, she is our Mother because of her co-operation in the Passion of Christ and of her special association with the work of Redemption. Pope Leo XIII writes: *As she is the Mother of Christ, she is also the Mother of all Christians, since on Calvary, amid the unspeakable*

---

[7] Leo XIII, *Octobri mense*.   [8] Luke ii, 17.
[9] Eph. v, 30.   [10] Pius X, *Ad diem illum.*

sufferings of the Redeemer, she brough them forth.[11]
There stood by the cross Mary His Mother who, moved by an immense love for us, and in order to receive us as sons, herself offered her Son to the divine justice, dying in her heart with Him, pierced by a sword of sorrow.[12]

Thirdly, our Lord Himself solemnly proclaimed and constituted her the Mother of Men as He was dying on the cross. Leo XIII leaves us no room to misunderstand the full significance of our Lord's words: *Mother behold thy Son; Behold thy Mother.* He insists that our Lord addressed St. John as the representative of the whole human race; *In St. John, as the Church has always understood, Christ indicated the person of the human race;*[13] *Christ from the cross bequeathed her and appointed her, as Mother to the human race;*[14] and he presupposes that our Lord is not merely announcing the dignity of Mary, but is giving her a function that is to be continually exercised in the future. He writes:

Mary has not brought forth, and could not bring forth, the children of Christ otherwise than in one faith and in one love; for 'Is Christ divided?'[15] *We are all bound, therefore, to live together the life of Christ, in order that in one and the same body 'we may bring forth fruit to God.'*[16] *It is necessary, therefore, that this same Mother, who has received from God the gift of giving birth to a holy progeny, should again bring forth to Christ as many as have been cut off by unhappy circumstances from this most holy unity. This is undoubtedly a result which she herself most ardently desires, and, on account of the most welcome garland of prayer [scil., the Rosary] which we offer her, she will invoke the help of the 'vivifying Spirit' more abundantly for them.*[17]

These are only, one might say, starting points. The

[11] Leo XIII, *Quamquam pluries*, 1899.
[12] Leo XIII, *Iucunda semper*, 1894.
[13] Leo XIII, *Adiutricem populi*, 1895.
[14] Leo XIII, *Amantissimae voluntatis.*
[15] I Cor. i, 13.
[16] Rom. vii, 4.
[17] Leo XIII, *Adiutricem populi*, 1895.

mystery runs through the whole of history and the whole of the spiritual life, so much so that we are tempted to go back and rewrite the whole of this book in order to give Mary her due place in each of its chapters. It is only in order to avoid confusion that we have reluctantly refrained from indicating her role at all stages of the spiritual life. But this much may be said, that wherever Christ is concerned in the spiritual life, there Mary is also to be found.

The first appearance of our Lady in the Gospel story is in the familiar scene at Nazareth where the angel Gabriel announced to her God's will in her regard. When God's will was made clear to her, there was no hesitation or reservation in her complete abandonment to His designs. *Behold the handmaid of the Lord: be it done to me according to thy word.*[18] To realize the generosity of this consent, we must remember that Mary knew well what it involved. She understood the Scriptures as no one else ever did; she was illumined by grace as no one else has ever been; she knew that the Messias was to be the Man of Sorrows who was to live and die in untold suffering. She knew also that the angel's embassy was to ask for her consent not merely to be the Mother of God, but also to be the Mother of the Redeemer and His Consort in the work of Redemption. Leo XIII tells us that even if Mary were not present at the pillar or in Gethsemani, she had known these sufferings long in advance.

> *For when she as God's handmaid consented to be God's Mother, she did so as consort* [consors] *with Him in His painful expiation for the human race. So that there is no doubt that she shared deeply in the cruel agony and torture of her Son.*[19]

So even then in her fifteenth year, this little maid of Nazareth was filled with a maternal solicitude for the whole human race. St. Thomas gives a further signifi-

[18] Luke i, 38.   [19] Leo XIII, *Iucunda semper.*

cance to her consent; for he sees in the Incarnation a spiritual marriage between the Son of God and human nature, and since marriage needs the consent of both parties, the angel sought the consent of Mary as that of all human nature.[20] She therefore spoke in our name as well as her own. Just as our natural Mother sends us to be baptized into Christ without waiting for our consent, so Mary, our supernatural Mother, pledges us in advance to live the life of Christ by our abandonment to the will of God. Is it not noteworthy that the one precept she gave to men was: *Whatever He shall say to you, do ye*? In fact, its significance can hardly be exaggerated, if we note that she is to give us life as a Mother, and if we remember that, *he that doth the will of God abideth for ever*.[21] That she was only teaching what was her own practice is clear from the extraordinary reply of our Lord to the crowd when He was told that His mother and brethren were seeking Him: *Who*, He exclaimed, *is my mother and brethren! . . . Whosoever shall do the will of God, he is my brother, and my sister, and mother*.[22] For her union with Him by the supernatural abandonment of her will to His was closer and more real than ever was her natural union with Him as His Mother.

We cannot here enter into the details of our Lady's life. She only appears at certain critical moments in the life of her Son. It is on Calvary that we would consider her, standing beside the cross, where, in the words of Benedict XV:

She suffered with her suffering Son, and almost died together with Him, and abdicating her maternal rights over her Son, she, in so far as was in her power, immolated Him for the human race, that justice might be satisfied, so that it may truly be said that she with Christ redeemed mankind.[23]

Recent popes have all indicated this close association

[20] *Summa* i, 26, 6, ad 4.   [21] I John ii, 17.
[22] Cf. Mark iii, 33, 35.   [23] Benedict XV, *Inter Sodalicia*.

between Jesus and Mary in the work of redemption and meriting grace for, as Pius X tells us:

> *Since Mary surpasses all in holiness and in union with Christ and has been taken into partnership* [adscita] *by Christ in the work of human redemption. She merits "de congruo," in the language of theologians, what Jesus merited for us "de condigno," and she is the supreme minister of the distribution of graces. By this communion of sorrows and of will between Mary and Christ, she merited that she should be a most worthy reparatrix of the fallen world and therefore the dispensatrix of all that Jesus won for us by His Blood and by His Death.*[24]

Thelogians are still discussing Mary's share in the Redemption. The title co-redemptrix has been applied to her, and she has a perfect right to it; but the title must not be misunderstood. It does not imply that Christ's work of Redemption was incomplete, or that there is a single part of the whole plan of Redemption that does not depend upon Him. Even the act by which we enter into our share of His grace, depends upon a grace coming from Him. The title means that God freely and without any necessity decided to associate Mary in the Redemption so that she should share in the glory of it. But every single act by which she co-operated drew all its value from the merits of Christ the Redeemer, and was vivified by His grace. Independently of Christ, Mary could contribute nothing to the Redemption. Everything she did was done through Christ, with Christ, and in Christ, in the unity of the Holy Spirit. In no one is the life of the Mystical Body of Christ so complete and so perfect.

Because of the fear of seeming to derogate in any way from Christ's position as Redeemer, there is as yet a

---

[24] Pius X, *Ad diem illum.*

Note: There is a difference between merit *de condigno* and merit *de congruo.* The former is based on justice and presupposes some equality between the work and the reward, or some promise by God; the second is rather a claim in equity, based on God's goodness; there is no question of strict justice. A soldier merits his pay *de condigno,* but has a claim to a D.S.C. only *de congruo.*

certain hesitation, and even difficulty, in formulating Mary's part in His work. One thing may be said. Apart from her own redemption, Mary has a role to play in all the rest of the work, so that no grace comes to us without her co-operation. Leo XIII writes:

> *She, who has been assigned so important a part in the mystery of man's redemption, was destined likewise to hold the same important place in the application of graces thus merited, there being vested in her a power almost boundless.*[25]

And the Holy Father selects from the titles *most rightly given to her*, the following: *Our Lady (Domina); Our Mediatrix; The Redemptress (Reparatrix) of the whole world; She who obtains for us the gifts of God.*[26]

Elsewhere Leo XIII makes his own the principle announced by St. Bernard that God willed us to obtain all through Mary; and, noting the fact that her consent to the Incarnation was given in the person of the whole human race, with which Christ was entering into a spiritual marriage, he continues:

> *From which one may no less truly and properly affirm that nothing whatever of that immense treasure of grace which the Lord produced . . . nothing is given to us except through Mary, for such is the will of God. And just as no one can come to the Supreme Father, except through the Son, so almost no one can come to Christ except through Mary.*[27]

The Holy Father makes his own the words of St. Bernardine of Siena:

> *Every grace which is given to this world comes by a threefold way. For it is given by God to Christ, by Christ to the Virgin, by the Virgin to us, in an ordered dispensation.*[28]

And he makes the strong statement:

[25] Leo XIII, *Adiutricem populi.*   [26] Ibid.
[27] Leo XIII, *Octobri mense.*   [28] Leo XIII, *Iucunda semper.*

*In her hands are the treasures of the Lord's mercies, for
God willed that she should be a source* [principuim] *of all
goods.*[29] . . . *For God willed us to have all through Mary.*[30]

We have quoted at length from these papal documents to avoid seeming to base our notions on the enthusiasm of piety or on sentiment. Compared with what some
of the fathers and doctors of the Church say, what we
have quoted above could be called understatements. It
it clear that the beginning of the formation of the Mystical Body was an intimate union between Christ and
Mary, in such a way that for its further development,
they formed, as it were, one principle, she always in
complete dependence upon Him. Medieval piety tried
to illustrate this fact by comparing Mary's part to that of
the neck of the body, joining it to its Head, from which
it was then thought all life and energy came. The metaphor, however, has not proved popular, nor does it seem
sufficient. For just as each action of any member of the
Body depends on Christ, for its initiation as well as for
its performance, so also, though not in the same way, it
depends on Mary. Every single member, therefore, must
be in vital contact with Mary. Mary's role is best described by calling her the mother of the Mystical Body,
even though she herself is its most important member.

There is a very close parallel between Mary's part
in the formation of the human body of Christ, and her
part in the formation of the Mystical Body of the "Whole
Christ." The human body is formed from the fruits of
the earth and the flesh of its animal inhabitants, from all
that can be regarded as food and drink. For the first nine
months of Christ's human existence, it was Mary's function to take these elements of food in the natural state,
prepare them as food, and, then consuming them, to
change them into her own flesh and blood, and thus
to minister them to the embryonic Christ, by whose
soul's action they were transformed into His own Flesh
and Blood. And even after that intimate physical union

[29] Leo XIII, *Diuturni temporis.*   [30] Leo XIII, *Iucunda semper.*

between Christ and His Mother had been severed by the birth of Christ, He still remained for a time dependent upon her very substance for His nourishment. When His growth as a child gave Him a fuller independence of His Mother, it was still her hands that transformed the raw materials and prepared His food, and cared for His growing body.

So it is with His mystical Body. The aim which Pope Pius X set himself at the beginning of his pontificate was *to re-establish all things in Christ, so that Christ should be all and in all.*[31] Shortly afterwards he set devotion to our Lady before the faithful, as a means to this end; and he writes:

For, there is no more certain and steady way of uniting all to Christ and of reaching that perfect adoption of sons so that we should be holy and immaculate in the sight of God, than by Mary. . . . For since it is the will of divine providence that we should have the God-Man through Mary, there is no other way for us but to receive Christ from her Hands.

And stressing the communion of will and of life that bound Mary to Christ, he continues:

There is no one more capable of joining men with Christ.[32]

Just as the fruits and animals of the earth are the food of the human body of Christ, so ourselves, our lives, and our actions, are the food of the Mystical Body. And just as the food of the human body of Christ was prepared by Mary, and made her own before becoming part of His body, so we ourselves, with out lives and our actions have to be prepared by Mary, and in some mysterious way made hers, in order to become members of the Mystical Body of Christ. There is, however, a great difference between the natural and physical order to which pertains the formation of the human body of

[31] Cf. Eph. i, 10; Col. iii, 11.   [32] Pius X, *Ad diem illum.*

Christ, and the supernatural and spiritual order to which belongs the formation of His Mystical Body. The manner of action is quite different and the duration is of an entirely new sort. When food is eaten in the natural order it is soon disposed of once and for all, and what is really nourishment in it is more or less permanently incorporated in those who consume it. Our incorporation in Christ is not permanent, in as much as it can be destroyed by the sin of infidelity; nor does our membership of His Body ensure that all our actions belong to Him as they should. This perfect incorporation of ourselves in Christ, even though it begins and is—in one sense—complete at baptism, is not fully perfected until the end of our mortal life. It is the work of a lifetime. Each single action has to be molded according to God's will and handed over to Christ.

Thus Mary has a continual part to play in our lives; and our relation with Mary is not sharply divided into the three stages of dependence that we indicated above. Her spiritual operations in our supernatural life, which correspond respectively to her co-operation in the embryonic, the infant, and the more developed stages of our Lord's human life, are performed both simultaneously and continuously where a member of His Mystical Body is concerned. In fact in all stages of the spiritual life, we are, in a measure, just as spiritually dependent upon Mary, as the divine Child in her womb was naturally dependent on her for the growth of His natural life. There are of course many services that Mary renders us that are better illustrated by what we may call her "housekeeping" activities. But they must never blind us to the infant-like —in fact, the embryo-like—dependence that binds us to our spiritual Mother.

We and our lives are the food of Christ's Mystical Body. But we are free agents. And our full co-operation is necessary for complete union with Christ. If one may be bold enough to summarize the lesson of a pope's encyclical, we would say that the lesson that Pius X teaches us, is: "That true devotion to Christ demands true devotion to Mary." And there is no better exponent of true devotion to Mary than Bl. Grignon de Montfort, whose canonization, we understand, is already (1945) assured. This true devotion to Mary consists firstly, in a complete and permanent consecration to her of all that one is, or has, or will be, or will have, in the natural and in the supernatural order, in time and in eternity; and secondly, in living in habitual and entire dependence on Mary by complete and cheerful abandonment to her maternal care. In this way we belong completely to her. She can dispose of the value of all our acts, our satisfactions, and our prayers, of all our spiritual and temporal treasures, even the prayers that are said for us; she can apply all to whom she will. She can use our prayers as she likes; for although we still express our "intentions," it is always with the understood condition that she may change each intention to her own. She may influence God's providence to do what she wishes with us; we are completely in her hands. We are all hers, and all ours is hers. What then is there to prevent her making us completely Christ's? Is not this consecration the perfect co-operation in her maternal office of uniting all things in Christ? Is not this the short cut to sanctity? Bl. Grignon's two little books will give the reader a fuller account of this devotion.[33] He promises us that "She will make our souls live for Jesus Christ, and Jesus Christ live in us."

But let us be clear that this promise is not attached to a mere passing act, such as the recitation of a formula. It requires a life of complete abandonment to Mary, and through her, to Christ. She herself has given us an example. For at every moment of her life, we find in her the perfection of faith, hope, charity, humility and abandonment to God's will. In that we have only to imitate her. And there is nothing in the life of Mary that in some measure we cannot imitate. We hear of no miracles, or of no extraordinary penances, in her life. Her external

[33] Bl. Grignon de Montfort, *True Devotion to the Blessed Virgin* and *The Secret of Mary*.

life can be summed up in three words: "Ordinary, obscure, and laborious." But her interior life is something that only God can know. For even that most intimate union of body and life that preceded the birth of Christ, was only a shadow of the complete union of heart and soul, which persisted throughout every moment of Mary's existence. From the very beginning of her consciousness —even, some say, from the very first moment of her conception—she gave herself completely, with every fiber of her being, to God, cleaving to Him in an utter abandonment of love and humility that cannot be conceived.

Mary then is our Mother—not merely in name or in sentiment, but in actual reality. In fact her motherhood of us in the spiritual order is something more real than the natural motherhood which gave us our human life. Devotion to Mary, then, is an integral part of Christianity, and essential for the spiritual life. It is not a question of a side chapel devotion which may be omitted at pleasure, and which is only something ornamental or, at best, just helpful for our spiritual life. It is an integral, one could almost say essential, part of true devotion to Christ.

Modern theology tends to divide her motherhood of the whole Christ, into two stages. The first concerns her share in the acquisition of grace, and in this respect, with certain reservations, she is called the co-redemptrix. The other concerns her part in the distribution of grace, and in this regard she is called the dispensatrix and mediatrix of all graces. Neither of these offices have yet been the subject of a solemn declaration of the Church. The doctrine, however, of the universal mediation of Mary, insofar as it implies that no grace is given to us without the intercession of Mary, is *proxima fidei*. That she is our spiritual mother, is *de fide*. It must be clearly understood that in making her thus a partner in the acquisition and distribution of the fruits of the Redemption, God was yielding to no necessity, for Christ is a sufficient and perfect Redeemer and Mediator. But he wished in the liberality of His Mercy to make Mary the associate of His Son, so that she might share in His glory and joy in Heaven. It was the perfection of her loving abandonment and faith-inspired humility that made it possible that a creature should be given such an amazing share in the divine work of restoration without any risk of injury to God's plan or detraction from His glory.

For us, too, a similar principle holds good. God wills to make us share in the work of our own salvation and to co-operate in the salvation of others. In fact, Christ Himself wills to share all His work with us; and so does Mary, the Mother of Christ. Since the first motive of all that work is the glory of God, humility is the first condition of our admittance into a share of it. The rest of our part consists in the loving performance and acceptance of God's will. This, too, is the very means by Christ to share in the Maternity of Mary: *Whosoever shall do the will of God, he is . . . my mother!* [34] By doing the will of God in humble love in the ordinary things of life we bring forth Christ in ourselves, and, through the Communion of Saints, in others also. The very acts which unite us to Christ, unite us to His Mother, and make us share in the work of each of them. As St. Augustine writes: "Every faithful soul doing the will of the Father with a most fruitful charity is mother to Christ, in those whom he quickens until Christ is formed in them." [35] If with St. Paul we can say we fill up those things that are wanting of the sufferings of Christ for His Body, the Church, so also we can say we fill up those things that are wanting of the sufferings of Mary for the Body of her Child, which is the Church. We are called to live in a close union of will and life and function with both Jesus and Mary. And the closer we keep to Mary, the closer we shall be to Christ.

There is nothing extraordinary required of us in external works. Our Lady is the perfect model of the Christian. But what a rebuke to our notions and to our standards! She had the best equipped mind that ever

[34] Cf. Mark iii, 35.   [35] *De sancta virginitate*, 5.

lived in Christendom. She was enlightened as no prophet
ever had been enlightened. She had a power of intercession of which no one can determine the limit. She had
a zeal for her Son's glory and for her Son's work, that
burned more fiercely than the zeal of all the great souls
of the Church. Yet what was her life? Ordinary—obscure
—laborious! The wife of a village carpenter, she takes
care to lose herself in the crowd. The Mother of the
far-famed Messiah, she appears but once in His public
life, between Cana and the Passion. The most enlightened and zealous member of His Church, she is invisible
to our eyes from the day of Pentecost. She gives but one
message to men in words, and preaches a lifelong sermon in obscurity and silence. All her desires seem to
have centered on her own effacement. Even the active
work of preaching Christ and teaching His doctrine she
left to others, although tradition has it that the disciples
found in her a gentle instructress and calm inspiration
for their ministry. There would be much more holiness,
as there would also be much more happiness, in the
world, if her Christian sons and, especially, her Christian
daughters, were to imitate her example.

It is just as impossible to come to an end of treating
of Mary as it is impossible to treat of her adequately.
We have relied principally upon papal documents for
our presentation of her place in God's sphere of things
and her claim upon our devotion. If we might presume
to state our own view, we would do so, not by appealing to Scripture or to the writings of the fathers and the
doctors of the Church, but, at the risk of scandalizing
the sober, by summoning to our aid the services of those
"inspired" men (for of course they must have been
inspired!) who wrote fairy-tales. For there is no fairy-
tale so improbable or so far-fetched as the truth; and,
while to those to whom the spiritual life seems a drab,
dreary, impossible burden, we would suggest the story
of *Beauty and the Beast*, while begging Christ's pardon
for any implication that the title may seem to contain,
to the others we would say if you would know the truth,

read *Cinderella!* For if there was ever a "Prince Charming," it is the Son of God come upon earth to seek His bride. And if there was ever a fairy god-mother who can and will make a fitting bride for Him out of the ragged kitchenmaid that we are—is it not Mary, the fairy god-mother of the whole Christ?

For that is what we must confidently expect from Mary, that she will transform us into a fitting bride for Christ. Let us never forget that she understands better than anyone else that what she does to us is done to her Son. Let no one then say he is too befouled by sin to go to Mary, Was any child ever too dirty for its mother to wash it? And if that child were Christ—and we are Christ in her eyes—and if that mother be Mary, is there any filth of sin which would deter her from joyfully cleansing the dirt and foulness with which we have befouled the Body of Christ? Nor need we be afraid that her immaculate purity will make her repel us. She is the Refuge of Sinners; and despite her purity, or perhaps because of it, she has a wonderful understanding and sympathy for the weakness of human nature. She is the Mother of Fair Love, and will give us a love of her Son that will more than atone for any sin. She might be called the throne of grace to whom we must go with absolute confidence. It is impossible to have too much confidence in Mary. The Church applies to her, the words of Scripture: *I was with him forming all things. . . . He that shall find me shall find life and shall have salvation from the Lord.*[36]

She is the *Mater Admirabilis*—the fairy god-mother, who will make us worthy brides of the Eternal Prince, the Son of God, to whom we are to be so closely united in the Mystical Body that "there shall be one Christ loving Himself."

[36] Prov. viii, 30, 35.

Christ Our Tremendous Lover

T HE whole plan of our Lord's life and the whole manner of His death are designed to show forth His love for men. Through love He became man for us, through love He worked for us, through love He lived for us, through love He suffered for us, and through love He died for us. With St. Paul, each of us can say: *He loved me and delivered himself for me.*[1] The whole plan of our spiritual life is a loving union and intimate partnership with Jesus in which we return Him love for love. We can picture that union in three ways: as the life of Christ in us; as our life in Christ; or as what we might call a "shoulder to shoulder" partnership with Jesus, a constant companionship of two lovers sharing every thought and every deed. Each of these pictures corresponds to a true aspect of the reality, the intimacy of which is so extraordinary that it defies description.

In this book we have started with the organic unity of the Mystical Body into which men are incorporated at baptism. We have considered the spiritual life as a development of that union and a removal of the obstacles to perfect harmony and unity caused by our self-love and self-centeredness. At the same time we had no hesitation in describing the spiritual life as a quest for God —for Jesus—regarded for the moment as apart from oneself; and there is no real contradiction in doing so. What we wished to emphasize is that there is no

[1] Cf. Gal. ii, 20.

intimacy or perfection of union between ourselves and our beloved that is not open to every soul. For love demands union, and only seeks the beloved to become one with Him. The very sacrament of Holy Communion is a pledge not only of the possibility of such union but even of our Lord's burning desire to effect it to an undreamt of degree. *Eye hath not seen, nor ear heard, nor hath it entered into the heart of man, what things God hath prepared for them that love Him.*[2] To stress the possibility of that union, we showed that it commenced even in baptism; and we have insisted throughout this book that the summit of sanctity, as Pius XI declared, is open to every Christian, and that nothing extraordinary is required to achieve it, contrary to what is often thought; for the essential points of the spiritual life which are necessary for every Christian, and which will suffice to make a saint are: faith, hope, charity, humility, and generous co-operation with and abandonment to the will of God.

Our Lord has left nothing undone to make that achievement *easy.* We have His own word for it, and surely we can take God at His word! *Come to me, all you that labor, and are burdened and I will refresh you. Take my yoke upon you, and learn of me because I am meek and humble of heart: and you shall find rest for your souls. For my yoke is sweet and my burden light."*[3]

As we have seen, He has lived our life for us. He has taken our sins and weakness upon Himself and blotted them out by the Cross. He has given us His own merits, His own life, His own strength, His very self. He has given us His own Mother that she might unite us to Him. He has forseen all the details of all our life and provided for every single one of them. To take but one example, He has provided for the happiness and the holiness of marriage, that great triumph of the commonplace, by first of all giving us an example—for He entered into a marriage with His Church, and loved Her and delivered Himself for Her—and then has given us Him-

[2] I Cor. ii, 9.   [3] Matt. xi, 28–30.

self in the sacraments that we might have the strength
and the means to imitate that example, for He is in each
partner to love and to be loved. He loved us and delivered
Himself for us; He has commanded us to love one another
as He has loved us, and then in the Blessed Sacrament
He gives Himself to us, daily if we will, with His own
power of loving so that we might fulfil His commandment. More than that, He has invented an eighth "sacrament"—one might say—in as much as He so identifies
Himself with our neighbor that not only is He in us to
love, but He is in our neighbor to be loved, for whatever
is done to the neighbor is done to Christ. Perhaps we
may now glimpse some shadow of the hidden meaning
in the extraordinary phrase of St. Augustine: *There shall
be one Christ loving Himself.*[4]

He has given us an example of complete devotion to
God His Father in adoration and love. He has sacrificed
Himself that the Father might receive a perfect sacrifice
of praise and thanksgiving, of adoration and satisfaction,
of atonement and impetration. He has made that sacrifice
ours for our daily use in the Mass. He offers us with
Himself in the Mass in a complete surrender of devotion
to God the Father, and then in the Communion of the
same Mass, He gives Himself in a complete surrender to
us, so that we may be able to live the Mass, and carry
out what we have promised. In the Mass He puts the
fruit of His whole life at our disposal; His adoration and
thanksgiving, His praise and satisfaction, His atonement
and impetration, are ours without limit, so that we may
walk with Him before God and be perfect. The more we
give ourselves to Him in the Mass, the more He gives
Himself to us in Holy Communion.

In giving Himself to us, He gives us His Holy Spirit
to dwell in our souls, as a permanent friend and source
of strength and light—as the soul, one might say, of
our soul—so that we might be completely one with Himself living in the unity of the same Holy Spirit. He has
made the whole spiritual life a partnership with Himself,

[4] *Epistola ad Parthos.* 70.

making us part of Himself, and reduced our share in the work of the partnership to a minimum. In fact, to repeat Father Clerissac's words: "It is our emptiness and trust that He needs, not our plenitude."[5] All He asks is that we put our faith and hope in Him, that we love Him with our whole heart, that we renounce our own pretended strength and our foolish plans by humility and abandonment; He will do the rest.

Truly He can say to us in gentle reproach: *What is there that I ought to do more for my vineyard, that I have not done to it? Was it that I looked that it should bring forth grapes and it hath brought forth wild grapes?*[6] There is a tragic note in His reproach; for it was for the sake of our happiness, rather than His own, that He loved us. He knew that He alone could make us happy. He knew the secret longings of our hearts better than we ourselves. He knew that to be without Him would be a grievous hell, to be with Him sweet paradise. He knew, too, that many souls would never understand the fearful suffering which eternal separation from Him would cause, and in showing to them the lesser sufferings of the fires of Hell, He hopes to deter them from ruining their eternal happiness, even though He sees the danger that they may regard Him rather as an angry and stern judge than as their ardent and merciful lover—as some one to be dreaded rather than to be desired.

Yet all that was not enough. During the centuries He has shown to some of His favorite friends that symbol of His love that we now know as the Sacred Heart. The Cistercian nuns, St. Gertrude and St. Mechtilde, have told us of the wonders of His love. But less than three hundred years ago, He came to His loving servant, St. Margaret Mary—and as Pius XI tells us in his encyclical on the Sacred Heart:[7]

Though He insisted on the immensity of His love, at the

[5] J. Clerissac, O.P., *Mystery of the Church.* Introd., p. xxvi.
[6] Isaias v, 4.   [7] Cf. A.A.S., I, vi, 28.

same time, with sorrowful mien, He grieved over the great number of horrible outrages heaped on Him by the ingratitude of mankind. He used the words—words which should be graven on the hearts of all pious souls so as never to be forgotten by them: "Behold this Heart, which has loved men so much, and has loaded them with every favor; and for this boundless love has had not merely no return of gratitude, but, on the contrary, forgetfulness, neglect, contumely, and that, at times, at the hands of those who were bound by the debt and duty of a special love."[8]

Elsewhere we read the further complaints made to St. Margaret Mary by our Lord: *If thou didst but know how I thirst to be loved by men, thou wouldst spare nothing that this might be accomplished. I thirst, I burn with the desire of being loved. Behold this Heart which has so loved men that it has spared nothing to testify its love for them, even to exhausting and consuming itself.* And telling her of the ingratitude and forgetfulness that has been the return He received for the extremes to which He had carried His love, He continues: *and this I felt more acutely than all I suffered in My Passion, in so much that if they rendered Me some return of love, I should esteem all that I have done for them as but little, and would do, if it were possible, more for them. But they have nothing but coldness and rebuffs for all My eagerness to do them good.* Is not this an echo of the tearful plaint over Jerusalem, *If thou hadst known. . . . And thou wouldst not!*

It is significant that this revelation of His desire to be loved and of His plan to use St. Margaret Mary as the means of spreading the devotion of love of the Sacred Heart, was accompanied by a mutual exchange of hearts, wherein He substituted His own Heart for that of the Saint. He first explained to her: *My divine Heart is so inflamed with love for men, and for you in particular, that not being able any longer to restrain within Itself the flames of ardent charity, it must spread them everywhere, through your means, and manifest itself to men*

[8] Pius XI, *Miserentissimus Redemptor.*

that they may be enriched with its precious fullness.
He then exchanged hearts with the saint and explained
that His Heart would supply for all she lacked, even
to the extent of giving her the power to offer Him the
reparation of love for which He thirsted. His reply to
her objection is enlightening. "But, O Lord," exclaimed
St. Margaret, "why dost Thou address Thyself to so
miserable a creature, to so poor a sinner, that by her
unworthiness she is calculated to hinder the accomplishment of Thy designs, when Thou hast so many generous
souls to execute Thy desires?" He replied: *Dost thou not
know that I make use of the weakest subjects to confound
the strong!—that it is generally in the most insignificant
and the poor in spirit that I manifest My power, in order
that they may attribute nothing to themselves?* [9]

These are but private revelations. But the devotion
they indicate has the authority of the Church, and Pope
Pius XI quoted in his encyclical the first words given
above. We have added, without attending to their order
or their exact authenticity, other expressions recorded
by the saint. Their value lies in the fact that they sum
up in an expressive way the whole Christian tradition.
The last reply above is an echo of St. Paul:

*But the foolish things of the world hath God chosen, that
he may confound the wise; and the weak things of this
world hath God chosen, that he may confound the strong.
And the base things of the world, and the things that are
contemptible, hath God chosen, and the things that are not,
that he might bring to naught the things that are: that no
flesh should glory in his sight. But of him, are you in Christ
Jesus, who of God is made unto us wisdom, and justice, and
sanctification and redemption, that, as it is written: He that
glorieth, may glory in the Lord.* [10]

In the encyclical which we have quoted, Pope Pius
XI lays down certain principles that are of great importance in our spiritual life, and are closely concerned with

[9] Cf. Bainvel, *Devotion to the Sacred Heart.*
[10] I Cor. i, 27–31.

what we have written in earlier chapters. The first is the principle of solidarity, by which our good works and sufferings are of avail for our fellow men.

A wondrous bond joins all the faithful to Christ, the same bond which unites the Hand with the other members of the Body, namely, the communion of saints, a bond full of mystery which we believe in as Catholics and by virtue of which, individuals and nations are not only united to one another, but likewise with the head itself, "who is Christ, from whom the whole body being compacted and fitly joined together, by what every joint supplieth, according to the operation in the measure of every part, maketh increase of the body, unto the edifying of itself in charity." [11] *Thus, too, was the prayer of which Jesus Christ Himself, the Mediator between God and men, at the hour of His death, made to the Father, "I in them and Thou in Me: that they may be made perfect in one."* [12] *As an act of consecration proclaims and confirms our union with Christ, so the act of expiation, by purifying us from our sins, is the beginning of such union; our participation in the sufferings of Christ perfects it, the offering we make to Him of our sacrifices for the welfare of our brethren brings such union to its final consummation.* [13]

The second relates to the influence which our deeds can have on the sufferings of Christ. The pope faces the question: *How can we believe that Christ reigns happily in heaven if it is possible to console Him by such acts as those of reparation?* He answers in the language of St. Augustine: *The soul which truly loves, will comprehend what I say.* And he points out that Christ was *bruised for our sins, . . .* so that:

Even sins committed now would be able of themselves to cause Christ to die a death accompanied by the same sufferings and agonies as His death on the Cross, since every sin must be said to renew in a certain way the Passion of our Lord, "crucifying again to themselves the Son of Man and

[11] Eph. v, 15–16.   [12] John xvii, 23.
[13] *Miserentissimus Redemptor.*

making Him a mockery." [14] *And if, in view of our own future sins, forseen by Him, the Soul of Jesus became sad even unto death, there can be no doubt that by His pre-vision at the same time of our acts of reparation He was in some way comforted when "there appeared to Him an angel from Heaven" to console that Heart of His, bowed down with sorrow and anguish.*

At the present time, we too, in a marvellous but no less true manner, may and ought to console that Sacred Heart which is being wounded continually by the sins of thoughtless men, since Christ Himself grieved over the fact that He was abandoned by His friends. For He said, in the words of the Psalmist: [15] *"My Heart hath expected reproach and misery. And I looked for one that would grieve together with Me, but there was none: and for one that would comfort Me and I found none."*

There is, then, no mere empty sentimentality in the notion of giving Jesus consolation and of living in close companionship with Him. If we ask what is the essential note of the reparation which Jesus asks for in setting the agonies of His Heart before us, we can find an answer to that, also in papal documents. Pius IX extended the feast of the Sacred Heart to the whole world, *to provide the faithful with an incitement to love and to repay with love the Heart of Him who had loved us and washed our sins away in His blood.* Leo XIII in the encyclical of 28th June, 1898, writes: *Jesus has no more ardent desire than to see enkindled in souls the fire of love with which His own Heart is consumed. Let us go then to Him who asks from us as the reward of His charity nothing but a return of love.* This is the burden of the whole encyclical, and all the papal documents center around this interpretation of the words of our Lord which they so often quote: *I came to cast fire upon the earth, and what will I save that it be enkindled?* [16]

To show how ancient is this doctrine of the personal love of Jesus, let us read the words which in the fourth century St. John Chrysostom put on the lips of our Lord:

[14] Heb. vi, 6.   [15] Ps. lxviii, 21.   [16] Cf. Luke xii, 49.

"It is not only in this way that I manifest My love, but also by My Passion. For thee, I was covered with spittle and buffeted, I stripped Myself of My glory, I left My Father and came to thee, to thee who didst hate Me, who didst flee Me, who didst not even wish to hear My name. I followed thee, I ran after thee; I caught hold of thee, and embraced thee. 'Eat Me,' I said, 'and drink Me.' It is not enough that I should possess thy first-fruits [a physical body like that of men] in heaven: that does not satisfy My love. I come once more to the earth, not only to 'mingle' Myself with thee, but to entwine Myself in thee. I am eaten, I am broken into pieces, in order that this fushion, this union, may be more intimate. When other things are united each remains distinct in itself; but I weave Myself into thee. *I want nothing to come between us: I wish the two to become one.*"[17]

That quotation alone justifies the title of this book, for God is indeed a tremendous lover. It also indicates the antiquity of a doctrine that reaches down to our day when St. Thérèse of Lisieux would exclaim: "For love is only repaid by love . . . it is love alone that counts!"

If we were to quote fully St. Bernard on this subject we should have to republish half of his works, for it is his constant theme. Two quotations must suffice: "You ask me," he writes, "for what reason and in what method or measure God should be loved. I reply: The reason for loving God is God: the method and measure is to love Him without method or measure."[18] And elsewhere he continues: "It is by this conformity of charity, that the soul is wedded to the Word, when, namely, loving even as she is loved, she exhibits herself in her will conformed to Him to whom she is already conformed in her nature. Therefore if she loves Him perfectly she has become His bride. What can be more sweet than such a conformity! What can be more admirable than this charity by which . . . thou art enabled to draw thyself nigh with confidence to the Word, to cleave to Him steadfastly, to interrogate Him familiarly,

[17] St. John Chrysostom, *In I Tim.* Hom, 15.
[18] St. Bernard, *On the Love of God,* 1.

to consult Him in all thy doubts, as audacious in thy desires as thou art capacious in thy understanding. This is in truth the alliance of a holy and spiritual marriage. But, it is saying too little to call it an alliance; it is rather an embrace. Surely we have then a spiritual embrace when the same likes and dislikes make one spirit out of two? Nor is there any occasion to fear lest the inequality of persons should cause some defect in the harmony of wills, since love knows nothing of reverence. Love means an exercise of affection, not an exhibition of honor. Honor is given by him who is awe stricken, who is astounded, who is terrified, who is filled with admiration. But none of these emotions has any place in the lover. Love is all sufficient for itself.

"Whithersoever love comes, it subjugates and renders captive to itself all the other affections. Consequently, the soul that loves, simply loves and knows nothing else except to love. The Word indeed is one who deserves to be honored, who deserves to be admired and wondered at; yet He is better pleased to be loved. For 'He is the bridegroom and the soul is His bride. And between a bridegroom and his bride what other relation or connection would you look for, except the bond of a mutual love? Such is the strength of this bond that it overcomes even the most intimate union which nature forms, I mean the union between parent and child. So much is evident from the words of the Saviour: *For this cause shall a man leave father and mother, and shall cleave to his wife.* You perceive how love, as it is found between bridegroom and bride, is not only more powerful than the other human affections, but it is even more powerful than love itself. It must be also remembered that this bridegroom is not only loving but is love itself. . . . God requires to be honored as a Father, and to be feared as a Lord, but to be loved as a bridegroom. . . . But, fear is slavish until it hath been emancipated by love. And the honor which proceeds not from love better deserves to be called flattery than honor. To God alone are due honor and glory; *but God will refuse to accept both the one and the other unless they are sweetened with the honey of love.*

"Love is sufficient of itself, it pleases of itself, and for its own sake. It counts as merit to itself and is its own reward. Besides itself love requires no motive and seeks no fruit. Its fruit is the enjoyment of itself. I love because I love, and I love for the sake of loving. . . . When God loves me He deserves nothing else than to be loved by me; He loves me in order that I may love Him, because He knows well that all who love Him find in this very love their joy and happiness. The love that is pure is never mercenary. Pure love derives none of its strength from hope, and yet suffers nothing from diffidence." [For, as the great Cistercian writes in *On the Love of God*: How should the soul that loves God seek any other reward of her love save God! If she seeketh any other, she assuredly loves that, not God."].

"This pure love is a love proper to the spouse and she that is a spouse is made a spouse solely by this. Love is the sole dowry and the sole hope of a spouse. This is all sufficing for her. With this alone the bridegroom is content. He requireth nothing else and she possesses nothing else. It is such a love as this that makes Him her bridegroom as it makes her His bride. . . . Let her then who is so beloved by Him, be careful to reciprocate His love. . . . If she loves with her whole being, her love is perfect and wanting in nothing. Wherefore . . . it is love of this kind that constitutes the spiritual marriage of the soul with the Word. . . . This spiritual embrace is nothing else than a chaste and holy love, a love sweet and pleasant, a love perfectly serene and perfectly pure, a love that is intimate, and strong, a love that joins two, not in one flesh, but in one spirit, that makes two to be no longer two but one undivided spirit, according to the testimony of St. Paul, where he says: *He who is joined to the Lord is one spirit.*" [19]

We could not resist giving this long quotation from

[19] St. Bernard, *Sermon on the Cant. lxxxiii.* Translation by Fr. Ailbe Luddy, O.C.R.

St. Bernard. Coming as it does from the Cistercian Abbot who dominated Europe in the first half of the twelfth century, and whose achievements and influence almost form the European history of his time, this passionate appeal for love, and for love alone, is all the more impressive. It was not a lack of good works or of achievement, a mere empty sentimentality, that dictated these words: "the bridegroom who is in love requires of His spouse nothing more than a return of love and loyalty." But the life of every saint manifests the same truth. God wants our hearts; nothing else will satisfy Him unless it come from our love. He said so Himself: *Thou shalt love the Lord thy God with thy whole heart and with thy whole soul and with thy whole strength. And these words which I command thee this day, shall be in thy heart, and thou shalt teach them to thy children, and thou shalt meditate upon them sitting in thy house, and walking on thy journey, sleeping and rising.*[20] And our Lord quoted this commandment, and added the completion of it—for it is the same love that is in question—*Thou shalt love thy neighbor as thyself.* And then He said: *On these two commandments dependeth the whole law and prophets.*[21] And He sums it up by the mouth of St. Paul: *Love therefore is the fulfilling of the Law.*[22]

Our Lord's appeal for love in the manifestation of His Sacred Heart is, as He said to St. Margaret Mary, "a last effort of His love." The results of the heresy of Jansenism, had injured the devotional life of many souls. Under the guise of a greater fervor, a more correct honoring of God, and a more genuine estimation of men's wickedness, this infection had separated men from God, had kept them from Holy Communion, and had turned them away from that tender, personal love of Jesus, which was the soul of the spirituality of the Middle Ages. Our Lord's revelation of his Sacred Heart came as an opportune means of combating this pernicious disease, of which not all the effects have yet disappeared. Whatever be the cause, there is still in the minds of many an incorrect idea of the relations which God would have exist between

[20] Deut. vi. 5–7.   [21] Cf. Matt. xxii, 37–40.   [22] Cf. Rom. xiii, 10.

Him and ourselves. The Blessed Sacrament of the Altar should be an eloquent testimony, as well as a powerful aid, to the intimacy of union that He longs to have with us. The passages we have quoted show the Christian tradition in this matter. And the whole teaching of St. Paul, proclaiming the unity of nature, of strength, and of spirit that is the beginning and the root of the life of every Catholic, makes clear the possibility of giving God a return of the love He so ardently desires.

For the love by which we love God is given to us by God Himself. It is in fact a special effect produced in us by the presence in our souls of the Holy Spirit, who is the subsistent love of God for Himself. As a great disciple of St. Bernard, William of St. Thierry, puts it: "Thou lovest Thyself in us, when Thou sendest the Spirit of Thy Son into our hearts. . . . Thou dost make us love Thee; or rather it is thus that Thou lovest Thyself in us. . . . We love Thee because we receive from Thee Thy Spirit. . . . Who transforms us . . . in perfect conformity with Thy love. This produces so great an attachment and union that . . . our Lord, Thy Son, called it unity, saying: *That they may be one in us . . . as I and Thou are one.* We love Thee, or Thou lovest Thyself in us; we by our affections, Thou by Thy power. And Thou dost make us one by Thy unity, that is by Thy Holy Spirit, whom Thou hast given to us." [23]

For that is the whole secret of God's love. He is in us that through Him and with Him and in Him, we may love Him who is now in heaven as well as in us; He is in us, that through Him and with Him and in Him, we may be loved by Him who is now also in Heaven. As one modern commentator summing up the doctrine of William of St. Thierry, puts it: "We love God through God, and all supernatural love constitutes, so to speak, one God loving Himself in Jesus Christ." [24]

Now, perhaps, we can form some idea of what underlies our Lord's impassioned entreaty for our love, and why He insists on offering us His Heart. The exchange

[23] *De contemplando Deo.*
[24] Mersch, *The Whole Christ*, p. 446.

of hearts that He made with St. Margaret Mary is only a special confirmation of the exchange of hearts—and of lives—which He makes with us in baptism and in Holy Communion. He gives us His own Sacred Heart that we may love Him with the love that is in that burning heart—that living flame of love that cannot contain itself! No wonder He complains of the coldness of our hearts! We in our self-sufficiency try to love Him with our own strength and with our own heart. He wants a love like to His own; and He offers us Himself so that we may use His love to love Him. His prayer to the Father is: *That the love wherewith thou hast loved me may be in them, and I in them.*[25] Thus the Two Persons of the Blessed Trinity are in our souls to help us to live and to love.

That is why we started this book with the doctrine of our incorporation in Christ, for that is both the beginning and the end of our love for God. It is by being in Him that we love Him, and it is by loving Him that we are in Him. In fact the whole question is summed up in a graphic phrase by St. Paul: *If then any man be in Christ; he is a new creature. The former things are passed away, behold all things are made new.*[26]

This "new creature" is no longer subject to our human limitations. It is the "Emmanuel"—"God with us"—a union of God and man, in which God's powers are at our disposal to sanctify us, and to make us capable of loving Him as He would be loved. It is the answer to the pagan poet's sigh—

"Ah! love, could'st thou and I with fate conspire
To grasp this sorry scheme of things entire.
Would we not shatter it to bits,—and then
Re-mold it nearer to the heart's desire."

That is what God does in the spiritual life. For the spiritual life is a conspiracy of love in which God and man unite to destroy the "old man" in us, to make all things new in Christ, to re-establish all things in Christ; —in a word, to remold us according to the desire of the Heart of God.

[25] John xvii, 26.   [26] Cf. II Cor. v, 17.

CHAPTER 24

One Christ Loving Himself

T HE spiritual life—that is, the real life of every Catholic—is a marriage with God. It is a marriage with God the Son, which begins for each one in the sharing of His nature at baptism, which grows in a loving intimacy and unity of operation during life, and which is intended to reach an ecstacy of consummated union in heaven. It is a union modeled on the union of the Three Divine Persons, who are one God. It is a union in which God is all, and we are nothing. It is a union in which God provides us with our dowry, with everything we need to fulfill our part. It is a union which in this life is based on faith, but in the next, on direct vision. It is a union of indescribable intimacy, yet one in which we never lose our own personal identity; for even in that sublime union of the Godhead where the Three Divine Persons are united in one Divine Substance, there is still a distinction of persons. It is, however, a union which perfects our nature and being, and elevates it to a new order by incorporation into Christ and by the indwelling of the Holy Spirit; so that the Scripture can say that in Christ we are *a new creature.*

It is above all, a union of love; a union with undreamed of possibilities, designed and achieved by the infinite love and loving ingenuity of God. When we shall see it in its truth and fulness, we shall either be raised up by the very knowledge to heaven in an eternal ecstasy of joy; or shall be hurled down with hell in our hearts into the unutterable bitterness of that which might have been and which is now forever lost by our own deliberate decision. For to be united to God is paradise, to be separated permanently from Him is hell.

Our life here below is given to us, moment by moment, to forge with God's help, link by link, that bond of love which is as strong as death. All else we achieve here below will either rot in the grave, or else will be burned away in the crucible of purgatory. The only thing that lasts is love—nothing else matters. And therefore God commands our love; and even after commanding it, God still pleads for our love. We are willing to love Him, but with reserves. He is not enough for us. He pursues us and seeks our love, but like the poet each of us can say:

> For though I knew His love Who followèd,
>> Yet was I sore adread
> Lest, having Him, I must have naught beside.

> I said to Dawn: Be suddèn—to Eve: Be soon;
>> With thy young skiey blossoms heap me over
> From this tremendous Lover.

We are afraid to let go of what we think we have or what we think we are going to have. And God in His loving ardor pleads with us, for love, for the love of our whole heart, and we turn away our ear, and drown the sound of His voice in the intoxication of pleasure, or of work, or of all or anything else, save the one thing necessary. And yet we find no peace. We hurry from one thing to another; we exhaust our ingenuity in devising new amusements to capture our jaded fancy; we plunge deeper and deeper into the mire of self-satisfaction; and we are further away from peace than ever. For our hearts are made for God, and they cannot rest till they rest in Him; He knows our hearts better than we do. And so in His love, like the Good Shepherd, He comes to seek us; He pursues us and He uses His providence to draw us away from all else, and to draw all else away from us, so that we may be driven to listen to His voice, and cast ourselves upon His Heart.

"And is thy earth so marred,
  Shattered in shard on shard?
Lo, all things fly thee, for thou fliest Me!
  Strange, piteous, futile thing!
Wherefore should any set thee love apart?
Seeing none but I made much of naught" (He said),
"And human love needs human meriting:
  How hast thou merited—
Of all man's clotted clay the dingiest clot?
  Alack, thou knowest not
How little worthy of any love thou art!
Whom wilt thou find to love ignoble thee
  Save Me, save only Me?
All which I took from thee I did but take
  Not for thy harms,
But just that thou might'st seek it in My arms.
  All which thy child's mistake
Fancies as lost, I have stored for thee at home:
  Rise, clasp My hand, and come."

  Halts by me that footfall:
    Is my gloom, after all,
  Shade of His hand, outstretched caressingly?
  "Ah, fondest, blindest, weakest,
    I am He Whom thou seekest!
  Thou dravest love from thee, who dravest Me." [1]

There is a perfect picture of our tremendous lover. Everything that happens to us is but the touch of "His hand,
outstretched caressingly," to draw us to Himself, to
mold us to His Heart's desire. What then have we to do?
  God gives His answer in the Canticle of Canticles:

Put me as a seal upon thy heart,
    As a seal upon thy arm,
For love is strong as death,
    Jealousy as hard as hell.
The lamps thereof are fire and flames.
Many waters cannot quench charity,
Neither can the floods drown it.

[1] Francis Thompson, "The Hound of Heaven."

IF A MAN SHALL GIVE ALL THE SUBSTANCE OF HIS
    HOUSE FOR LOVE
HE SHALL DESPISE IT AS NOTHING.[2]

That is God's desire—that we give Him all the substance of our house—for love—and count it as nothing. And that is God's desire for every single soul. All He asks is love; and the love that He asks for is the love that He Himself is willing to give us.

Because this love, because this whole new life, comes to us from God; that is the reason why we so insistently and categorically assert that the basis of the whole spiritual life is humility. It was our Lady's humility that attracted God's regard, and was the foundation of the "great things" He did for her. It is humility that will make Him do "great things" for us. The whole spiritual life comes from God, and is infused by Him, and the only thing in us that puts a limit to its increase in us is our pride; for it is pride that makes us appropriate the glory that really belongs to God, and which He would obtain for Himself by His sheer mercy in endowing us with His Holy Spirit and making us one with Christ.

All then that is necessary for any Christian in order to seek the summits of divine love, is to live in faith, hope, charity, humility, and willing abandonment to God's will. The teaching of the popes, the tradition of the whole Church, as we saw, proclaim that all God seeks is our love. He does not ask for miracles, for great achievements, for extraordinary success, for outstanding personal development. The only thing He asks is so extraordinary—for it is a love entirely beyond our powers —that we must rely upon Him to give it to us Himself; hence no one need despair of achieving it.

If one ask for more practical details, all we can do is sum up what we have already written. There is absolutely no need to do anything beyond the ordinary obscure things of the ordinary obscure life which was shown to us by the Holy Family in Nazareth. What must be done

[2] Cant. viii, 6. 7.

is to make each act of that ordinary life an act of extra-ordinary, superhuman, supernatural love. That is done, by diligently acquiring and daily nourishing a knowledge of our Lord and of ourselves, and of the relations that He wants to have existing between us. We have to read daily, and we have to reflect daily. Like our Lady, we must *keep all these words in our heart.*[3] Like her too, we must keep in personal contact with Jesus by prayer. We must pray often and intimately, with our heart more than with our lips, and cultivate a prudent recollection in our thoughts. To this prayer we must add the frequent use of the sacraments; thus shall we ourselves and our daily work be sanctified. Holy Communion should be approached as often as is reasonably possible. And Holy Communion is but the complement of the Mass. We give ourselves to God in the Mass, and He gives Himself to us in Communion. We must live according to that offering of ourself and according to the union of Holy Communion, by a life of ready devotion and generous abandonment to God's will. For the rest, all that is needed is that we make the ordinary things of our ordinary life one long act of love of God by purity of intention and fraternal charity.

As we said, there is no need for anything extraordinary. Whatever we do for God is unacceptable to Him unless it comes from love, and it is the love that prompts the work that He seeks, more than the work which love achieves. Purity of intention should be our aim; for that is what He asks when He says: *Put me as a seal upon thy heart, as a seal upon thy arm.* We must try to do all that we have to do, in union with Him and in service of Him. He must be the principal agent in all our works, and He must be the principal end of all that we do. In particular, we must be careful to see Him by faith in everyone of whom we speak or with whom we come in contact. Whatever we do to our neighbor, whatever we say about our neighbor, is done to Him or said about Him. We can always find Him in our neighbor, for

[3] Cf. Luke ii, 51.

He takes to Himself lovingly all that is prudently done to the least of His brethren.

Here we must be careful to observe His disposition of things. There is an order in fraternal charity; it begins at home, and we must not give away what is not ours to give. There is a tendency to express our fraternal zeal in the corporal works of mercy, and this is but the age-old Christian tradition. But we must remember that our chief duty to our neighbor is a spiritual one. The supernatural must come before the natural, and supernatural works are only done by supernatural means. Therefore our first and best service to our neighbor is to sanctify ourself, by a life of loving union with Christ.

There is no limit to be put to our love, but our love must put a limit to our exterior works. It is the interior life that matters. As St. Thomas writes:

Man's good, his justice, consists especially in interior acts, in faith, hope, and charity, not in the exterior acts. . . . Man should place no bounds to his charity, but on the other hand, he should in his exterior acts, employ a discretion governed by charity.[4]

Some indication of the errors to which we are liable can be gathered by observing human love in married life. Self-will and an obstinate refusal to accommodate oneself to the will of one's partner is an obvious lack of love. Infidelity is still worse. True love cannot divide itself in its own order; it must find its all in the beloved. Still, the waywardness of weakness and the faults of frailty can be forgiven by love, precisely because it is love. But there is one thing that love, precisely because it is love, finds most difficult to forgive; there is one thing that causes love, because it is so deep a love, intense anguish; there is one thing which repels love and casts it down completely like waves shattered into fragments and thrown back from the unyielding and relentless cliffs; and that is, self-sufficiency. Love of its nature

[4] In Epist. ad Rom. xii, 12.

is dependent, and calls for dependence. Love wants to give, and nothing can be given to the self-sufficient.

And so, if there be one way better than any other in which a loving heart can make reparation to the wounded Heart of Jesus, it is by a cheerful acceptance of one's own poverty and insufficiency—it is by living a life of genuine humility. There is no more acceptable gift of love to God, there is no greater comfort we can offer His agonizing Heart, than to cast ourselves on His mercy in our complete poverty and powerlessness, joyfully accepted and gladly acknowledged, so that all may come to us from Him. For in very truth if He is not our All, He is not our God.

It is here that many souls err. They see the spiritual life as a service of God, and so it is. But they imagine that the principal value of their service is found in the results they achieve; whereas in God's eye the results —the increase from their sowing—are the fruits of His goodness and His grace and of His Son's merits and sufferings. As far as that particular soul is concerned, it is rather the love that should inspire the service, that God is seeking. And to make things worse, it often happens in the service of God, that those who are seemingly zealous for His service are really serving themselves. They are pursuing their own career. Their zeal is not so much for God's glory as for their own. They resemble those modern wives who insist on having their own career. They are living their own life—not the new life of union with Christ.

The prototype of all careerists is Judas. He seems to have been one of the ablest of the apostles, one who felt that he was sure to rise to high estate in the new kingdom which all the apostles understood Jesus was to found on earth. He was the minister for finance in the apostolic college, a man of affairs and prudence. Gradually pushed into the background by Peter's rise to favor and thwarted in his desire for advancement, he began to realize that our Lord's policy was not going to lead to the temporal greatness on which he had counted. Christ was an impractical idealist! He was deliberately setting a course that would bring Him in conflict with the authorities and openly spoke of His crucifixion. He spoke only of love and suffering. When the mother of John and James asked for preference for her sons in the future kingdom, Jesus could only speak of a chalice of suffering which was all He had to share with His friends.

And so this prudent man decided to cut his losses. After all, he argued, a man must look after himself. If Jesus would not see reason, well, he himself would have to make other provisions for his own future: there were other fish in the sea . . . and so on. And his mind was soon filled with all those other good and sound reasons that men use to stifle their conscience when they are deciding to betray their friends. . . . And just at the very hour when our Lord was pouring out His Blood in the sacramental offering of Himself at the Last Supper and delivering Himself up to the Agony in the Garden, in order to make superabundant provision for the eternal happiness of Judas, that worldly-wise mercenary was selling his lover and his God for thirty pieces of silver. . . . And, even then, if he had only known the Heart of this tremendous lover, it would not have been too late. *If thou also hadst known . . . and thou wouldst not!*

For it would seem that if Judas had turned to Jesus in sincere sorrow, but also with confidence, relying on the goodness of His loving Heart and forgetting the wretchedness of his own, he would not only have been forgiven—that is certain—but he could even have become one of God's greatest lovers and saints; for God's mercy is over all His works, and Judas would have been the saint of God's mercy. Whether that be correct or not—it is only a personal opinion—the story of Judas has a lesson for us all. God's plans for our sanctification are never quite what we expect them to be; and are often quite contrary to our own ideas, no matter how well we are acquainted with God's ways. He always hides His sanctifying work from our eyes, for He must preserve in us that humility and poverty of spirit which is essential for sanctity. Even though we avoid the error of Judas of expecting temporal success instead of eternal love; still we must not expect to see *our* plan for our own sanctification being realized instead of God's plan. His plan for us is His secret—a lover's secret—and we must trust His love. In fact, our trust in God, especially when we see our own unworthiness, is the greatest compliment we can pay Him.

But whatever else we do—even though we go so far as to imitate Judas in his crime of betraying God— let us, for God's sake as well as for our own, avoid his still greater crime of thinking that our sins are too great for God to forgive. That is the blasphemy of blasphemies! No matter how great, how numerous, how malicious are our sins, even if we had spent every moment of our life in deliberate mortal sin against God, still one single act of love of God for His own sake can destroy every single sin on our soul; and even if our love be but imperfect, even if our sorrow arises rather from love of ourself—inasmuch as we deplore our supernatural loss —than from love of Him, still He is waiting for us in the sacrament of penance, to forgive us and to change our imperfect sorrow into love of Him, making us His friend by grace. No sins in our past, of which we are willing to repent, are any barrier to our reaching the summits of sanctity.

The reason is because our sanctification is from God and from His mercy. Listen to our Lord's words on the night He was betrayed: *For them do I sanctify myself, that they also may be sanctified in truth;* and consider St. Augustine's explanation of His meaning:

What else can He mean but this: "I sanctify them myself, *since they are truly myself.*" For they of whom He speaks are His members, and the head and body are one Christ. . . . That He signifies this unity is certain from the remainder of the same verse. For having said: "For them do I sanctify myself," He immediately adds: "In order that they too may be sanctified in truth," to show that *He refers to the holiness that we are to receive from Him.* Now the words "in truth" can only mean "in me," since Truth is the Word who in the beginning was God. . . . "And for them do I sanctify myself," that is "I sanctify them in myself as myself, *since in me they too are myself.*" "In order that they may be sanctified as I am sanctified," that is to say "in truth which is I myself." [5]

Quia et ipsi sunt ego: "since they too are myself"!

That is why no one who is willing to love God, is prevented from reaching the heights of holiness and all that is essentially connected with it. Because if anyone is willing to love God—and by that very fact one does love Him—our Lord can say of him, "he too is myself"; and He has sanctified him in Himself and has already won the holiness that such a one is to receive from Him. By truly loving Christ we become members of Christ, and if we do His will by keeping His commandments, the Father and He will come and make Their abode in us.

The whole Christian life, then, is Christ and His love. We ourselves live and love no longer, it is Christ who lives and loves in us. In Christ we are loved, and Christ is loved in us. In us Christ loves the Father, and the Father loves Christ in us. Christ in us loves our neighbor, and in our neighbor we love Christ. Christ in the husband loves the wife, and in the wife the husband loves Christ. So also Christ in the wife loves the husband, and in the husband the wife loves Christ. Christ is our supplement, our complement, our All in fact, both in loving and being loved. "And there shall be one Christ loving Himself." For "Christ is all and in all." [6]

. . . . .

Let us go back now to the scene with which we commenced this book. That scene where our Lord weeps over His beloved city, is but typical of His sorrow at the folly of all men who reject Him. His complaint is but one of the many expressions we read in Scripture of His frustrated love. *And when he drew near, seeing the*

[5] *In Ioh.*, 108.   [6] Cf. Col. iii, 11.

city, he wept over it saying: *"If thou also hadst known
and that in this thy day, the things that are to thy peace
. . .*[7] *O that thou hadst hearkened to my commandments! Thy peace had been as a river, and thy justice
as the waves of the sea.*[8] *If thou didst know the gift of
God and who He is that saieth to thee, give Me to
drink!*[9] [Did He not say to St. Margaret Mary, I thirst
to be loved? *Jerusalem, Jerusalem . . . how often would
I have gathered thy children as the bird doth her brood
under her wings . . . AND THOU WOULDEST NOT!*[10]

Perhaps in light of what has been written above, we
may begin to see what was breaking our Lord's Heart as
He looked out over the world on the eve of His Death
and saw all those "who *would* not." His whole Passion
and Death were vividly present to His mind, as if they
had already been accomplished. He saw as if already
accomplished, not only all that He had done for us, but
also that He had done not only all that was necessary,
but more, much more than that. He had left His Father
in heaven and had become man for us, *emptying Himself, taking the form of a servant.* He had not only shared
our nature, but He had shared our life.

He had even gone further. In some mysterious way,
He had taken on Himself the shame of our sins, and had
accepted in Himself all the effects of our rebellion against
God. So much so, that in some extraordinary way, He
found Himself rejected and deserted, as it were, on the
cross by His Father in heaven. He had been numbered
with the wicked and, in St. Paul's graphic phrase, had
become *sin for us, that we might be made the justice of
God in him.*[11] And the anguish of soul, in which He
could exclaim *I am a worm and no man, the reproach of
men and the outcast of the people . . . O God, why
hast thou forsaken me,*[12] is made all the more bitter
by the knowledge of the futility of His sacrifice for
some, because of those who would not give Him their
love. *What profit is there in my blood, whilst I go down*

[7] Luke xix, 41, 42.   [8] Isaias xlviii, 18.   [9] John iv, 10.
[10] Luke xiii, 34.   [11] Cf. II Cor. v, 21.   [12] Ps. xxi, 7 and 1.

to corruption? [13] Who can fathom the agony of His Heart as He saw that our happiness was already won, that everything was ready for the marriage, that only our consent and love were necessary, *and we would not give it!* He had lived our life for us at the cost of His own and it only needs our love to make all He has done for us our own, and we *will* not love Him.

We will not believe in Him. He has promised us everything, if we leave what we think we have, and cleave to Him by love—"a hundredfold in this life and eternal happiness in the next"—and we will not believe Him. He has assured us that every single thing that happens to us is under the loving hand of the Father who will not let even a sparrow fall on the ground without His providence; yet we will not believe Him. He was raised up from the dead to glory so that our hope might be in Him, and yet we will not put our trust in Him. We hope in our own goodness, not in His.

Nor will we even love Him. We will not give Him our whole heart, lest having Him we should have naught besides. We want to live our own life, to be the author of our own sanctification. We do not want to be like the rest of men. We spend our days in seeking distinction, for we will not admit that the commonplace is the gate of eternal happiness. We go here and go there, we do this and do that, in order that we may talk about it, and be talked about. We seek "the bubble reputation in the fool's mouth," not knowing *the fool hath said in his heart, there is no God.* We will not look beyond the opinion of this world and lift our eyes to the reality of the next. We live and hope and love as if there be no God, as if we were alone, as if we had no hope save in what we achieve for ourselves. We insist on planning everything and on doing everything ourselves. We will not deny "ourself" and love Him. We are too busy arranging for our happiness to listen to Him, whereas He has already made all the arrangements necessary for our happiness.

[13] Ps. xxix, 10.

God sees that it is not good for man to be alone. And He had made Himself a help to us like unto ourselves. With the co-operation of Mary, the most wonderful person of His creation, He makes us one with Himself, for it is written *Behold a virgin shall conceive and bear a son, and his name shall be called Emmanuel—God with us.*[14] For in Christ we are one with God.

But this union with God demands our co-operation, and that is why our Lord and lover Jesus Christ weeps over our refusal to hearken to Him and to be gathered under the wings of His sanctifying love and His saving grace. There is no true happiness for us except in union with God. Nothing else on earth can satisfy our hearts; nothing else can give our life any real meaning. The extremes to which our Lord has gone to provide for our salvation and to awaken our love for Him show how earnestly and how urgently He desires our happiness. His plan for our renewal in Himself which we have attempted to outline in this book speaks for itself: but most eloquent of all is the Crucifix. So urgent did He consider our need, so ardently did He desire to save us that He being God, came down from His place in heaven, became man and lived and suffered and died for the love of us. "What greater reason," writes St. Augustine, "can we assign for the coming of our Saviour than His longing to manifest His love for us?"

If we would but be convinced that there is but one answer to the riddle of life and if we would accept our vocation to divine union as the sole end of our life, then immediately everything falls into perfect harmony; the whole scheme of things down to every detail of our lives acquires a new meaning, for all things have been accepted by the will of our Redeemer and made to co-operate in leading us to union with God. All things work together for good to those who love God, for it is His purpose and plan to re-establish all things in Christ.

What then have we to do? We must realize that God is our tremendous lover, that He is our all and that

[14] Cf. Isaias vii, 14.

He has done all our works for us. We must believe in God, and not in ourselves; we must hope in God and not in ourselves; we must love God and not ourselves. As St. Augustine told us, there is one man who reaches to the extremities of the universe and unto the end of time. We have to enter into this one man—this one Christ—by faith, hope and charity. We have to find our all in Him. He is our full complement and our perfect supplement. No matter how weak we are, He is our strength; no matter how empty we are, He is our fullness; no matter how sinful we are, He is our holiness. All we have to do is to accept God's plan—to say as Christ said coming into the world: *A body thou hast fitted to me; behold I come to do thy will, O God.* We have to accept the self, and the surroundings, and the story, that God's providence arranges for us. In humility we must accept our self—just as we are; in charity, we must accept and love our neighbor just as he is; in abandonment, we must accept God's will just as things happen to us, and just as He would have us act. Faithful compliance with His will and humble acceptance of His arrangements will bring us to full union with Christ. For the rest, let us gladly glory in our infirmities, that the power of Christ may dwell in us. In our weakness and in our love we shall thus become one with Him, and there shall be one Christ loving Himself.

For Christ is all, and in all. He is the Alpha and the Omega, the Beginning and the End. No one can truly love, except Christ loves in him. No one can be truly loved, except Christ be loved in him. It is only by Christ and with Christ and in Christ that we can love God; and God Himself loves us in Christ for He has chosen us in Christ before the foundation of the world, unto the praise of the glory of His grace in which He hath graced us in His Beloved Son.

For God made all things for His glory, and Christ is the glory of His substance. God willed to glorify Himself by His mercy, and ours is the misery that calls down His mercy. Our holiness in spite of our misery is the glory of His mercy, for Christ is our All. Let us then be filled with Christ, and by a life of love become one with Him, through Whom, and with Whom, and in Whom, in the unity of the Holy Spirit—the Love that is God Himself—is all the Glory of God.